A BUDDHIST VISION FOR RENEWING SOCIETY

First printing 1981 1,500 copies
Second printing 1986 2,000 copies
Third printing with Addenda 1994 2,000 copies

© 1994 Sulak Sivaraksa

ISBN 974-7493-41-1

Painting on front-cover by Prataeng Amcharern
Painting on back-cover by Taweesak Uchugtanond
Cover design by Thongtip Suthakorn
Text design by Song Sayam Co.,Ltd.

Baht 250
Distributed by:
Suksit Siam 113-115 Fuangnakorn Rd.,
Opp. Wat Rajabopit, Bangkok 10200
Fax 662-222-5188

A BUDDHIST VISION FOR RENEWING SOCIETY

Collected articles by a concerned Thai intellectual
S.Sivaraksa

Thai Inter-Religious Commission For Development
Bangkok 1994

SĀDHU DHAMMARUCĪ RĀJĀ
SĀDHU PAÑÑAṆĀ NARO
SĀDHU MITTĀNAMADDUBBO
PĀPASSĀKARṆAṂ SUKHAṂ

A good ruler is delighted in righteousness.
A good person is endowed with wisdom
A good friend does nor betray his friends.
Happiness is achieved by not doing evil.

THE JATAKA BOOK XVIII 114(222)

IN FOND MEMORY OF MY LATE FATHER

NAI CHALERM SIVARAKSA

my first friend and teacher

who had me educated in both a Protestant and a Catholic school, following his footsteps, but made sure that I was properly instructed in the traditional Buddhist atmosphere of a Thai monastic order.

This kingdom was known as Siam until 1939, when its name was changed to Thailand. Then it reverted to the original name again in 1946. Two years after the coup d'état of 1947 it was decreed that the country would be called Thailand, and it remains so officially. Ironically the kingdom has since been ruled by one dictator after another— with very brief liberal democratic intervals. The name, Thailand, signifies the crisis of traditional Siamese Buddhist values. By removing from the nation the name it had carried all its history is in fact the first step in the psychic dehumanization of its citizens, especially when its original name was replaced by a hybrid, Anglicized word. This new name also implies chauvinism and irredentism. For this reason, the author of this book refuses to use it.

CONTENTS

ACKNOWLEDGEMENTS

The articles contained in this volume were kindly edited by David W. Chappell in 1978, and the Centre for Religious Studies, University of Toronto, accepted the manuscript for publication then. However, whereas the Centre will have the publication typed and bound in a limited edition, the copyright for further printing remains with me.

Since my *Siam in Crisis* met with a certain degree of success, some friends feel that *A Buddhist Vision for Renewing Society* also should be published in Bangkok, hence this edition.

I should like to thank David Chappell, whole heartedly first of all for being instrumental in my being invited as a Visiting Professor at the University of Toronto, and then for editing this volume. Last June, David again invited me to teach at the University of Hawaii and to take part in the Buddhist-Christian Conference on the Future of Humanity.

I should also like to thank Bill Bradley, great-grandson of the physician who was also the first publisher in Siam, for writing a contribution to this volume, which adds value beyond my own writing.

After having edited *Siam in Crisis* for me, Harold Gross again was kind enough to read the proofs of these articles.

Jim Riley played an important role in getting me invited to deliver lectures at Michigan State University in 1977 and 1978. He also edited two of the ones which appear in this volume. At the printing stage, he happened to be in Siam and was able to help me again in 1981.

Robert J. McCloy went to College with me in the fifties and we have been in touch ever since. After the October *coup* of 1976, I was stranded in London; he and his family looked after me, my wife and many other Thai friends for a long time. Recently he and his wife came to Bangkok for the first time. Yet he found time to read the proofs of this book for me.

Lastly, I should like to thank all the friends and colleagues who invited me to deliver lectures which appear in this volume. Most of their names do not even appear here. I should also like to thank the editors who published or reprinted the articles prior to their appearance here.

I trust that the articles herein are worth your efforts in trying to read them. I shall always welcome suggestions, reaction, or criticism from my readers.

S. S. S.

EXPLANATORY NOTES TO THE THIRD EDITION

A Buddhist Vision for Renewing Society, a collection of Sulak Sivaraksa's articles and lectures prior to and during his exile in North America in 1977-1978, was edited by David W. Chappell. It was first published by Thai Wattana Press, in 1981. It was reprinted by Thienwan Press in 1986.

Meanwhile quite a number of books by the same author have appeared in print, some of which have more than one edition: *Religion and Development* (1976,1981,1987); *Siamese Resurgence* (1985); *A Socially Engaged Buddhism* (1988); *Siam in Crisis* (1980,1990); and *Seeds of Peace* (1992). Some of these books have been translated into Sinhala, Italian, German and Japanese.

As a result, there seems to be no need for another edition of *A Buddhist Vision for Renewing Society.* However, since there is a constant demand for the book, we feel obliged to reprint it. In doing so, we chose to add later lectures by the author which did not appear in the other volumes, as well as ask William J. Klausner to introduce Sulak Sivaraksa to new readers who may not have had a chance to read his other works. His introduction greatly adds to what was said of Sulak by William L. Bradley in the first edition.

We have also included a citation from the Naropa Institute, which kindly gave our author the Founder's Award in Boulder, Colorado, on 7 September 1993 as well as the recommendation for the Noble Peace Prize by the American Friends Service Committee.

We should like to thank the author and the above mentioned people and organizations for allowing us to print their work. We should also like to thank Mr. Nibondh Chamduang, Ms. Ladda Wiwatsurawech, Ms. Wendy Wank and Mr. Kenneth MacLean for overseeing this edition.

Anant Wiriyapinit
Executive Secretary
Thai Inter-Religious Commission for Development

PREFACE TO THE THIRD EDITION

Twenty years ago, *Siam Through a Looking Glass: A Critique,* the first collection of Ajahn Sulak's writings in English, was published. In the introduction to that volume, I wrote of the author: "He sometimes seems to be spoiling for a fight ... He is always provocative... and is firmly convinced that the body politics will ultimately flinch under the stings of the gadfly critic and slowly but surely reform itself." Twenty years later, Ajahn Sulak continues to be testy, provocative, intellectually stimulating and an irrepressible gadfly on the Thai body politic. Despite periods of disappointment, frustration and even repression, he has faithfully adhered to the injunction written on the page opposite to the dedication in *Siam Through a Looking Glass*: "This, above all, to thine ownself be true". He has maintained his intellectual integrity and principles although the decibel level of his critiques may often appear about to break through the sound barrier.

Ajahn Sulak remains the quintessential intellectual, a "tester of life", agitating for fundamental changes in values and styles of life. Much like Ralph Waldo Emerson's ideal "Scholar", Sulak has avoided the pitfalls of either marching to the "regimental music" in the corridors of power or withdrawing from society into an ivory tower.

From the day Ajahn Sulak returned from his studies in Wales and Middle Temple in London, he has, with his singular panache, offered alternative visions to those, both within the leadership elite and population at large, obsessed with what Ajahn Sulak perceives to be the false gods of unrestrained economic growth, commercialism and westernization. In his writing, his teaching, his involvement with NGO's — such as the Co-ordinating Group for Religion and Society, ACFOD, International Network of Engaged Buddhists, and the Thai Inter-Religious Commission for Development (the publisher of this present volume) — and his initiatives in the planning and implementation of innumerable seminars and workshops, Ajahn Sulak has, in one form or another, challenged the Thai body politic to engage in self-appraisal while offering alternative models and visions. His prescriptions are rooted in the Buddhist values of compassion, tolerance, social justice, harmony with nature, self-control, self-sufficiency, frugality and tranquility of spirit.

Since the second printing in 1986 of *A Buddhist Vision for Renewing Society,* Ajahn Sulak has not diminished his frenetic pace. During this period, he authored several Thai books as well as works in English. Among the latter are *Religion and Development; A Socially Engaged Buddhism;* and *Seeds of Peace.* He also was co-editor of and contributor to the following publications: *Radical Conservatism: Buddhism in the Contemporary World; Searching for*

Asian Cultural Identity; and *Buddhist Preceptions for a Desirable Society.* In 1988, he founded and became Director of Santi Pracha Dhamma Institute and the Thai Inter-Religious Commission for Development. He also traveled extensively, and, in the last seven years, has continued to mesmerize foreign audiences with both his wit and acerbic critiques. He has lectured and participated in conference, seminar and workshop discussions in leading centres of learning in Europe, the U.S. and Canada, South America and Asia.

Ajahn Sulak seems indefatigable. One marvels and wonders where he finds the time to get into trouble. However, he manages to do so. Alas, while in Thailand in August 1991, he delivered a lecture at Thammasat University which led to charges of slander against the then ruling military junta and accusations of *lese majeste.* The case is presently being adjudicated in the Thai courts.

Many regret that Ajahn Sulak has felt it prudent and advisable to spend so much time abroad. He often seems to be more honored abroad than at home— witness his recent nomination for the Noble Peace Prize. His heroic and lonely struggle against authoritarianism in the sixties and early seventies in Thailand often seems to be forgetten as new anti-establishment critics with their own unique brands of charisma emerge. One so quickly forgets the changes in the socio-political environment which, at present, unlike earlier decades, more readily allow intellectual flowers to blossom.

This third edition of *A Buddhist Vision for Renewing Society* addresses issues and themes which have consumed Ajahn Sulak's intellectual attention from the moment of his return from his studies in England in 1962 to the present. In the first section of this book, Ajahn Sulak analyses the role of intellectuals in Thailand and his own place in the intellectual ferment. Following this, the author critiques western concepts of development rooted in the imperatives of economic growth and materialism. Ajahn Sulak implores his readers to consider the need for a new definition of development focused on Buddhist values. His call for a spiritual dimension to development is a constant refrain in all his writings as well as in his community service initiatives. The next section touches on the need to understand the idealism and yearnings of the younger generation in the struggle for a more just and equitable society. At the same time, reform in education is perceived as a necessity. Another constant concern of Ajahn Sulak, the need to understand and follow the Buddhist principle of non-violence (*ahimsa*), is dealt with in the last part of this section. The final section of the book addresses the interconnection between religion and development. Ajahn Sulak has been the foremost lay spokeman for a responsible community service role played by the Sangha, and his rationale for this position is outlined in the articles in this section. However, the author moves beyond his own religion, Buddhism, and the concern over its contemporary relevence as he discusses the need for a spiritual dimension, whatever one's religion, in all forms of development, whether they be social, cultural, economic or political.

This third printing provides an opportunity for readers to become familiar with Ajahn Sulak's views on issues which have been of major concern to him throughout his very productive life. One may not always agree with his opinions, and some may well be shocked by his presentation. However, very few could fail to be both challenged and informed by this inimitable, unbridled gadfly.

William J. Klausner
Chulalongkorn University
20 August 1993

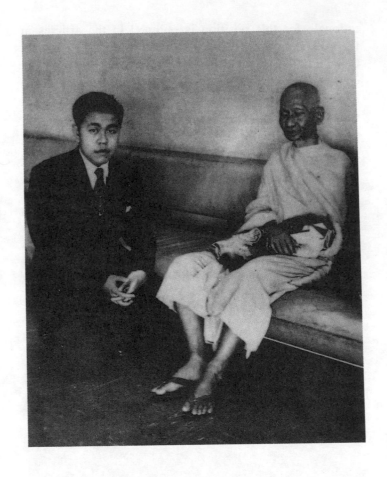

The author with his guru, Ven. Phra Bhadramuni, late abbot of Wat Thongnopakhun, Thonburi, whose birth centennary is being commemorated from 15 March 1993 - 15 March 1994.

SULAK SIVARAKSA

AN APPRECIATION

The road that Sulak travels is one with few companions, for he is an intellectual in a land of pragmatists. As such he walks in the footsteps of a sparse but distinguished company of seers who have deepened their country-men's understanding of the Thai ethos, and in so doing have contributed as well to the universal culture of mankind. Within the past decade Thailand has lost three such interpreters of her culture: Prince Dhani Nivat, who kept alive the classical traditions of the ancient monarchy; Prince Wan Waithayakorn, a key figure in the formation of the United Nations; and Phya Anuman Rajadhon, a philosopher and social critic *extraordinaire*.

Now these are gone, and their successors, who reached maturity after the Revolution of 1932, are giving way to a new generation of intellectuals whose entire lifetime, except for a few brief interludes, has been spent under military rule, and more often than not under martial law. Unlike their predecessors, they cannot look back to a time when Thailand was ruled by a benevolent albeit inept monarchy, while the relatively tranquil agrarian culture of their childhood has been disrupted both by rapid modernization and a massive U.S. military presence during the Vietnam war.

Thailand's long and futile experiment with democracy had barely begun when Sulak Sivaraksa was born in Bangkok in March, 1933. He grew up in comfortable surroundings and at the age of nine entered Assumption College from which he graduated in 1952. It was not unusual for Assumption's alumni to continue their studies in Europe or the United Kingdom, and thus Sulak matriculated at St. David's University College in Wales. Following his graduation in 1957 he studied at the Middle Temple in London, and in 1960 qualified for the bar. He remained in London until 1961, serving as a translator and broadcaster for the BBC and assistant lecturer in the Thai language at the University of London. In 1962 he returned to Bangkok to become editor of the Social Science Association Press of Thailand and its journal, the *Social Science Review*.

So much for the externals. Since the reign of King Chulalongkorn in the latter part of the nineteenth century it has been customary for Thailand to send its most promising young men and women to western universities for higher education. Today there are thousands of Thai students in the United States alone. Most of these return to secure, prestigious positions in the civil service or to business slots that require bilingualism. The normal career path for Sulak, therefore, would have been employment in a legal firm with an international clientele, or assumption of a position in one of the more important government ministries. How did it happen that Sulak chose a course so different from that of his contemporaries ?

Perhaps the answer lies in a combination of chance

and personality, or in other words, Sulak's *karma*. Chance made it possible for Sulak to become editor of the Social Science Press just at a time when Thai social scientists were ready to take over the management of research on Thailand from foreign scholars. Until the formation of this Association very little of the published works on Thailand had been written by Thais. Sometimes their names appeared as research assistants on the journal articles of foreign experts, but seldom did they have sufficient funds to conduct their own research, or a scholarly journal in which to publish the results. Sulak was the right man for the right job at the right time.

Another person in that position would probably have built it into the university system in such a way that it became a part of the gigantic government bureaucracy. This would have provided Sulak with security and in creasing influence within the establishment. Sulak, however, chose to maintain the freedom of an outsider while exerting his influence on the inside. He gives the clue to this decision in his essay on "The Role of Siamese Intellectuals," written for the Philippine journal, *Solidarity*, in 1971. Referring to the intellectual community in Thailand as a tiny group, he distinguishes between three types: the Royal Traditionalists, who are conservative, the Social Technicians, who are liberal, and a third group that is conservative regarding cultural values and progressive in respect to social change. While he does not mention names, M.R. Kukrit Pramoj, a leading journalist and former Prime Minister in the civilian government of 1975, would represent the first type, the cadre of foreign-trained economists and social scientists within government ministries and universities would represent the second group, and Dr. Puey Ungphakorn, former Governor of the Bank of Thailand and Rector of Thammasat University, would represent the third type. Likewise, so would Sulak.

In that essay Sulak declares that while the intellectual does not play a leading role in Thai society, he can have an influence. This he can do, writes Sulak, "by persevering as well as maintaining close contact with members of the younger generation in our universities, which are but grand civil servant schools." This precisely describes the role Sulak has chosen for himself. As a journalist with strong ties outside Thailand, Sulak has maintained his freedom from the bureaucracy. As an informal teacher of idealistic university students, he has exerted leverage upon the establishment.

By so defining his role as *guru* outside the formal educational structure, Sulak has pursued a course that is traditional to Thailand. In the Thai social structure, teachers are born and not made, and teacher-student relationships do not depend on institutional structures but rather on the peculiar chemistry of interpersonal relationships. More often than not it is the student who seeks the teacher, and the bond between them endures throughout a lifetime, transcending all intellectual and even ideological barriers that might come between them in a different type of social order. An outstanding example of this bond is the enduring relationship between Pridi Panomyong, the founder of Thammasat

University, and those who studied under him. Despite his exile in the People's Republic of China, and the cloud of suspicion that hangs over him because of the mysterious death of King Ananda in 1946, and despite the fact that few of his loyal students agree with his socialist doctrines, he is still their beloved teacher *(acharn)*, whom they will always respect and love.

It is this kind of intellectual that Sulak has become: one of a tiny company of those who show their patriotism by deliberately remaining outside the establishment and gently but pointedly criticizing it for its failure to serve adequately the spiritual as well as the material and social needs of the Thai people.

Sulak's message resembles that of the prophets of ancient Israel, combining adherence to traditional religious values with the call for structural social reform. Remember that he and his contemporaries have endured four decades of false hopes for the democratization of their nation. Proud that Siam was able to preserve her sovereignty throughout the colonial period, they are humiliated by the role that Thailand played as junior partner to the United States during the Indochina war, and like most Thais profoundly disturbed by the social disruptions that occurred during the American presence on Thai soil. While not intrinsically opposed to modernization, they see its effects as beneficial only to a small segment of society and deleterious to the great majority, which is to say the farmers and the industrial proletariat.

We see in Sulak's writings a constant attempt to come to terms with modernization, and an increasing pre-occupation with religion as a means of dealing with this problem. Two influences seem to have been at work on him: the one indigenous and the other international. On the one hand he has been profoundly influenced by a learned monk in the south of Thailand, Buddhadasa Bhikkhu, who has reinterpreted the traditionally individualistic teachings of Theravada Buddhism to include important elements of social activism customarily associated with Mahayana. On the other hand, as a member of an international body of intellectuals, Sulak has been influenced by Gandhian and Quaker social theory based upon the principle of non-violence.

In combining these two elements Sulak provides an option to the path of violent reform advocated by a small but significant body of student intellectuals, many of whom have joined the communist-supported Thai Liberation Front. Sulak's way is even more difficult than that of the revolutionary, because it requires patience of its practitioners, while it stirs up suspicions on the part of those who are satisfied with the *status quo*. In a nation governed by martial law, any form of social protest, no matter how non-violent its nature, may bring reprisals. Thus it was that Sulak's bookshop, which has been a classroom for many of the student leaders in the early 70's, was ransacked in the conservative coup that overthrew the democracy in 1976.

What course will Thailand follow in the years ahead? At present there is breathing space for a laissez-faire ruling elite because of the enlightened leadership of her present military government that has learned from its early mistakes, and Thailand's good fortune that her communist neighbors are in deep trouble and therefore cannot concentrate on the communization of their capitalist neighbor. It seems unlikely that under present conditions the Thai people will take seriously Sulak's admonitions to start down the path of Buddhist socialism practised by her Theravada neighbors, Sri Lanka and Burma. But over the long term, Sulak's influence may be felt by the young people who will reach maturity a decade hence: those who must learn to live with reduced material expectations and a greater concern for one another's well being in an over-crowded nation, on an over-populated planet. And perhaps even those who fear almost any form of social change in Thailand will recognize in Sulak a friend rather than a foe, because his teachings of moderation, compassion, and passivity are designed to bring badly needed reforms without violence and anarchy to a nation that prizes moderation and respect for order above all other values.

William L. Bradley

THE EDWARD W. HAZEN FOUNDATION
NEW HAVEN, CONNECTICUT

EDITOR'S INTRODUCTION

I first met Sulak Sivaraksa in 1977 when he was in exile, a fugitive from arrest by the Thai government. In September 1976, Sulak had left home honourably enough. He was one of only two representatives from South-east Asia to be asked by the Smithsonian Institute to speak at their conference entitled "The United States in the World" as part of the American bicentennial celebrations. Returning to Siam via England, he read in the *London Times* that there had been a political coup at home, the Thai democratic government had fallen, and among those arrested by the new regime was Sulak Sivaraksa!

Although this turn of events was a blow to Sulak and to the concerns that he represented, it was a gift to the West. During the next eighteen months he became an invited guest at numerous universities in North America to lecture about contemporary Siam. In addition to his frequent side trips, he became a visiting professor at the University of California at Berkeley in the spring of 1977, and at Cornell University in the fall, followed by an appointment at the University of Toronto for the 1978 spring semester.

In the summer of 1977 Sulak delivered three Berry Lectures for the Department of Religion, University of Hawaii, two of which are published here: "Buddhism and Non-violence" and "Buddhism and Development – Is Small Beautiful?" In addition, in March 1978 at the University of Toronto, Sulak participated in a conference on "Buddhism and Christianity in Crisis" in which he presented a paper entitled: "Buddhism and Society: Beyond the Present Horizons."

In 1973 when Sulak was forty, his admirers honoured him by compiling and publishing some of his writings that had been translated into English, entitling the volume *Siam Through A Looking Glass: A Critique*. Now in his 48th year—being the fourth Siamese cycle of life — Sulak is having another volume compiled by his admirers, this time in the West and focusing on his writings in the last five years.

Three articles in this volume appeared in *Siam Through A Looking Glass*, viz., "Cultural Freedom in Thai Society" and "The Role of Siamese Intellectuals" (see #1 and 2, Chapter I), and "A Thai Image of Japan" (#4 in Chapter II). It is interesting that all of the remaining articles (except for "Thai-US Relations" #3 in Chapter II) in some way deal with Buddhism. To a certain extent this reflects the interests of the sponsors and editor of the volume. However, it also highlights the increasing way in which Sulak has been interpreting contemporary crises in spiritual terms, and finding in his religious heritage a source for challenging and healing social, economic and political injustice.

Sulak is embedded in the web of his times. In Siam he is a journalist, editor, concerned intellectual and an active Buddhist. Because I have wanted to preserve some of the immediacy of the events which provoked these writings and the engaging style of Sulak, I have largely left the articles in their original form and only added explanatory prefaces where they seemed necessary.

Throughout the volume I have used "Thai" as an adjective to refer to the people, language and culture, and preferred the traditional word "Siam" to refer to the nation. This is in response to Sulak's constant reminder that "Thailand" (sometimes translated as "Land of the Free") was chosen and imposed on the Thai people in 1939 by a military dictator who weakened Thai culture by trying to westernize Siam, even to the extent of including an English suffix ("land") in the name of the country.

William L. Bradley, President of the Edward W. Hazen Foundation, has a long acquaintance with Sulak and the circumstances of modern Thai history. We are indebted to him for writing the "Appreciation" that begins this volume because he shows the nature of Sulak's role and contributions within the cultural tradition of Siam.

Sulak Sivaraksa: The Eye of the Storm

In Western circles Sulak is a delight—charming, witty, urbane and gracious to others. He is thoroughly popular with students and secretaries as well as with the learned and powerful, all of whom seek him out. He listens appreciatively and quietly to views totally opposed to his own and is always helpful and thoughtful. However, his reputation in Siam is somewhat different. In December 1975, the *Bangkok Bank Monthly Review* published an interview with Sulak which was prefaced thus:

> *Sulak Sivaraksa is barrister-at-law, publisher, critic, lecturer, traditionalist — and thoroughly unpopular. Rightists call him an out-and-out communist, while he disappoints Leftists (and his rightist detractors) by rejecting communism and most aspects of doctrinaire socialism. His position forms an eye of quiet, of commonsense wisdom, in the midst of the intellectual storm now raging. His very unpopularity is a recommendation that he be listened to. He presents no ideal solutions, but his thought is wide enough to contain the best in tradition with the best in progressive thinking.*

Why is Sulak so unpopular in certain circles? In a phrase, because among strongly divided and desperate factions he is a "passionate moderate"—open to all but beholden to none. He refuses to be swept away by any movement (economic, ideological, moral or political) which neglects or is unfair to some segment of society. A supporter of the young, he understands but avoids their rhetoric, and rejects their call for revolution. On the other hand, he refuses to stand still and accept the status quo when it demeans or oppresses others. Idealistic, active and vocal, against injustice, he has often seemed offensive. As he himself explained in the above interview:

XXIX

Many Thais, like the English, feel that certain things are better not mentioned in public. In polite British society sex, anatomy and bodily functions are taboo; we Thais have a similar delicacy when it comes to the nitty-gritty of corruption, rivalry, greed and oppression. Nice folks do not talk or write about that sort of thing; at least they did not until recently.

Sulak has been one of the earliest and most outspoken critics, and has received political persecution because of it. But he is much more than that, as a brief outline of his recent activities will show.

Sulak's father was a businessman of Chinese and Thai ancestry. In the gradual acculturation process, the Chinese family name became Indianized to Sivaraksa. Sulak was born in 1933, and remembers Siam when land was available for the asking, fish and rice were plentiful, and society was centred in the village and family. Siam had been led into the modern world by strong and enlightened Kings and Princes who were balanced by a Buddhist legacy of compassion and righteousness. Although Siam was never colonized, Thai leaders had become more and more influenced by Western models of economics and culture.

Sulak himself did not escape this process of Westernization. Like every Thai boy Sulak spent a number of months in a monastery; and might have remained there except for the concern of his father. Accordingly, he was sent off to a western Christian school, Assumption College in Bangkok, and then spent nine years in

Great Britain where he became a barrister, broadcaster and language teacher. However, when he returned to Bangkok in 1962 and discovered that the governing authorities now expected him to wear Western clothes and to teach English, he resisted. Turning instead to the publishing business, he became active as an editor and writer. Listening to the voices of Thai poets and protestors, he saw all too clearly that although Siam had never been colonized, its ruling elite had been thoroughly seduced by the "western wisdom" of industry and materialism. The idyllic world of his youth had been replaced by ugly signs, urban slums and political corruption.

Sulak's response to this desecration was to become active in sponsoring societies to preserve and perpetuate traditional Thai culture. For example, up until 1972 he served as editor of *Our Future*, the journal of the Society for Conservation of National Treasures and Environment. On the other hand Sulak encouraged workers, farmers, students, Buddhist monks and whoever would listen, to organize to heal their newly divided society and to bring about social justice—a rather radical activity often branded as communist. Although the government forbade the establishment of new periodicals, Sulak's concerns became expressed through re-orienting the content of an academic journal called *Social Science Review* that he edited.

From the mid-1960's Sulak met secretly with students to discuss the problem of communicating the concerns of the people to a ruling class that had become isolated because of Western luxury, bureaucracy and loss of identification with traditional Thai culture. This problem was then compounded when the elite became frightened by communist insurgency in South-east Asia and rigid against any criticism as a threat to their own survival. Nor did Sulak endear himself to the government when he educated young Buddhist monks from the rural areas about community development in the face of exploitation by the new economic elites. Buddhist compassion had to adjust to find solutions to these new problems, he argued. How did one help tenant farmers who had to pay their produce to city landlords for the right to work the land once owned by their fathers? What could be done for those who fled to Bangkok only to experience another gift of progress, viz., slums!

Sulak's activity among farm leaders and labour organizers took him throughout the countryside, while his courses in the School of Economics at Thammasat University kept him in touch with students and future government leaders. The growing crisis came to a head in 1973 when a mass popular protest toppled the government. Now was a chance for youth and democracy instead of the wealthy elite supported by the army and police.

This experience of hopeful and chaotic democracy allowed Sulak freedom to participate in a wide range of activities. He became Managing Director of the Komol Keemthong Foundation. It was named after an idealistic young village teacher who was killed by communists and was supported by Protestant Christian groups for its work in training Buddhist monks to be leaders in community development. Sulak by now was editor of the annual Thai Buddhist publication, *Visakha Puja*, but was also being increasingly sought out by Christian groups as a resource person. He had helped the Roman Catholic Pro Mundi Vitae compile its report entitled *Thailand in Transition: The Church in A Buddhist Country* No. 48 (1973). In 1974 he gave a lecture at a Conference on Human Development of the Asian Council of Catholic Bishops at Quezon City, Philippines. In 1975 he was a member of the Coordinating Team of the Asian Cultural Forum On Development, an interdenominational and international group. In 1976 he was invited by a Protestant college, in Chiang Mai, to deliver their Thompson Memorial lectures on "Religion and Development."

However, a dark cloud of death began to overshadow the hope of those days as more and more community organizers and labour leaders were assassinated. Sulak began a periodical called *Seeds of Peace* to develop a coalition to stop the killing. He joined with others to form the Coordinating Group for Religion and Society to plead for reconciliation while bringing relief to the suffering.

As mentioned above, a coup finally occurred and Sulak was not able to return to Siam without fear of arrest. Nevertheless, he sought to address the problems of his homeland in the lectures he delivered in the West. Increasingly, he invoked the cool waters of Buddhist compassion and mindfulness as a way to dampen the strife and to bring relief. More forcefully than before we see Sulak revealed not just as an activist for peace, but as a peaceful activist. Tranquil, mindful and un-afraid, he appears as the eye in the storm (as the *Bangkok Bank Monthly Review* described him) or as a calm lake whose surface reflects the changing sky but whose clear depths provide a deep source of renewal reminding us that the sky isn't everything. Through his constant and unattached mindfulness, Sulak offers us a Buddhist path through the storm. He reminds us that we are not alone and windswept under a modern sky, but have streams of tradition to nourish our roots. He offsets the compulsiveness and divisions caused by the lure of progress by recalling both East and West to their spiritual heritage and noblest ideals. Because he works at being calm, clear and unattached, Sulak has also been able to be compassionate and courageous in his activities. As his friend Thich Nhat Hanh might remind us, in this troubled world the miracle is not to find someone who can walk on water, but someone who can walk mindfully and calmly upon this earth. Sulak Sivaraksa is that kind of person.

Sulak himself defies limiting categories: a Thai tradi-tionalist, he is sought out constantly by Western acade-mics, foundations and religious leaders; a thoroughly modern man, he is most critical of the destructive greed and exploitation bred by Western capitalism; a barrister, writer, editor and publisher who has been also a professor in the School of Economics of Tham-masat University, he advocates Buddhist mindfulness and equanimity beyond gain and loss, fame or disrepute. A kind and courageous man filled with personal warmth and charity, his social and political statements excite hope in the weak and angry persecution by the strong. For us in the West, his writings offer a unique glimpse at a Buddhist grappling with social problems. Through him we can sharply see the destructive seeds inherent in Western progress. Because of him we can find a way out, a method of giving humanity a chance, a Buddhist vision for renewing society.

David W. Chappell

DEPARTMENT OF RELIGION
UNIVERSITY OF HAWAII AT MANOA
HONOLULU, HAWAII

Sulak Sivaraksa with H.H. the Dalai Lama
at the World Parliament of Religions
in Chicago, 3 September 1993

I

THE ROLE OF A CRITIC IN THAI SOCIETY

A GADFLY AT HOME

Editor's Introduction

The articles in this chapter serve to illustrate William Bradley's outline of the role played by Sulak Sivaraksa in contemporary Siam. The first piece is a very personal statement by Sulak sketching modern Thai problems and is remarkable in showing how conscious Sulak is of the objectives and methods that he has chosen for himself. Specifically, it describes his role as editor of the *Social Science Review* and his work with young people, and is the best place to see Sulak's own assessment of himself.

The second article describes Thai intellectuals and places Sulak between the traditionalists and the progressives. Although penetrating and constructive, Sulak breaks with Thai tradition by his blunt criticism. We can readily see why he often provokes a storm of controversy, even though he has chosen a modest path for himself outside of the power structures.

THE ROLE OF SIAMESE INTELLECTUALS

Siamese intellectuals have been referred to as a tiny group of people who provide for Siam the most articulate, persuasive, precise and perhaps accurate definition of Siamese society and the Siamese experience. They also have a serious commitment to improve that society. Occupationally, they are the Kingdom's major living writers, educators, technocrats, members of Parliament and intellectual leaders of the Buddhist monkhood. They seem to enjoy a certain degree of freedom to write and to speak in public, whereas this right is denied to the majority of the population. But however much they try, they cannot manage to help solve the most fundamental problems of the society in order to bring about the rule of law, social justice and an honest government which really cares for the welfare of the common man. The reason is obvious: as long as the Siamese ruling cliques come into power through military *coup d'état* as they have since 1932, and as long as they can control the affairs of state by the use of military strength alone, they see no point in paying any serious attention to intellectuals, except those who are willing to serve them. But once you are in their service, what you can hope to achieve is very small indeed. No oligarchy ever changes any society fundamentally, because change means a decrease in their power.

A few intellectuals who choose to be outside the establishment can be critical of the government as long as the political elites feel secure about their position.

When there is a threat to their security or a split among the political leadership, intellectuals who hold different views from those of the government are either silenced or brought into a certain faction of the ruling cliques. After the 1958 "revolution" more than 200 artists, writers, journalists and editors were put in jail without trial on the charge of being communists. Some still remain there, while others have been released. A few are now advisors to the government, although there has been no basic change of regime since then.

Among the intellectuals themselves, apart from their personal rivalries, there is a great diversity of views. Since their numbers are small to begin with, these differences further weaken their position in Siamese society. However, one can safely divide the intellectual community into two leading groups: the Royal Traditionalists, or Conservatives, and the Social Technicians, or Progressives. The latter are on the whole members of government agencies — hence there is not much of a dissenting voice heard from this quarter. They are concerned with bureaucratic organization, the concept of public planning and the educational and economic systems of the country. One can find them in the National Economic Development Board, National Educational Council, National Research Council, National Institute of Development Administration and the Bank of Thailand. Related to this group is a small number of University professors, who are also civil servants, military intellectuals in the Command and General Staff College, as well as a few persons in the office of the Prime Minister. Most of these people, educated abroad, believe wholeheartedly in the economic development of the country. They claim that the present economic stability and the material progress of Siam are due to their efforts. Hence they support strong economic and political ties with the USA, which eventually placed Siam in the position of being an American junior ally in South-East Asia. This so-called "progress" hides the fact that the poor are becoming worse off than before, since the rich are reaping most of the benefit out of a short-term economic prosperity. Since US inspired anti-communist propaganda contributed to slowing down the development of an effective trade union movement, employers have taken the opportunity to exploit the workers. The Siamese Progressive Intellectuals have failed entirely to improve the economic situation of the peasants. Nor have they helped to reorganize the out-of-date judiciary, not to mention the military-bureaucracy. The majority of the people are still, therefore, at the mercy of provincial administrators, who are very centrally orientated. The present planned development era means more funds will be spent on upcountry projects — but the peasants will also be paying higher taxes. The result is that at present there is now more hatred towards administrators than ever before. Also, commercial exploitation through advertising in the mass media makes the country people desire more than they actually need. The farmers, who are 80% of the population, cannot produce enough to buy all the goods now easily available to them on credit purchase. No wonder, therefore, that land which used to belong to the peasants themselves is now in the process of changing hands to the rich merchants. The genesis of subversive movements exemplified by local terrorists in the North, North-East and the South may more often than not be found in the material "progress" in the society, which remains feudal in many respects.

The Royal Traditionalists, on the other hand, are concerned with the glorification and maintenance of Siamese art forms, literary styles, history, poetry, manners and even grammatical forms. They have often been accused of being narrow nationalists who live in the past and refuse to have anything to do with the present day problems. It is quite true that some of these Conservative Intellectuals care very much about preserving Siamese cultural heritage, while they do not seem to pay as much attention to the avant-garde poets and writers of today. One must bear in mind that in this age of rapid national development, old ruins in ancient cities must give way to road building, temples for shop houses, canals and public parks for parking lots and trees for an ugly concrete jungle. Without this group of intellectuals, Siamese society would become even less livable.

Like their counterpart the Progressives, the Conservative Intellectuals are not helping to solve the most fundamental problems of Siamese society either. Yet, as most members of this group remain outside government agencies, they can be very vocal and critical of the establishment. For the past few years the cabinet has followed a fairly tolerant policy towards strong criticism. But never once have they acted on a suggestion offered to them by an outsider, however sound and practical that suggestion may have been. This frustrates some intellectuals, particularly older ones, who become very cynical. They see no point in what they are doing and no hope for the future of Siam either, especially if they disagree fundamentally with the Progressive Intellectuals who work inside the establishment and contribute to an even greater social injustice within the country. Some have given up intellectual pursuits entirely, and find solace in superstition or astrology.

The more practical among the intellectuals, however, are those who feel at home both among the conservatives and the progressives. Professionally he may be a civil servant, like the Governor of the Bank of Thailand, yet in such a position he can often be very critical of the government in public. And in such a case the man should be a progressive. Indeed most of the Social Technicians look up to him as their spiritual leader. Yet he fully supports the conservatives in their endeavours to make traditional culture meaningful to modern Siamese society.

If the intellectual is an outsider—say, an editor of a magazine—he cannot hope to achieve anything at all by mere writing. What he should do is not only to maintain his integrity as an independent writer of some depth, but he must also know his counterparts in the different government departments well. He can collaborate with them on certain lower echelon decisions. In such cases working from within the system, then, small achievements may result such as making the Government accept family planning as a national policy, or declaring Ayutthaya, the old capital, as a historical monument worth preserving. But however hard one tries to make the government pass the law on land reform, one despairs of success, for this law touches the fundamental issue of the oligarchy's wealth and therefore their survival.

In general, the intellectual does not play a leading role in contemporary Thai society. But if one is not too ambitious and not too impatient, each intellectual can perhaps contribute something constructive to his society. By persevering as well as by maintaining close contact with members of the younger generation in our universities, which are but grand civil servant schools, one hopes to keep intellectual ideas alive among the new leadership which, one hopes, will be able to bring about fundamental change to Siam, while also having enough sense to preserve some of the lofty heritage which is unique to Siam.

CULTURAL FREEDOM IN THAI SOCIETY

Mr. Chairman,

You ask me, as you have done members from other countries, about the condition of culture in my country and my role in maintaining and demanding cultural freedom. Before answering this question, I wish to ask you first to bear in mind that Siam is absolutely different from other countries represented at this meeting. We Thais are in the habit of boasting that we have never been subjects of the rule of any Western country. It is admitted that this is something to be proud of, but, conversely, not having been a colony means we have not been exposed to the worthwhile aspects of independence as practised in the West. Thai society is still feudalistic, a society in which everybody must think alike and act alike, making individuality virtually a fluke.

Money and power are therefore the paramount wishes of all persons, for each is a factor dependent on the other. Thai society, at present, is furiously in pursuit of these two ideals. Whoever is outside the circle of affluence and power, if he is poor and lives quietly as such, well and good for him; if he expresses views antagonistic to persons in the two circles, though the views be in the common interest, in the interest of a minority or merely creative, the person expressing them, may well be branded a traitor to his country, a Communist, or a person who cannot be trusted in anything.

Though Siam has been thoroughly exposed to Western society we have adopted only the outer shell without probing the core. Even our universities are under the mandate of the government, while our newspapers exist in a realm of fear because the press officers are invested with the power to close any newspaper at will. It is not necessary to mention how numerous the newsmen are who sell themselves to politicians and merchants.

This does not mean, however, that there are no newsmen who fight for the freedom and prestige of human beings, but such men suffer from the oppression of investors, those in power and the rich in Siam, who join together harmoniously to make money. This practice was most pronounced during the development era of the past two decades, when the power wielders gained more wealth and the rich gained more power, and while the welfare of the common people was sorely neglected. The National Assembly of Siam came into being at the pleasure of the power wielders who reserved the privilege to dissolve it any time they wished and re-establish it according to their whim.

The present Constitution, the drafting of which took more than a decade, has only just been promulgated. Even then, the Constitution still stipulates blatantly that the power-holding clique may continue to remain in power on and on. Even in the Upper House, the power wielders fill the seats with civil servants and heir cronies who are not government servants.

The elected representatives also, with the exception of a small number, use the National Assembly as a tool to gain personal benefit, working in league with the government rather than working for the betterment of the general public or thinking of the future. True, we have an opposition party which to a large extent is sincere in its endeavours, but whose policy and social values when closely considered can be seen as little different from those of the government.

In effect, there are virtually no influence groups in Siam except merchants who team up closely with politicians to make money. There are also soldiers whose delegated responsibility is over other soldiers but who, in fact, have considerable power in society and politics. Apart from these, academic and religious associations, and farmers' groups once established, find their activities limited to small areas and operate more for their own amusement. All are afraid of clashing with those who wield political power. Furthermore the law in Siam prohibits these associations and foundations from involving themselves in politics. A municipal ordinance also contains a provision prohibiting the municipal assembly from having anything to do with national politics. The law also prohibits religious persons from tangling with politics, stipulating that they must concern themselves with sacred matters only. Therefore no matter how much the state works to promote religion, if government officials should misappropriate ecclesiastical funds and squander them, all the clergy can do about it is only to look on helplessly.

To summarize, Thai society is a society of government officials. Even monks who hold ecclesiastical ranks may be viewed as government servants; they all receive stipends from the government. Social value is therefore based an bureaucracy, an institution which has influence over executive, legislative, judicial and academic fields.

Though Thai courts of justice are free and worthy of respect, Thai judges, in general, have ideas which are antiquated. They are not creative enough to bring about the reformation of the court system to be compatible with the time and era. Thai judicial procedures and Thai laws are not compatible with present day Thai society, but nobody takes the trouble to consider this most important matter; hence the stagnation of social reforms over the ages.

According to the condition of society heretofore enumerated, how can a person, such as me, engage in much of a role? The thing I try to do is merely to show the various sectors of society what social problems the country is facing. Even to do this is a difficult task because the mass media in general distort facts and publish only meaningless and nonsensical reports as if they are afraid to report facts.

The rest of the mass media is operated by the government. For instance, at one time Thais were not told how many American soldiers there were on Thai soil until the fact was known by every other person in the world. This is only to give an example. Whoever dared to report this information faced possible charges of subversion or of attempting to destroy friendly relations with allied countries.

To me just to report merely that a situation exists is a worthwhile and necessary act as long as a story is presented from all angles, both pro and con. Whoever believes in freedom must do so, but I do not see any newspaper in Siam that does this. The conservatives report only what is damaging to the "liberals" and the "liberals" return the assault against the conservatives. At least both sides have followings, making the persons who report facts from many sides, supplemented with suggestions and comments, partyless, and thereby shunned by all sides.

My personal opinion is that the most important institutions for Thais are the monarchy and the clergy, because they have been objects of worship and adoration by Thais from ancient times. But even they must be reformed to become leading institutes of wisdom and thought, both cultural and social, even while playing minor roles in politics. When such is my thought, then I must present it openly, because I believe it is necessary that society undergo revisions and change all the time.

The change should be geared toward improvement guided by reason and everybody should be free to make his own judgements. But then the royalists and the religionists, of whom there are many, and who have considerable influence, accuse me of being a Communist who aims to destroy the age-old institutions of the country. Even the creative work I am engaged in, in conjunction with members of the Royal Family and the Sangha universities, are accused of being only a front I am using to conceal my true intention which is the work of destruction.

From the examples I have mentioned, you will know that I want to see alterations in Thai society. At the same time I also want the valuable things of the past to be conserved. To achieve my goal I have adopted the method of being myself, exhibiting succintly my social values, through the medium of journals, by publishing my own views and opinions as well as those others whose thoughts may differ or even conflict with mine. The journal of which I used to be editor was partially supported by grants from the Asia Foundation, and therefore I was accused of being an American lackey, an accusation which is delightful to me because nobody can be the lackey of both the U.S. and the Communists simultaneously.

The fact that this journal has been able to weather the storms and survive for eight years now is indeed a miracle. Coincidentally the government has showed its magnanimity even to inviting me to deliver addresses via the radio every two weeks despite the fact that the radio station belonged to a company in which the Department of Public Relations held major shares. Extensive freedom was allowed in the gist of the speeches. Furthermore, when later I published a journal along the same line for a private company, no matter how strong the articles I published, I was never summoned by the police for reprimand or persecution, despite the fact that friends of the same profession as mine had to face many unpleasantries.

What I had said seemingly implied I held good views of the current government, so much so that some people thought I was a partisan of the government. In the social system of partisanship, the kind that would not allow a person to be his own self like this, such allegations are unavoidable. I would like to add that the government allowed me to remain in Thai society because it has only contempt for the Thai mass media.

But when there is serious challenge to their clique or when they feel that their stability is shaky, they muzzle the newspapers which are unaligned with any particular cause as was the case recently when a monthly journal was closed for no apparent reason. If they want to, even the journal which I am editing can be closed at any time they wish without any difficulty whatever. Moreover, when a major publisher senses the mere indication of a threat to one of his publications he will promptly dissolve that sector of his business without delay, in order to preserve his business in other sectors because of higher income derived therefrom.

Even if the *Social Science Review* itself were ordered closed, only a handful of people would decry its demise. The majority of the people who have kindred social values would not feel the effect of the closure at all. The struggle for the freedom of other people, the demand for the right of the people with whom we do not have common agreement, has not yet become the tradition in Thai society.

At least let me brag that the thing I have endeavoured to do all along is to implant this idea in people, namely, to agree to listen to those with whom we differ, to agree to exchange ideas freely with one another despite the fact that once upon a time there was a martial law proclaimed and even now the "orders of the Revolutionary Party," which constitute a vital obstacle to freedom, still loom dominant; orders which forbid political assembly, forbid establishment of new associations as well as the opening of new journals.

We, however, fought and gained success in stages, using bookstores, temples, and other places for meetings and conferences when opportunity favored. Because the Thai educational system has a tendency to follow established social norms instead of seeking new values applicable to new situations, our objective in conducting meetings and writing is to lead society more than to follow society. Therefore we are more critical than subservient in our activities. Because I advocate reform more than revolution the young people in our group cannot bear me. They think I try to conserve antiquated social values too much. Some say I am only good at talking but hopeless at accomplishing deeds — not having any successful piece of work to show to date. These young people are impatient and want to see changes quickly.

I admit that I believe in working within the system to improve things by committing myself to involvement with the particular institution. Because of this reason I willingly involve myself in the Buddhist universities, projects of the religious associations, academic associations and in social service work. All these projects are long range and therefore results cannot be immediate and so I cannot deny accusations of not gaining success in anything.

I venture that the work of changing society must proceed very slowly, and the person doing this work must be a person with great patience. He must be dedicated, eschewing praise, and must hold firmly to his beliefs at all times. Only after he is able to apprehend the core problems of society will confidence be created which will lead to change. This kind of change, though slow, is more beneficial than killing which is the result of revolution.

Buddhism teaches me to be patient, though by nature I am a person with an impatient temperament. Buddhism teaches me to be obliging and charitable to my enemies, though by nature I have in me the element of wanting to annihilate my enemies. Buddhism teaches me to be humble and to serve society though I am ambitious and imbibed with perhaps too big a head. I adhere to the Buddhist social values as my guiding force in performing my work, no matter how deficient I am. In accordance with what I have mentioned before, my work does not have much influence. I have the burden of having to earn a living. If I make a good income then I am accused of abandoning society. When my income drops then people say it serves me right. Irrespective of the fact that I do not want to be a hero, by profession and work I have perforce become the target of the general public who have social values different from mine.

For this reason I feel alone and lonely: what with people not understanding my true object, what with the obligation to have to face enemies who masquerade in the guise of friends as well as those who declare their enmity openly. My joining in work with various organizations while striving to preserve my individuality is harder than by simply withdrawing into myself. They want us to become like them, to be their partisan and to have views similar to theirs in every respect.

If I should think of becoming rich, it would not be difficult, if I think of seeking power, the task would not be difficult; all I have to do is to bow to the parts of society which hold both, but I do not care to usurp their power or wealth. I only wish to make them see that they should use their wealth and power in the right and proper way for the common interest. If they do not see it this way, the new generation which understands social problems will oppose them on their own. If the young generation is wise and not impatient it will follow my method. If circumstances are allowed to remain as they are longer, there may be a revolution.

II

UNDERDEVELOPED — OVERDEVELOPED

A CRITIC ABROAD

Editor's Introduction

Japan and the United States are two dominant forces in Southeast Asia and their policies and ideas are readily accessible. Sulak Sivaraksa offers a voice from the other side. While generally critical, he is appreciative of the potential for good in both Japan and America. After all, Sulak has a long history of Western education and close affiliation with Western agencies, foundations and churches. As a voice from the Third World, he offers three powerful themes: (1) Modernization for Southeast Asia has brought luxury for a few, poverty and oppression for the majority, and general urban ugliness, social chaos and cultural disintegration. (2) No matter how necessary some form of modernization is, we must not tolerate its destructive and divisive side, nor trust its representatives to be all good and all knowing. (3) Modernization has limited benefit, whereas Japan, America and Southeast Asia have rich spiritual legacies which need to be inwardly taken to heart if we are to live in harmony and fulfillment, and which could offer alternate models for social and human development... if we would only cultivate them.

As Chapter I has made clear, an ongoing concern of Sulak has been to raise the consciousness of Buddhist monks in order to help them respond in a Buddhist way

to the changing economic problems that laity are facing
in their communities. However, he has also played an
active role in the Christian community where he is a
frequent panelist and lecturer on these themes. For
example, the Asian Bishops' Conference, the Student
Christian Movement, the World Council of Churches,
and others have invited him to speak to their meetings.
In February 1976, he delivered the ninth Thompson
Memorial lectures at a Protestant college, in Chiang
Mai. These lectures, entitled *Religion and Development*, are a major theoretical statement by Sulak
and have just been published in a translation by
Francis Seeley, who had given an excerpt of them in
Dialogue n.s. III. 2, Colombo (May-Aug 1976) and
in *Seeds of Peace* 2, Bangkok (1976). It also
appeared in *Questioning Development in Sontheast Asia*
(Singapore 1977).

The last article that follows in this section partially
draws on these lectures, but provides new emphases
and further reflections. The article was delivered a
year later as one of the Berry lectures for the Department of Religion, University of Hawaii, in June 1977
when Sulak was in exile.

THAI - US RELATIONS

It is difficult for a Thai, or Siamese, to take an un-biased view of the United States of America. For my father's generation, America was the land of freedom and democracy. Shortly after the 1932 coup d'état, which claimed to establish a constitutional monarchy to replace the old 'absolute' monarchy, 18 persons were arrested by the Government for having planned a counter-coup to bring back the ancient regime. They were all sentenced to death. Before being shot, one proclaimed that he would like to be reborn in the United States, the promised land, which Siam could never claim to be.

Prior to that date, when all the great European powers expanded their empires into this part of the world, the British and the French in particular tried hard to divide Siam into parts and to establish protectorates over our territory. Although our country remained independent throughout, we granted extra-territorial rights to all the great powers, including the USA and Japan. Citizens of these countries, including their Asian subjects, would have cases adjudicated in consular courts, not in Thai law courts, and import duties on all luxury goods were restricted to 3 % only. Our country was in fact regarded by all the great powers as an unequal partner, since we were not 'civilized' i.e. we were not progressive enough materially. Had the Japanese not defeated the Russians, they, too, would have been treated as we and the Chinese were.

We had to adopt western methods and technologies

so that we would be on a par with them, and advisers and experts had to be employed in the fields of governmental, legislative and judicial administration, in the fields of finance, commerce, communications, public health and education.

Our canal system was no good; roads and railways had to replace it. Our temple schools and hospitals were out of date; missionaries were therefore invited to lead the way in establishing modern schools, hospitals and printing and publishing houses. American missionaries seemed to lead the way in most of this. Even Thai newspapers and typewriters were started by American missionaries, who were God-fearing men, and who tried their best to apply their scientific knowhow in the service of mankind. Although they made very few converts, their efforts were greatly appreciated.

In 1928, when American missionaries celebrated the centenary of their arrival in Siam, there was even a speech from the Throne to thank them, and the celebration took place in the presence of the Buddhist Prince Patriarch and senior monks in the Buddhist hierarchy—not to mention a very large gathering of the public. Missionaries themselves said that they could not find such a spirit of tolerance anywhere else.

Further, former kings even gave them land and contributed financially to enable them to build churches. Some missionaries who taught English to King Mongkut were granted permission to preach the gospel at his own temple, for the King was a Buddhist monk for 26 years prior to ascending the throne in 1851. The wife of a later-generation missionary made a lot of money by writing a best seller *Anna and the King of Siam* mixing fact with fiction (This became *The King and I*).

In 1856, Townsend Harris, the US envoy, drew up a treaty of friendship and commerce with Siam, similar to the one which Sir John Bowring had signed on behalf of Great Britain in the preceding year, whereby we had to grant extra-territorial rights but managed to maintain our independence. A missionary, Rev. Stephen Mattoon, became the first American Consul in Bangkok. Indeed, up to the Second World War, the only Americans, whom the Siamese knew well, were mostly missionaries.

When M.R. Seni Pramoj was appointed Siamese Minister to the USA before the Second World War, he had to travel to Chiang Mai, the northern Thai capital, where American missionaries had their headquarters, to acquaint himself with Americans. Although occasionally missionaries involved themselves with diplomacy and politics, they did not seem to forget their higher duties while engaged in such affairs, for they seemed always to await the indications of Providence and sought to be guided by their own consciences—not by the maneuvering of their Government.

The American government at that time appeared to us to be the only government which was steadfastly friendly, with no indication that it was trying to take advantage of a small kingdom like ours. My father, who was employed by the British American Tobacco Company, always spoke very warmly of his employers. He never felt that there was anything wicked about the company in the way youngsters nowadays feel about multinational firms.

Although he admired the British, he could not stand their snobbery and he never trusted the British government; on the other hand, he never hated them as he did the French, who had brought gunboats right into Bangkok to force us to cede part of our kingdom to their Indochinese empire.

During the First World War, it was the American Administration, which persuaded the Royal Siamese Government to join the Allies against the Germans. Siamese voluntary troops were sent to Europe. Even a neutral power like the USA had joined the Allies to be on the side of righteousness, so we, as protectors of the truth, did likewise.

The reason Siam joined in the war was that right was at stake, for the Germans regarded Might as Right. Luckily, the Allies won the war and right was triumphant. Even the Siamese Prince Patriarch preached sermons on the birthdays of the King of Siam for two consecutive years on "Right is Right" and "The Triumph of Right."

As a consequence of the War, American advisers to the Siamese Ministry for Foreign Affairs—mostly professors from Harvard Law School—helped the Thai Government to alter previous treaties with the Great Powers. Dr. Francis B. Sayer, son-in-law of President Wilson, in particular, performed a great service for the

Thai by persuading the American Government to give up extra-territorial rights in Siam, and other great powers followed suit.

For this service, the Thai felt very grateful to Dr. Sayer, whom the King created a Thai nobleman with the title of Phya Kalyanamaitri (A Good Friend) and to the American nation, for without their lead none of the other great powers would have been willing to sacrifice what they had taken away from us almost a century ago.

With the end of extra-territorial rights, it meant that we were independent in all respects and we were treated by the great Western powers as an equal partner. Thanks to the Americans, Siam had gone a long way along the progressive road of the advanced nations!

Indeed, it was in the USA, in 1930 that the Siamese King, the first to make a state visit there, announced his intention that he would grant a constitution to his people. And it was American advisers to the Siamese Foreign Ministry, including former advisers like Dr. Sayer, who advised the King that the Thai public were not yet ready for democracy.

When democracy came to Siam in 1932, it was forced on the King by the Thai military and civil servants who were mostly educated in Europe. The new political elites preferred to model the Thai political future on the regimes of Germany, Italy and Japan. As a result, during the Second World War, Siam declared war against the Allies.

Luckily, the Siamese Minister in Washington D.C., who is now our Prime Minister (M.R. Seni Pramoj), refused to hand over the declaration of war against the USA and the United States took the attitude that no state of war existed between the two countries. This could not be said for Great Britain and France, both of which wished to punish us severely after the war.

Again, the Americans came to our rescue, and not only was our independence secured, but we were also allowed to join the United Nations soon after the war was over, as if we had been on the victorious side. (We had been a member of the League of Nations after the First World War.) Dr. Sayer was appointed a Thai member in the International Court of Justice and has continued to act in this capacity ever since.

With this historical background, it is difficult for an older generation Siamese to regard the American nation and people as anything but having been friendly and helpful to the Thais all along. Although our best brains had been trained more in Europe than in the United States, the Rockefeller Foundation had been helping us build strong medical and agricultural schools here locally.

Prince Sitthiporn Kridakara, known as the father of modern Thai agriculture, though he had never been to the USA, used American textbooks and methods to improve local farm products. The present King's father and mother were both educated in America where they first met, and the King was even born there! For a country with such a strong monarchical attachment, no greater compliment could be imagined.

For the younger generation, born after the Second World War, all the historical links seem to have faded away. To them, American governments, one after the other, do not appear as helpful to the Thai and as altruistic as they appeared to the generation before them.

It is true that immediately after the War, the American government, especially in the person of her first Ambassador in Bangkok, Edwin Stanton, tried to be fair to the Thai, but not long afterwards she began to care for her own aggrandizement. She only paid lip service to democracy, freedom and equality.

She regarded herself as the leader of the Free World, yet she was willing to employ all kinds of unscrupulous tactics, which she hypocritically accused the Communists of using, in order to save the so-called Free World. Was her real fear Communism ? Or was Communism a pretext that the American public were being conditioned to fear, so that those with vested interests could use such tricks to preserve their brand of free trade, which is the worst kind of capitalism.

Capitalism reached the peak of ugliness in this part of the world only after the Second World War, when the latest technologies in all fields made trade and advertising an effective partnership in exhorting everyone to work more in order to want more, to produce more, to waste more natural resources and to destroy natural environment. Never before has the gap between the rich and the poor, the powerful and the powerless, become so polarised. The more the rich developed materially, the more the poor suffered.

In the long run, both the rich and the poor suffered socially, culturally and spiritually. Yet there seems to be no solution to all these dilemmas. Even though development appears not to help, there seems to be more development. Education creates more unemployment and frustration, hence we must have more schools, colleges and teachers. Public health does not seem to cure or prevent disease, so let us have more hospitals and medical services so that many of our trained medical doctors and nurses will be serving in the United States.

As American experts failed to solve their own problems at home, they were exported to solve problems in the developing countries, so that we would be developed in the American image. Since the USA failed to keep Communism away from China, she had to, at all costs, keep it away from Southeast Asia. With such determination, by hook or by crook, the American Government recruited junior allies for the "Free World."

Hence all these allies then became American puppets, full of corrupted officials, and were usually dictatorial or quasi-dictatorial. They could neither become free nor let their citizens enjoy freedom. Such regimes are actually the best breeding ground for Communism. Anywhere where the poor get poorer, without enjoying full participation in governmental affairs, and where their grievances are not remedied justly and rapidly, and yet where their expectation is high materially, is an open door for Communism.

Since the USA could not get rid of the Communists in China, she created South Korea to prevent them spreading further. And governments such as those in South Korea and in the Philippines are the kind the American Government really likes to have as junior partners. At best her junior allies could be allowed to be as prosperous and as democratic as Japan—with American troops always present within the country.

U.S. policy towards South Vietnam was the same as in the case of South Korea. Now it did not work in Vietnam, nor did it work in any Indochinese state, so it seems to us that she would like to treat our country as another Vietnam or Korea. ASEAN would be shored up as a hostile neighbour of the Indochinese states, so that the USA could have a great deal of political influence in saving 'the free world' by maintaining troops or radar stations in Siam, which would become like South Korea, the Philippines or at least like Japan.

Such a junior partner would never be allowed to develop herself for the sake of her own self-respect, in her own image, for her own self-interest. Whatever this junior ally does, through the powerful elites in the country, she must maintain the links with American and Japanese vested interests.

At least in our own case, it was an American government which supported three successive dictatorial regimes from 1947 to 1973. Without initial American support the regimes would not have lasted. In fact, it was Field Marshal Pibulsonggram who had proclaimed himself a dictator and declared war against the Americans at the outset of the Second World War and who had been declared a war criminal after the war, who came back to power undemocratically in 1947.

This time the American Government gave him full support, for he was willing to send Thai troops to Korea and to recognise South Vietnam. When he tried to back out from the Americans by trying to contact the People's Republic of China in 1957, the US Government allied itself with the new military elites and pushed him out of power by helping to put Field Marshal Sarit Thanarat in his stead.

From then onwards American experts penetrated within many Thai Government agencies, even in the provinces, and we developed our country in the American image in most respects. Our educators and administrators, our soldiers and policemen, were trained en bloc in America or by Americans. Our officials were even trained to suppress our own people! Development means more roads upcountry, which means that the rich can buy more land in the distant provinces. Development means officials have more access to the people in the rural areas, which means more dissatisfaction with officialdom. Without Parliament and without the free press, there was no real leadership developed in the open.

Our universities and colleges were only set up for preparing future civil servants and entrepreneurs who would rather maintain the status-quo, so it was only the subversive elements in the jungle who gained ground. Hence American troops and air bases were needed in the country, to fight in Vietnam, Laos, Cambodia and of course to fight against the insurgents within the kingdom. All this led to more Communist insurgency.

In the towns, the US presence has had catastrophic effects on Thai culture. The Thai elites became greedy and corrupted. The best way to earn money was through working with the Americans, who had a lot of money they did not have to account for. The rich and the powerful got the bigger share from dealing in weapons and heroin to catering for Rest and Recreation for the soldiers from Vietnam as well as smuggling PX goods to flood the Thai market.

The poor and the beautiful could also earn something through manual work and sex. As a result, we are now known for our prostitutes, for cheating and corruption. Every town now must have a night club, as every college must have at least one teacher who has been educated in the USA. How all these will benefit us, I do not know. And to be fair, we should not blame all this on the Americans. But without an American presence to the extent already indicated, would all this have been possible?

One good element, however, is that there have always been some American friends in the tradition of Mr. Mattoon and Dr. Sayer. They included former Ambassador Stanton and members of the American Friends Service Committee. They worked with us in letting the world know how wicked it was to ave foreign troops in such a country as ours; how bad it was for military and financial aid to be given with so many strings attached.

Yet the people in America cared so much about themselves and the big problem in Indochina that our voices were not usually taken seriously. Again, thanks to some of our American friends, we have been told that citizens of the USA comprise about 6% of world population, but they consume almost 50% of the world's natural resources.

To pattern ourselves after the American way of life, as our forefathers did, would be to us impossible, and unethical. Besides, to the younger generations the USA is no longer the land of milk and honey. Even democracy does not seem to work there—not to mention the exploitation of the minorities and the abuse of freedom. It is not even safe to walk in the New York Central Park in broad daylight! Yet these facts are not known among the older Siamese generation, particularly the rich and the powerful, who still cling to a superficial idea of the American system. Some of them have already put money in American banks and bought houses in the USA. If the worst comes to the worst, they can always survive comfortably. The present Prime Minister told me about ten years ago that we Thai must be grateful to our American friends, who had helped us so much in the past. In any small way, such as allowing American troops to be in our kingdom, we should do so, in order to express our gratitude. After all, the troops would boost our morale, and it would benefit our military materially also. We no longer talk about our own self-reliance and our own proud Thai dignity.

Being a junior ally for three decades has made us childish and helpless, and look down upon ourselves.

Of course Americans with vested interests in Bangkok—CIA or otherwise—exploit the situation cleverly. They penetrate our military, our civil service and our mass media—not excluding the court and learned societies. Even some assassinations and defamations are believed to be carried out with full American support.

Although President Ford once announced a policy of understanding towards US friends who may feel the need to accommodate to the new situation in Indochina, yet American officials here know how to manipulate the situation in this country to make it very difficult for those of us who would like to make some policy adjustment vis-a-vis our Indochinese neighbours. For instance, everyone knows very well that cutbacks in outright grants of US military aid are occurring all over the world as a part of a general American policy decision. These cutbacks can be interpreted to some of our military people as if they are a special US reaction to Thai anti-American moves. In this subtle way the US has the power to make it impossible for us to run own affairs, and time is running out.

The policy adjustment referred to, in fact, simply means that we would like to have sovereignty over our kingdom (not excluding American military bases) and they would also help us restore our relationships with our Indochinese neighbours. It was precisely in such matters that the Americans of our fathers' generation helped us so tremendously.

At this stage in Siamese-American relationships, we do not expect the Americans to go out of their way to help us as their forefathers did. In fact, it would be ironical if they did. What we expect of America right now is to leave us alone. Having been defeated in Indochina and having dragged us into the arena, we would be very grateful indeed if they would only allow us to chart an independent course involving a degree of accommodation with our neighbours.

Certainly there is ample evidence that the Thai society, having been taught to follow her great American ally for three full decades, has become very weak, culturally and spiritually. We need to undergo some rather far-reaching reform in order to resist the challenge of bloody revolutionary change.

But if our American ally does not even allow us this flexibility and her officials in Bangkok use all kinds of tricks and manipulation, we shall not likely be able to reform ourselves adequately. Only through our own efforts of reform could we be allowed to remain the only free and non-Communist country adjacent to Indochina.

If our friends in the USA still believe in what the Founding Fathers said in the American constitution of two centuries ago, they could perhaps help us, by putting in more effort to learn about and publicize the kind of manipulation that American officials—CIA or otherwise—carry out at home and abroad. Concerned American individuals, religious leaders and liberal academics ought to make friends with local people in a more meaningful way and to be real watchdogs over their politicians who seem to work closely with financial tycoons.

If you think it right to develop your own country towards peace and justice in your own way, could you not restrain your public servants to allow us, a very small kingdom in a far away land, to develop our way of life in our own land?

Let the past teach us to begin the new era by respecting one another. Real friendship can only be created out of respect and understanding, not by mere convenience, interference or manipulation. What was well begun in the field of Thai-American relationships, has been strained recently. It is not too late to put the wrong right, if the US would only admit her mistakes and put forth a genuine effort of goodwill towards her smaller and weaker friend.

A THAI IMAGE OF JAPAN

I have been in Japan now for exactly one month which is the right time for a journalist like myself to feel he knows everything. Were I to stay on longer, I would, of course, be in a state of doubt and perplexity about my so-called knowledge of Japan. You know the well-known journalistic saying that one who visits a country for a week can write a book about it. If he stays on for a month, he can write an article about it. But, of course, if he lives in a country for a year, he doesn't know what to write. So I am in the right stage for writing an article or giving a lecture about Japan.

Mr. Chairman, I have been told by some members of your staff that I should be provocative. That I can be, for provocation is my usual talent. Especially, since I am due to take leave of you all by mid-day tomorrow, I can afford to be very frank and suffer no consequences for what I shall say tonight. But having reflected on your kindness and on the friendliness extended to me by my Japanese friends here, I was wondering whether I should be blunt, or should I be more cautious. However, as George Bernard Shaw once said, if you are in a state of doubt, speak the truth. The truth, then, I shall be speaking, or, at least, the truth about Japan as I see it. As you all know, truth sometimes hurts, but I hope you will understand that I say it with sincerity and goodwill, although I might not be able to put it in neat, diplomatic language.

Some of you who have read my curriculum vitae must have noticed that I am a member of the Siam Society, which is the oldest learned and non-profit establishment in Bangkok. Its motto is "Knowledge Creates Friendship," and I adhere to it; but in order to derive knowledge, one must seek the truth, even though stating the truth in plain words may sometimes cause embarrassment, especially in an after-dinner speech, and a foreign relations dinner at that. Please, therefore, endure it and bear in mind that when I criticize Japan and the Japanese, at the same time I also criticize the Thai people and the Thai Government no less. I only hope that His Excellency the Thai Ambassador does not leave the room in a fury before my speech comes to an end.

In Siam—please take note that I never use the word "Thailand" which is an ugly, mongrel, hybrid word, half English and half Siamese — in Siam I am known as a prophet of doom. I hardly see eye to eye with the Thai Government, nor does my view represent that of the majority of the Thai people. So the Thai image of Japan which you will be listening to will really be my image of Japan, purely subjective and as prejudicial as a journalist can make it.

Apart from being a journalist, I am also a teacher. I teach political philosophy at one of our universities and the first lesson one teaches, of course, is that the term "political animal" is a misunderstanding of Aristotle. What he meant was that man is an animal who lives in a polis — a city state. The term "political animal," I am sure, is well-known to us all whether one studies political philosophy or not, but the term "economic animal" was unknown to me until I came here.

The International House kindly arranged for me to attend the Siamese speech contest by Japanese students, which took place a day after my arrival in Japan. There, for the first time, I heard Japanese students criticizing their countrymen, especially the traders in Southeast Asia, as "economic animals." And I thought how appropriate it was to use such a term, although Aristotle may not approve of it. Let me explain why I felt such a term was applicable to the Japanese overseas. Before I came here I hardly had any direct contact with Japan and the Japanese. The image of Japan I have back home is merely one of advertisement signs — big, ugly, and everywhere. A watch company built a clock tower for our university, not for the benefit of our students or faculty members but to have their advertisement signs there. Another company built an overpass on our street, not to help the pedestrians but to advertise their goods. I have slides here with me taken at random in Bangkok and if anyone is interested in seeing them, you will realize how ugly our city has become with cheap Japanese advertisement billboards. Of course, it is not your fault alone. It is as much the fault of the Bangkok municipal authorities who allow such things to happen.

Apart from the advertisement signs everywhere, both in the cities and in the countryside, what else does the average Thai see of Japan? What image do we have? The answer is that what we know of Japan is Japanese imported goods — ranging from vehicles of all kinds, radio sets, television sets, to all sorts of luxuries and unnecessary things in life. In spite of the fact of a 50 percent unbalanced trade deficiency at Thai expense, Japanese firms are still trying to mint as much money out of our country as possible.

Again, I simply cannot blame only the Japanese. Were our politicians honest statesmen who carry out affairs of state for the benefit of our people at large, these are things that might never happen. It's very easy to put an end to, or at least put a quota on, undesirable imported goods. Yet, the Japanese traders know full well that in Southeast Asia many politicians and bureaucrats are corrupt. So they take every advantage of this corruption by bribing these officials. The traders are, I fear, both short- sighted and unethical.

I know some European and American firms exploit this situation also. But they do it in a more scrupulous manner. At least some of the firms feel that they have to do a certain amount of bribery in order to get business done, whereas their Japanese counterparts go out to bribe their way through business without any kind of regret whatsoever.

And in Japanese business, the Japanese must benefit as much as possible. The products are made in Japan, they are shipped by Japanese steamers, insured by Japanese insurance companies, advertised by Japanese advertisement agencies, sold by Japanese wholesalers and, of course, they are bought by the Thai people. No doubt the Japanese have some Siamese retailers and they employ local or, rather, native staff who are badly treated by any international standard. Again, this is mainly our own fault. In a country where the word "trade union" is a synonym of communism, and the country is so anti-communist, the laborers are obviously at the mercy of their employers. Yet big Japanese companies lack big enough hearts to be compassionate toward their fellow Asian employees. No wonder they never have first-rate Thais working for them. Even those who have been educated in this country would rather work for other companies than for Japanese unless they can't help it.

Discrimination among Asians is sometimes worse than racism between East and West. A Siamese student told me the other day that he studies engineering here. Before each vacation some engineering firms send circulars to his university asking senior undergraduates to work temporarily during the vacation in the establishment. But the circulars always add that foreign students are not wanted. I have been told not only by Siamese but also by other Asian students that the Japanese treat their Asian fellows as unequal partners. Indeed, they regard other Asians as inferior to them, whereas they regard Westerners as superior.

On this score, the Thais are exactly the same as the Japanese. I feel that these two countries suffer the same fate, for these two countries were not colonized and in order to remain independent we must prove to the West that we follow their mode of living, their thought, and their civilization. Why should one look at our Asian neighbors? Why should one have any business with them, since they were not masters in their own houses? We would rather deal with London, Paris or Washington D.C., than with Rangoon, Phnom Penh and Manila. This kind of self-conceit is still lingering on with us Siamese of this generation.

Among our fellow Asians, we only admire the Japanese who, we feel, are nearer to the mark of the Western paradise than we are. And I'm sure the majority of the Japanese feel and know that they are catching up with the West. In some fields they are even better than the West. Yet, using the Western yardstick by which Japan is measuring her achievement, she has no time to pay any respect to her more unfortunate Asian neighbors. Of course, she has to pay lip service to fellow Asians. In fact, they are there to be exploited.

Three decades ago, they were exploited politically and militarily. Now, they are exploited commercially and economically. Japan has not yet learned the lesson that those who exploit must themselves capitulate sooner or later. The world, in fact, is not divided into East and West, communist or non-communist, but it is divided into the haves and the have-nots. Japan is now with the haves. She is now the second largest economic power in the world. So, she would rather associate herself with her rich counterparts, and like most rich countries and people, Japan shows off her wealth in a foolish, extravagant way. Hence, the Olympic Games, hence the Exposition 1970, and hence the world conferences of big organizations hosted by Japan. These are all on a big national scale—"Come and see our riches."

On another scale, there are streams of Japanese tourists everywhere who behave exactly the same as their American brethren, who trot all over the globe spending money everywhere, going by Japan Air Lines, eating Japanese food, using Japanese guides, talking Japanese all the time, and returning home no wiser.

It would be more beneficial if this type of "tourist" would stay at home and watch television or films and pay attention to all the explanations contained therein. But how can you stop rich people from spending their money? We can only educate them to spend their money wisely. Most rich people not only look down upon poor people, but they also feel that they must help the poor, the unfortunate poor, not for altruistic reasons, obviously, but merely for their own benefit and psychological well-being. Hence, military aid and economic aid which are detrimental and dangerous to both the donors and the recipients.

Japan is now, I'm afraid, in that kind of a rich man's dilemma. She has to take a leading role in the Asian Development Bank, as her American partner does in the World Bank, and she is gradually brought in to play a leading role in several international and regional cooperation schemes. She doesn't like it yet. That is why one often sees members of the Japanese delegation sitting silently, smilingly, and sometimes sleeping at international conferences. Japanese delegates are well-known for not understanding English at international conferences. They will not sign any agreement since they say they do not understand it. But any statement which is profitable to Japan, the delegates readily understand and sign without any hesitation.

Whether Japan likes it or not, she will have to play more and more of a leading role in international affairs. Her wealth doesn't permit her to do otherwise, but as long as her mind, her spirit, and her yardstick are viewed vis-a-vis Western norms, she will commit every error and follow in the footsteps of the West. She is now giving scholarships to foreign students who come to Japan, without any clear and critical thinking about it, as well as giving aid to developing countries, sending so-called experts to those countries, and now even sending peace corps men to help the unfortunate. Japan has not yet learned that the United States has done much harm with her AID program, has not learned that the U.S. has played her role as a rich man, on the whole, foolishly and selfishly. Of course, there are some exceptions—some aid programs are quite good, but on the whole, I mean what I say.

Japan will never learn this lesson until she stops trying to catch up with the West. What does it mean to have more GNP? What does it mean to become the first economic power of the world? When prices keep going up, people always want more things which they do not really need, and they become more restless, rush to work, compete in their work and hardly have time to relax and enjoy life.

One must also bear it in mind that economic advantages have been derived at the expense of the poorer countries and in those countries, too, their mode of living used to be much simpler. They had very few things and they ate very simple meals and, of course, they spent less time at work and more time at leisure.

Now, with these advertisements, all sorts of billboards, and mass media communication and exploitation, these simple people are made to want more, to work more in order to spend more for the things which they do not really want but they must have in order to catch up which the Japanese. In this dilemma, who benefits? Are the rich who make more money out of the poor any better off when they learn from their bank statements that they now have more money than previously? Or should the rich feel that we ought to do our best to bridge the gap between the rich and the poor, in order that social justice will prevail not only within the country but throughout the world? If the rich don't feel and act in this way, the poor peoples and countries will sooner or later demand something more than money from them, and when this happens, call it communism or what you will, it will be a dangerous state of affairs both for the rich and the poor. There will be tension and strife such as now exists between the black and the white and the older and the younger generations in America.

Although Japan doesn't have problems with a racial minority inside the country, she already faces youth problems and, from what I could gather, the older generation on the whole does not understand the problem either, or at least they do not try to understand it, for to understand the demand of the young means admission of the failure of the old. Yes, most members of the older generation of Japan have failed to guide the aspirations of the newer and younger generation.

This doesn't only happen in Japan; it happens everywhere that political leadership and economic leadership have become united for their selfish ends. What these people really want is to have money and power without taking any moral responsibility whatsoever.

Among junior allies of the U.S.A., ranging from Great Biitain, West Germany and Australia, to all the so-called "free countries" in Asia, the politicians in power look to their American leaders to guide them, to defend them, and to aid them. Had the Americans the moral courage and wisdom to lead the world, the young might not have rebelled, but as there is no real leadership in America either, and as the Americans have proved their failure in China, Cuba, and Vietnam, the young Americans themselves cannot look up to their elders any longer. Yet, political leaders among the so-called free world still cling to Washington as, indeed, Rome's junior allies kept on following Rome even during her declining period. The reason they did so, of course, was because they got material benefit out of it, not because it was for the benefit of the people at large.

Most Siamese used to look to Japan with great admiration, especially at her scientific and technological achievements. And politically, I thought, she was in a unique position to play quite a positive role internationally vis-a-vis China and the U.S.A. But the closer I look at this country, the more disillusioned I become. As long as Japan is content with being an economic animal, she will blindly follow in the U.S. footsteps, getting more and more involved with Taiwan and all the U.S. so-called "puppet governments." Of course, it starts economically at first, and then when America is no longer on the Asian scene— and one hopes she will not be here much longer —Japan, obviously, will be for her Asian neighbors the number one target of hatred. Then Japan may have to resolve to play a political and even a military role again, despite the fact that she doesn't want that now.

When one says that history repeats itself, one means that a person or country which doesn't learn lessons from past events will normally commit the same mistakes again. I can see this quite clearly now in Cambodia where there is a threat that Siam will intervene and if this is done the Siamese will make the same mistake as our ancestors did over a hundred years ago, although the Americans were not there then.

By saying this, I do not mean Japan will start another great war. What I mean is that, despite what all my Japanese friends are saying, militarism is a possibility in this country, especially if this sort of leadership is continued much longer. Japan may now be a democratic country, but democracy can only survive if the country has strong and positive leadership. Otherwise, it becomes mob rule. And in Japan, where herd instinct has a much stronger force than individualism, when the time comes, people will easily be led by a dictator, benevolent or otherwise.

I know that there are many Japanese who are dissatisfied with the present situation. Some have even become outspoken about their country and people. Ex-ambassador Kawasaki is not the only such critic. Yet, I have not found anything constructive in these criticisms. The reason is that these critics, too, are much too Western-oriented. Kawasaki is perhaps the arch example, for he even wrote *Japan Unmasked* in English, and I gather that he is more at home in a Western context than that of Japan. In the book, he merely sets aside almost all of the positive elements of traditional Japanese values. For example, he says that Buddhism is now dead in Japan. I wonder how seriously he studied the subject before he said that. And I'm sure he's not the only one among modern writers and thinkers who feel this way.

I have been talking to quite a number of university students who often demonstrate against the government. Good for them. And I regard them as one type of social critic, too. They do not find anything positive in the traditional culture of Japan, either. This, indeed, is very sad. There is nothing worse than a person who doesn't know about himself, who doesn't appreciate the good things in himself, and who does not really know the bad elements in himself.

Perhaps I make too strong and too generalized a criticism when I say that Japanese intellectuals seem to know so much about Western progress and so little about themselves. Dr. D.T. Suzuki wrote as long ago as 1934 that "We must somehow find ways, the sooner the better, to compensate all such losses inevitably arising from science, machines, and capitalism."

I don't think that the Japanese have found a way to do that yet. In order to find a way, Japan must follow Herbert Spencer's advice. It was published in an appen-

dix to Mr. Hearn's famous *Japan : An Interpretation.*
Spencer said that Japan should be "keeping Americans
and Europeans as much as possible at arm's length."
Of course, Spencer was an American.

I don't mean that we must go back to the closed door
policy, in spite of the fact that we opened our doors
because we were forced to by the West. Commodore
Perry came here at about the same time as Sir John
Bowring went to Siam with gun-boats. No, we can't
put the clock back.

Nor should we, nor can we deny Western science and
technology. But, can we accept it and at the same time
keep the West at arm's length? Do not judge ourselves
by their standard. Do not ape their fashions. Learn
something about them. Learn something from them.
But do not hasten to put their approaches into practice
uncritically. Democracy, freedom, demonstrations,
socialism, communism and what not may be all right
for Western societies, but the trouble with the West is
that they try so hard to export all of these to us too,
as they did with their gun-boats and their Christianity
in past centuries.

What is wrong with us Siamese as well as with the
Japanese and, indeed, with most other Asians, is that
we accept all these too easily in order to prove that we
are superior, to prove that we are equal to the West.
Hence we have all been subjected to Western intellectual
imperialism, while political imperialism has come to an
end. Soon economic imperialism, too, will have to go.
But the East, the Japanese in particular, will not be

able to play a very positive role unless and until they get rid of Western intellectual imperialism.

In the West, no doubt due to the Protestant ethic, people have to compete to survive; they have to rush to get there first. One can see now that with such ethics, such a society becomes more and more unlivable — hence hippies, hence the quest for Zen in the West, hence the slogan of "keep cool and go slow."

What the new generation in the West is seeking we already have here in the East, at least in Japan, but we ignore it. We do not bother about it. It would not really be a bad thing to take time and go slow. I think the Japanese read far too much and what they read is usually of Western origin. I think they ought to read less and think more. It wouldn't do them any harm to be a little detached from society, to be a little detached from themselves in order to conserve inner strength, and then one can contribute much more positively to society in the long run.

Kingsley Martin once said that it doesn't really solve human problems to rush to the moon. The future of mankind rests with moral commitment, personal, national, and international. Unless we have time to think about our own destiny and commitment as well as that of others, about misery and poverty, we shall never come to the crux of the problem. Many rich people are really poor at heart. Many people who lead a gay life are really trying to escape from their inner misery, and if they never look within they never find themselves. If they do not know about themselves, they cannot lead their lives properly. And if they cannot lead their own lives properly, they simply cannot lead others. I hope that new leadership will emerge in Japan, leadership which knows more about itself, about its society, and its traditional values. Only with this new kind of leadership in the political, economic, academic as well as in the intellectual arena, could Japan or indeed any rich country play a more positive role internationally; for if a country is not motivated by selfish goals, and such a country has some spiritual depth and cultural value, she can contribute something positive to her neighbors whom she regards as equal partners and friends.

This is not wishful thinking on my part, for I agree with Watsuji Tetsuro who said some time ago that "Japanese culture has a multi-structure. The old element is not lost when a new one is introduced, but the new is added to the old." At present, the Japanese may seem a little too enthusiastic about Western progress and materialism, at the expense of their older and deeper treasures, Buddhism and Confucianism. The day will come, the sooner the better, when Japan will be enjoying her cultural and spiritual depth. She will then be in a good position to play an international role with wisdom and compassion. Thank you.

BUDDHISM AND DEVELOPMENT
IS SMALL BEAUTIFUL?

The Venerable Buddhadāsa Bhikkhu, a famous Siamese Buddhist monk, once remarked that the word "development" in its Pali or Sanskrit equivalent means "disorderliness" or "confusion," and in Buddhism "development" refers either to progress or regress. In a similar vein, Ivan Illich once told me that the Latin word *progressio*, which is the root idea of "development," can mean "madness" also.

When we look at what is happening in the world today, where national development is being so much emphasized, especially in the so-called underdeveloped or the developing world, it is difficult to contradict what these two religious leaders were implying. The further development has proceeded, the more it has resulted in the rich becoming richer, while the poor remain poor or become even poorer — and the rich are still not happier. Nature and the environment are deteriorating day by day. Animal life and other natural resources are increasingly wasted for selfish purposes to such an extent that some of the world's leading professionals, who organized the Club of Rome, have prophesized that unless mankind makes some fundamental changes in its world view, continued development may result in the ruin or destruction of the world within this generation or the next. Is this overly pessimistic?

In fact, development may be viewed from either of two aspects: quantity or quality. This does not mean that the two are mutually exclusive, for quantity and quality are quite inseparable. But the question is, which one is to be viewed as basic and which one as secondary?

Accepting quantity as the basic factor, one can measure the results of development in terms of physical things, things that can be measured or touched such as the increase in income, factories, schools, hospitals, buildings, food, clothing, the labor force, etc., assuming that these are all good things, and that the more the quantity increases the more the quality automatically is increased. But the question is, is this a correct assumption? As I have suggested, it is now clear that it is not correct.

Accepting quality as the basic factor, one can measure the results by looking at human beings themselves. But one must view people in relation to their full potentiality. It is not correct to say that when people have enough to live on without starving and are free from disease, that they have sufficiency, even though they may lack freedom and liberty; or to say that it will be quite satisfactory if only *most* of society can be developed in a material or quantitative sense. Is it not true that those who have become excited about the successes of China or Russia have not considered people in their wholeness? I don't want to belittle those two countries, especially China, which has developed so far materially. We must admit that China has had no small success. But if you say that such societies have also been successful in the matter of the quality of human life, I would have to disagree. Most of those who praise such societies have no desire to go and join them, unless there is no other option. To put it another way, development through socialistic communism only becomes possible when no other way is open, for people want to realize their full humanity. The four Buddhist "requisites" (food, clothing, shelter and medicine) help only to keep one alive. But people want and need to go further and search out their own abilities as far as possible, and then to use these hidden abilities to the fullest extent, through social or institutional structures for the general welfare. To put it in religious terms, this has to do with the sacredness or the special quality which man has. In this view development must at every step take into account the essence of humanity. It must deal with the question, "What is man, and what should man be?" Development in this sense will not overlook the need for the four requisites, for they are necessary for life itself. But they are not sufficient. Emphasis should not be put on luxuries beyond the four requisites, while some fellow humans still do not have enough of the four requisites to sustain life. Emphasis should be placed on the *quality* of human life, moving beyond the supplying of the bare necessities of living, to bring human life its highest fulfillment.

The problem in qualitative development lies in the difficulty of identifying and measuring qualitative results. Planners on the whole, whether in the East or the West, do not want to take the time to study the complicated problems having to do with ultimate goals of humanity. They excuse themselves by saying it is a problem of metaphysics or of religion, as though ultimate goals are beyond the ability of common people to discuss or understand. Philosophers and theologians or religious leaders are not without fault in this, as they do not give sufficient attention to using language that common people can understand, or they show obvious disdain for non-religious people, while at the same time they evidence little interest in the development plans of experts in other fields. Or they simply occupy themselves with things that have little to do with the life and death matters of people. They spend their time on trivia and on the outward forms of religion, emphasizing this or that aspect of theology or of ceremony, and some even make their religion into a business.

Because of the failure of development to take quality into account due to the difficulty of assessing results, and because of the refusal to examine the essence of true humanity, development generally is simply a matter of quantity. The greater the development in society, the more complex society becomes, until development requires people with highly specialized knowledge who find it difficult to be interested in the wider problems of humanity. Even their language becomes so technical that only their own inner circle can understand it. (In this respect those who set themselves up as religious experts are no different from other experts.) What is worse is that it is possible for these experts to measure results in terms of their own success, in their own profession, with scarcely any consideration given to whether or not society has been bettered or not. For instance, success in religion is measured in terms of the number of churches or temples built, their beauty, the income of the religious organization, increase in membership, and the quantity of material published, without necessarily taking any note of possible change in the basic humanity or character of the members, their self-sacrifice, or their true neighborly love, not to mention any improvement or deterioration in matters of the mind or purity of spirit. In the field of educational development, success is spoken of in terms of the increase in the number of students and schools, and the expansion of curriculum, with no method of determining to what extent, if any, the studies are helpful to the students. In the medical field, what seems to count is the number of doctors and hospitals, or the public health budget. This or that country is held up as an example of medical leadership because of heart transplants or kidney transplants, or the prevention of this or that disease, without taking note of the fact that in that country everyone has become a patient and no one has any ability to take care of himself. They have become totally dependent on doctors. A simple headache or a slight fever, and they must rush to a clinic or the hospital. Even an argument between a man and wife requires the services of a psychiatrist. Moreover, it can be asked, to what extent is modern medicine responsible for the population explosion? In the field of transportation, success is measured in terms of speed. Some people have to spend most of their time traveling, while many more people don't even have a chance to leave their village. Yet there is no consideration given to the question whether it is beneficial or detrimental to leave one's village or to be able to go where one wants to go.

Even worse is the fact that economists measure success in terms of increased production, and so must turn to industrialization, to the profit motive. And it is the economists who are most influential in development planning. As a result development becomes supremely a matter of economics and politics. For economists see development in terms of increasing currency and things, thus fostering greed *(lobha)*. Politicians see development in terms of increased power thus fostering ill-will *(dosa)*. Both then work together, hand in glove, and measure the results in terms of quantity, thus fostering ignorance *(moha)*, and completing the Buddhist triad of evils. This is illustrated by the fact that almost every country aims to increase the gross national product, to increase the trade balance, to increase exports, to expand its industry, to expand building construction, etc. As for *people*, they are considered only as the labor force and as consumers. So people have value only as a means to make the numerical statistics of success look good on paper. No consideration is given to the fact that those people must endure tyranny, and are taken advantage of, while nature around them and their own style of living deteriorate. Take as an example the construction of a new industrial plant in a developing country for which modern machinery is brought in from abroad, with foreign experts brought in to run it;

it is financed from abroad, but *local* laborers are used, who must work hard at boring tasks for a small wage, while the factory spews out wastes night and day. Who profits from this? Does this type of development reduce the poverty of the worker or not? How much does it help to bring about social and ecomomic equality? Does it contribute to the peace and well-being of society as a whole and to the conservation of the natural environment? Of what value is it, apart from the fact that the foreign investors, along with a few local investors who usually have political interests at stake, accumulate wealth, while oppressing their own countrymen and obstructing them from having economic and political power on, or near a level with their own? The tourist industry and the hotels should ask themselves these same questions. But to even ask these questions is considered to be obstructive to development and progress. For it is difficult to measure how much so-called progress might be an impediment to a true human society, or might destroy the old culture and the quality of life. Economists and politicians usually give the matter no thought, but they continually mouth phrases about how concerned they are.

It may seem that I am not being fair to the economists, although I have taught philosophy in the Faculty of Economics at Thammasat University in Bangkok, but I would like here to show the weakness of some basic theories of that school of economists which emphasizes "development" and which measures results in terms of mathematical figures having to do

with the gross national product, the gross domestic
product, and the per capita income. If there are
any economists here, please forgive the limits of my
exposition.

When economists or members of any National Economic Development Board announce that the Gross
National Product (GNP) has increased by 8% they are
quoting a figure which amounts to taking the year's
production and services increase of 10% and subtrac-
ting the year's population increase of 2%. If the
increase holds steady over a few years, then the economists will say the country has reached self-sustaining
growth. This method of figuring is used as the basis of
Rostow's theory in regard to "take-off," and is used
in development planning.

The question we need to ask is whether it is legiti-
mate to average this increase out in terms of per capita
income, as is done. For instance, when the GNP
increases by 8% it may be that 80% of the increase
goes to only 10% of the population, while the other
90% of the population divides up the remaining 20%.
This is what usually happens in the developing countries, so that the rich get richer and the poor poorer.
But economists of this school maintain that a better
division cannot yet be made, that it is not yet possible
to take justice or economic equality into consideration.
If we did, there would be no economic progress, and
self-sustaining economic growth or the take-off point
would not be reached. So it can be seen that in such
countries as Siam, the Philippines, Korea, Malaysia,
and Singapore, equal opportunity is lacking to a great

extent. While a few are at ease, the majority are poor, because the economists argue that for fast progress to be made it is necessary to keep the laborers and the majority of the people down, in order that foreigners and capitalists will be willing to invest. For they must keep costs low and make a fast profit if they are to continue to invest. When this happens the gross national product will increase.

This type of thinking is inescapably related to capitalistic thought which holds that the more goods increase, with the least interference, the greater the progress. Capitalistic business has only this as its goal. The goal is to make the highest profit possible by keeping the money in the hands of a few, in order to make larger investments, in order to produce more things. So production and consumption are emphasized. Advertising becomes important in order to increase greediness, and usually lust is a part of the advertising also, since greed and lust usually strengthen each other. So almost every type of advertising, in addition to luring people to want unnecessary things, will include sensual pictures.

This kind of development is always accompanied by some kind of incentive to make people want, to thirst, to desire; and the desire is usually for worldly or material things. If people were temperate in their desires, being satisfied in the material sense with the four Buddhist requisites, or a little more which might be necessary for life, in order to give them the opportunity to develop their potentialities — with each one wanting to help the other as was typical of our Buddhist village life in former times, then capitalism would fail. Is not this the reason that western imperialism, which went to Asia along with capitalism, looks down upon the former Asian way of life as backward and uncivilized — because that kind of life provides no incentive to buy foreign goods, nor is it anxious to exploit natural resources to the maximum?

In the light of this, is it putting it too strongly to say that it is impossible for anyone who loves a peaceful life and contentment, and has an honest desire to help others, in other words anyone who takes his religion seriously, to approve national development on capitalistic lines?

By taking one's religion seriously I mean, by getting down to the heart of religion, not simply being strict about non-essentials and presenting a false front, like those Buddhists who won't slap a mosquito but have no compunction about loaning money out at exorbitant interest, or those Christians who go to church every Sunday while they use crooked business methods, even taking excessive profit from the sale of grain to feed orphans, or those Moslems who refuse to eat pork but defile themselves by devious dealing and lasciviousness, and give support to politicians who cheat the people by various devices. Is it not because of hypocrites such as these that young people turn away from religion? As one Hindu said, his father was very dishonest, but that was all right, since he was very religious — making pilgrimages, praying, and bathing in the Ganges to wash his sins away.

Religious truth is the pinnacle of religion, but it must have morality or decency as its base. Otherwise, religion is indeed an opiate, or a mask for evil people to use in reaping profits from those who are more stupid than they are.

When an economic system, based on a capitalistic market economy, requires increasing greed, both in the producer and in the consumer, can any religion encourage it?

The producer must find a way to invest his money that will bring him the greatest return, without regard to the disappearance of natural resources, or to the fact that he may be producing luxury goods. While 80-90% of the people in the world do not have the basic necessities of life, if it is possible to realize a large profit by using natural resources to produce luxuries for 1% of the people, this type of developer is only too happy to do it. When one part of the world has an overabundance of corn or wheat, they gladly burn it to raise the price even higher. Especially in developing countries, one can see the emphasis given to the hotel industry, tourism, and places catering to the physical pleasures of man, rather than to agriculture or the production of the basic requirements of food, clothing and medicine, because the more advanced nations maintain control of the markets.

The capitalistic system aims for profit, not for the general welfare of the public. Capitalists may indulge in some philanthropy, as long as the majority of the people remain under their control. But since profit is their goal, they must take every advantage they can, beginning with taking advantage of the workers and finally taking advantage of the consumers. The extent to which advantage is taken varies. In countries where labor unions are strong, where the government officials are fairly honest and efficient, and where the consumers keep up with the producers by their own organizations to test quality against price, the producers must have a higher ethical standard. In countries where these conditions do not exist, the proportion of dishonesty is higher.

Consumers ordinarily have modest desires unless they are especially stimulated to want and to buy. But in a capitalistic system the mass media are used to stimulate desire for things that are not really needed. Consumers are forced to choose between brands which in fact may be identical. The consumer becomes a victim of advertising. The claim that capitalism gives freedom to the people, by providing freedom of choice, is less than true. For advertising companies determine in large part what is to be sold, and they together with the multinational corporations deceive the people in such a way that they scarcely realize they are being duped. This is not real freedom. In countries under a dictatorship, at least the people know that the government is propagandizing them, for the propaganda is usually quite crude. But deception is more difficult to perceive when it is based on the encouragement of greed, either by using fancy decoration or by advertising methods. In such countries, wherever electricity is brought, no matter how poor a family is, it feels it must buy a television set. TV plays a most important part in the deception of the public, since it is held up as a status symbol. It is pictured as improving the way of life, so that people will sell their land if necessary to buy a TV. This is but one example of tricks to induce people to buy; time payment is another.

People seem to measure development in terms of their own personal increase in new and expensive goods.

Because greed is the boss in this type of development, it causes an increase in cross-purposes and conflict; people increasingly take advantage of and oppress one another; cheating, swindling and crooked tricks inevitably follow. This is the truly materialistic way of life. Yet many nations admit with a rueful smile that this is also the way of development.

It is true that there are ways to correct the bad image of capitalism to some extent, at least since the time when Maynard Keynes of England attempted to improve its image by injecting some socialism. He tried to reduce the lust for things and to give some purpose beyond profit to the capitalists, so they would use at least part of their profits for the benefit of society. But capitalism was still capitalism. Even though the capitalists helped their neighbors to some extent, their basic purpose was selfish, and they only tried to disguise the fact a little more than formerly. Their way of life still emphasized physical pleasure and prestige, only not quite so obviously as before.

Can this way of life be accepted by one who turns for refuge to the Buddha? Whether or not we accept Weber's theory, it is a sad fact of history that capitalism grew and prospered first in Christian society. And the more capitalism flourished, the further that society separated itself from Jesus Christ. Today capitalistic society has begun to flourish in Buddhist society. Though our Thai forebears were forced to accept it, yet we, or at least those of our number who now hold the reins of power in Siam, have gladly accepted capitalism, even to the point where they have laid the plans for development along capitalist lines, and it is now a question as to whether or not they are any longer Buddhist, regardless of what they say.

What is worse is that the majority of religious leaders, whether sons of the Buddha or followers of Christ, have flocked into the capitalist camp.

We should note plainly at this point that it is not only the capitalist system that has been increasing the gross national product as its goal of development. The socialist countries of Eastern Europe use the same standard as capitalist societies in measuring the results of development. And why shouldn't they? Their eldest sister, the Soviet Union, took the lead.

In terms of human values, countries that take their refuge in materialism, no matter to what ideological camp they belong, scarcely differ in their end results. Eric Fromm has said, "The Russians think of themselves as the representatives of socialism, because they use Marxist ideological terminology, not realizing how closely their system resembles the fully developed capitalist system. We in the Western camp, on the other hand, believe we are the representatives of an individualism which encourages each person to take the initiative, with a humanitarian ethical system; thinking that these are our ideals. But we fail to see that in truth many of our own social institutions closely resemble those of the communism which we detest."

Development which has quantity as its basic goal has many weaknesses as we have pointed out. It is not that economists are not aware of the weaknesses. As Keynes once attempted to correct the weaknesses of capitalism, so more recently the United Nations Social Development Research Institute has sought ways by which income might be more nearly equalized throughout society. It is an admirable effort and should be encouraged. But to date it has failed.

The institute mentioned above has listed about seventy-seven items which can be assumed to be important in development, including such things as long life, sufficient vitamins in the diet, the number of pupils enrolled in school, the number of people who use electricity, the numerical ratio of buildings to people, the opportunity of access to radios and television, the amount of agricultural produce in relation to the number of male farm workers, the use of currency in exchange for food, etc. It is held that the more improvement and expansion in these items, the greater the development. This means that the institute is attempting to turn the members of the United Nations away from their pre-occupation with increasing the national income as the goal of development, and to lead them to make a more just and equitable distribution of the income.

This is a real step forward, yet it still does not go beyond the usual quantitative definition of development. Measurements are still made in terms of quantity. None of the seventy-seven items can be used to measure life qualitatively. And this method does not take into consideration the means used in increasing production, but simply assumes that the more production the better, as long as there is a just distribution.

So we can say that the error in development lies in making quantity its goal, in continually trying to measure results in terms of materialism and "modernity." This type of thinking has its roots in Western Europe at the time of the industrial revolution. But the question is not asked as to whether this way of life is really desirable or not. Rather the social order of the Westerner is simply accepted as the goal, as the model to imitate, and the only question asked is how many years will it be before a country like Siam will catch up with England or Japan or Russia or the United States?

I am glad to say that leading thinkers, including economists, now see more clearly that this type of development solves no problems. The United States, which once was the land of dreams of the free world, is full of social injustice and poverty within, and takes unfair advantage of countries outside its boundaries.

It has food to throw away, and with only 6% of the world's population, it consumes almost 50% of the world's irreplaceable natural resources. At the same time, the rich become drug addicts, crime increases, and the old Christian values are given up. This seems to be happening all over the country that once was held up as the prime example of this type of development.

It is evident that our world is caught up in a cycle. Especially in quantitative development, the further it goes the more problems appear, faster than they can be solved, and the technocrats are not able to stop the spiralling because (1) they are afraid that if the quantity is not increased everything will come to a standstill. Or all the systems will go haywire leading to possible ruin. For instance, the population will increase and there will be insufficient food, leading to clashes. Actually in this regard there is enough food, if it were distributed equitably and used without waste. The problem is that those who have the surplus refuse to share it, because (2) they want to maintain the status of the rich. Their hope is that by increasing production most of the poor will receive a portion of the increase, continually raising their standards. But our nature is such that once we ourselves have become more comfortably situated, even though we see some injustices appearing, we don't get much excited about them if they don't touch us too much. Besides, if we do something about them, we might get hurt.

Is it not for these reasons that development has worked out in such a way that the gap has grown between the rich and the poor, and between the wealthy nations and the poor nations? In Siam, since development planning began, a few wealthy people in Bangkok have become continually wealthier, while the people of the northeast have become poorer, not to mention conditions in other parts of the country. And up until now, there has been no indication (including the present dictatorial regime which is a swing from the former democracy) that my country is considering a change in its development policies, but it goes blithely on following the blueprints of the capitalist economists. If anyone raises objections to these methods or this type of thinking, he is labelled a rabble-rouser, a proponent of communism, or else he is accused of disloyalty to the Nation, Religion and the King. Is it not time that we should speak the truth, and especially those who hold themselves to be religious? We must be honest, and if we are honest, we must admit that this type of development has not added to the happiness of the people in any real human sense, but on the contrary has taken a form that to a greater or lesser extent is permeated throughout with crooked deceptions. Moreover, we must not forget that the increase in production through the use of modern machinery to exploit natural resources cannot go on forever. Oil, coal, and iron, once they are gone, cannot be brought back.   As for the forests and some wild animals, when they are depleted, if they are to be brought back, it won't be in our time or our children's time. Production on a grand scale not only uses up the raw materials, it also destroys the environment, poisoning the air and the water, the fish and the fields, so that people are forced to ingest poison continually. But we do not need to expand further on how man takes advantage of his fellowman.

In short, any country that feels itself so inferior as to call itself developing or underdeveloped, cannot and should not try to raise itself up through this kind of quantitative development in order to put itself on a par with those nations which brag that they are developed.

It cannot do so because, as Everett Reimer has said, if every country be like the United States, "the oil consumption would be increased fifty times, iron one hundred times, and other metals two hundred times. And the United States itself would have to triple its use of these materials simply in the process of production itself." There are not enough raw materials in the world to do this, nor would the atmosphere be able to take the change. The world as we know it would come to an end.

You will, no doubt, surmise that I do not agree with that form of development which aims at quantity, and even not that form of development which has as its objective the improvement of the quality of human life, yet still stresses material things, In reality, the latter, too, diminishes the quality of human life.

It is not only that materialism fosters violence, but modern applied science also destroys the values of time and space. To a materialist civilization, time means only that which a clock can measure in terms of work-days, work-hours, work-minutes. Space simply has three dimensions which are filled with material things. That is why Buddhadāsa says development means confusion, for it assumes the more the merrier, the longer one's life the better, with no thought of measuring the real value of a long evil life as against that of a short good life. This is contrary to the teaching of the Buddha, who said the life of a good man, however short it may be, is more valuable than that of an evil one, however long he lives.

As a matter of fact, it is only religion, which puts material things in second place and keeps the ultimate goals of development in sight, that can bring out the true value in human development. For even in the matter of judging the value of development, from the point of view of ethics and morality, it is difficult to keep material considerations from being the sole criteria.

From the Buddhist point of view, development must aim at the reduction of craving, the avoidance of violence, and the development of the spirit rather than of material things. As each individual progresses, he increasingly helps others without waiting for the millennium, or for the ideal socialist society. Cooperation is better than competition, whether of the capitalist variety which favors the capitalist, or the socialist variety which favors the laborer.

From the standpoint of religion, the goal can be attained by stages as evil desires are overcome. So goals are perceived in two ways. From the worldly standpoint, the more desires are increased or satisfied the further development can proceed. From the religious standpoint, the more desires can be reduced the further development can proceed.

Western civilization erodes Christianity, or at least real Christian spiritual values, and becomes merely capitalistic or socialistic, aimsing to increase material goods in order to satisfy craving. The capitalist variety wants to raise the material standard of living of other groups, if possible, providing the capitalists themselves can stay on top. The socialist variety reverses it and wants the majority, or those who act in the name of the majority, to oppress the minority or those who are opposed to them.

The value scale of Western-type development emphasizes extremes. The richer the better; the capitalists apply this to the wealthy, and the socialists to the laborer. The quicker the better. The bigger the better. The more knowledge the better. Buddhism, on the other hand, emphasizes the *middle way* between extremes, a moderation which strikes a balance appropriate to the balance of nature itself. Knowledge must be a complete knowledge of nature, in order to be wisdom; otherwise, knowledge is ignorance. Partial knowledge leads to delusion, and encourages the growth of greed and hate. These are the roots of evil that lead to ruin. The remedy is the threefold way of self-knowledge, leading to right speech and action and right relations to other people and things (morality), consideration of the inner truth of one's own spirit and of nature (meditation), leading finally to enlightenment or complete knowledge (wisdom). It is an awakening, and a complete awareness of the world.

When one understands this, one understands the three characteristics of all things from the Buddhist point of view: their unsatisfactoriness, their impermanence, and their lack of a permanent selfhood.

True development will arrange for the rhythm of life and movement to be in accordance with the facts, while maintaining an awareness that man is but a part of the universe, and that ways must be found to integrate mankind with the laws of nature. There must be no boasting, no proud self-centered attempts to master nature, no emphasis placed on the creation of material things to the point where people become slaves to things and have no time left for themselves to search after the truth which is out beyond the realm of material things.

In 1929, Max Scheler formulated a remark which is just as true today as then. He said,

We have never before seriously faced the question whether the entire development of Western civilization, that one-sided and over-active process of expansion outward, might not ultimately be an attempt using unsuitable means — if we lose sight of the complementary art of inner self-control over our entire underdeveloped and otherwise involuntary psychological life, an art of meditation, search of soul, and forbearance. We must learn anew to envisage the great, invisible solidarity of all living beings in universal life, of all minds in the eternal spirit — and at the same time the mutual solidarity of the world process and the destiny of its supreme principle, and we must not just accept this world unity as a mere doctrine, but practise and promote it in our inner and outer lives.

This is indeed the spirit of Buddhist development where the inner strength must be cultivated first; then compassion and loving-kindness to others become possible. Work and play would be interchangeable. There is no need to regard work as something which has to be done, has to be bargained for, in order to get more wages or in order to get more leisure time. Work ethics would be not to get ahead of others but to enjoy one's work and to work in harmony with others. Materially there may not be too much to boast about, but the simple life ought to be comfortable enough, and simple food is less harmful to the body and mind. Besides, simple diet could be produced without exploiting nature, and one would then need not keep animals merely for the sake of man's food.

In *Small Is Beautiful*, E. F. Schumacher reminds us that Western economists go for maximization of developmental goals in a material sense so that they hardly care for people. He suggests Buddhist economics as a study of economics as if people mattered. He says that in the Buddhist concept of development, we should avoid gigantism, especially of machines, which tend to control rather than to serve man. With, gigantism, men are driven by an excessive greed in violating and raping nature. If these two extremes (bigness and greed) could be avoided, the Middle Path of Buddhist development could be achieved, i.e., both the world of industry and agriculture could be converted into a meaningful habitat for man.

I agree with Schumacher that small is beautiful in the Buddhist concept of development, but what he did not stress is that cultivation must first come from *within*. In the Sinhalese experience, the Sarvodaya Shramadana movement applies Buddhism to the individual first. Through cultivated individuals a village is developed, then several villages, leading to the nation and the world.

The guideline for the movement is the use of the Four Sublime Abodes *(Brahma Vihāra)* to develop each individual. The steps to be taken are as follows:

1) *Mettā:* Loving kindness towards oneself and others. We all desire happiness. We should try to be happy. Through the precepts and meditation, a happiness state could be created. The mind will feel amity and harmony with oneself as with others. It renders assistance and benefits without ill-will, without the malice of anger and of competition. Once one is tranquil and happy, this tranquillity and happiness could spread to others as well.

2) *Karuṇā:* Compassion can only be cultivated when one recognizes the suffering of others and wants to bring that suffering to an end. A rich man who does not care for the miserable conditions of the poor lacks this quality. It is difficult for him to develop himself, to be a better man. Those who shut themselves in ivory towers in the midst of an unjust world cannot be called compassionate. In Mahāyāna Buddhism, one should vow to become a Bodhisattva who will forego his own nirvāna until all sentient beings are free from suffering. So one should not remain indifferent, but must endeavour to assist others to alleviate their suffering as much as one can.

3) *Muditā:* Sympathetic Joy is a condition of the mind which rejoices when others are happy or successful in any number of ways. One feels this without envy, especially when a competitor is getting ahead.

4) *Upekkhā:* Equanimity means the mind is cultivated until it becomes evenly balanced. It becomes neutral. Whether one faces success or failure, whether one is confronted with prosperity or adversity, for oneself or for others, one is not moved by it. Whatever one cannot do to help others, one is not disturbed about it (having tried one's best).

The Four Sublime Abodes should be developed step by step from the first to the last. Even when one is not perfect, one must set one's mind toward this goal, otherwise one's dealing with others will tend to be harmful—to oneself and to others—one way or the other.

Having developed oneself toward happiness and tranquillity rather than toward worldly success and material progress, then a Buddhist is in a position to develop his community, starting with his family and his village. He must first be awake before he can awake others. An individual who is awake is called *Purisodaya.* By sharing his awakening with others, the whole village could become awake—*Gamodaya.* Once several villages awake, the whole nation could perhaps be saved from materialism and Western economic development models. In the case of Sri Lanka and Burma, when proper efforts are put along these lines, the chance is greater than in the case of Siam, which lost so much confidence

in the Buddhist heritage (especially among the ruling
elites). The Western developmental process has been
accelerated far too much during the last two decades.
But, of course, if Siam could free herself from being a
junior ally of the USA, and also be saved from Communist aggression, she too could have a good chance to
opt for the Middle Path of development and become a
Desodaya, an awakening nation. The hope for several
nations to awake so that the world could be saved and
we would reach the state of universal awakening for all—
Sarvodaya — at this stage is very remote. Yet, we must
not despair, and we must live in hope and practise what
we can.

In the Buddhist experience of Sri Lanka, the driving
force to develop from the village level upward comes
from the Buddha's teaching of the Four Wheels. As
a cart moves steadily on four wheels, likewise human
development should rest on the four *dhammas*, namely,
Sharing, Pleasant Speech, Constructive Action, and
Equality.

1) One must share *(dāna)* what one has with others – be
   it goods, money, knowledge, time, labor, or what
   have you. This is still practised in most village
   cultures. Sharing does not mean giving away what
   one does not want, or giving in order to get more.
   We should strengthen the Buddhist concept of *dāna*
   practised in the villages and spread it to counteract
   the invasion of materialism and the new value system
   of competition – by sharing, by giving freely rather
   than by buying and selling. In Ceylon, they share
   labor, with Buddhist ceremonies in the background,

as the Siamese still do in remote villages where they find such fun in work.

2) Pleasant Speech *(Piyavācā)* not only means polite talk, but means speaking truthfully and sincerely, regarding everyone as equal. This too is strong in village culture, although villages have received glamorous propaganda treatment by politicians and advertisers, who are full of deceit and make one buy things one does not really need, or make one hope for something which is not really possible.

3) Constructive Action *(atthacariyā)* means working for each other's benefit. Here Schumacher's recommendation for intermediate technology and the proper use of land would be relevant.

4) Equality *(samānattatā)* means that Buddhism does not recognize classes or castes, does not encourage one group to exploit the other. So Buddhist socialism is possible, without state capitalism or any form of totalitarianism.

The development toward Buddhist socialism means that equality, love, freedom, and liberation would be the goal. A Buddhist community – be it a village or a nation – would work for harmony and for awakening, by getting rid of selfishness of any kind – be it greed, hatred or delusion. Such a development would entail truth, beauty, and goodness – be it big or small.

III

RELIGION AND SOCIAL JUSTICE

A BUDDHIST RESPONSE TO TERRORISM

Editor's Introduction

In the fall of 1973 (as predicted by Sulak on page 18 above) the military dictatorship fell because of a popular outpouring of protests in Bangkok, and a democratic regime was established. But all was not solved. Democracy can be chaotic, and those who wanted to regain power (the rich and military leaders) had their own means of retaliation, namely, assassination. As Sulak himself observed (in an interview in the *Bangkok Bank Monthly Review*, December 1975):

> By comparison with many other countries in the world, Siam now seems to enjoy an admirable degree of freedom of expression, but the impression is deceiving. Compare Siam with the Philippines and Malaysia where the regimes are openly oppressive and where dissidents are quickly jailed. The Thai Government has not, it is true, clamped down on protestors or closed newspapers, but one must not ignore the fact that over 20 farmers' leaders and other activists have been assassinated over the past year or so.

> I would prefer that the Thai Government were to emulate the Philippines and Malaysia, locking people up, closing papers. Under such circumstances at least you know where you stand. In Siam at present one feels very insecure. One cannot blame

Kukrit or the Cabinet; no one knows who is doing it. All we know is that it is a group that is threatened with the loss of its privileges. Without a clear-cut hierarchical chain of command, one cannot tell where the orders are coming from. For me these assassinations, up and down the country, are much more barbaric, sinister and unintelligent than the open, systematic controls imposed in some other nations ...

These movements [among industrial workers and farmers] existed even before 1973, and I was involved in their formation. They were there for a long time, but they were suppressed, so we met illegally, tried to make use of the universities, working under the auspices of various organizations. Now they have the opportunity of becoming legal, open and above-board, and now their leaders are being shot, killed, assassinated.

They are learning a very hard lesson. If only those in authority would try to understand. These people are not hard-headed, and their demands are very understandable. They have been extremely patient, they have refused to take up arms, and now they are accused of being communists; they have not only been accused, but they have been shot without trial, throughout the country and particularly in the North ...

We ought to be able to understand each other, to tolerate and to talk each other's language, to preserve our Thai-ness, our sense of humour. But there is no sense of humour in those who are shooting the farmers. This frightens me and prompts me to suspect that we are losing our sense of direction, our common sense that has got us through so many difficult periods in history. However, I am convinced that we are not all that wicked, nor all that stupid. Siam has always found a way to get through; we do not like extremes, you know.

By 1976 the killing had increased and Sulak played an active role among Buddhist and Christian leaders to take counter-measures. The "Declaration" printed below from *Visakha Puja* B. E. 2519 (1976) is the result.

In late 1976, the government itself had fallen, and Sulak was arrested in abstentia. The next summer, while still in exile, he presented a fuller explanation of his Buddhist position on non-violence as part of the Berry Lecture series, Department of Religion, University of Hawaii.

The first article in this section, however, was delivered to religious groups and reveals Sulak siding with the ideals of the young and being extremely harsh with the failings of their elders.

SOME ASPECTS OF YOUTH IN ASIA

There are certain basic points about Asia that are important to bear in mind, although most of us here are Asians. First, Asia is 80-90% rural, which means that 9 out of 10 Asians spend their time tilling the soil and caring for life's basic needs, enduring the hardship of status quo existence. Those of us in the establishment know or care very little about the rural youth. Above the villagers stand the political and economic elites, born of a colonial past and collaborators today with foreign interests. The life of the privileged elite and the life of the commoner cannot be compared. The elite youth is much cared for, since most of them are our children, or children of our friends and relatives. When we say that the number of secondary school students in the world doubled in fifteen years between 1950 and 1965, and the number of college and university students registered a phenomenal increase of 61% from 1960 to 1965, we mean specifically this category, since peasants' children, for the most part, do not continue beyond primary education. Most of the latter, in fact, remain illiterate. If they are no longer able to endure farming, they are driven to migrate into a worse condition in the slum areas of big cities, where unemployment and drug situations await them. To see the contrast in this very city, one only has to visit Forbes Park and Magsaysay village.

As for the educated youth, most countries have taken concrete steps towards formulating and implementing programmes for them. However, in most cases, those initiatives have been taken on an ad hoc, sporadic basis, mainly to meet the demands of the vocal sections of the citizenry. There has been very little effort to integrate the young people into the main stream of society.

It is natural that the younger generation with some education should question the decision of their elders, since policies in almost every sphere of life will effect both their present and future lives. Unfortunately, there has been an element of suspicion on the part of elders, the establishment and governments in dealing with young people in almost every Asian country.

We of the older generation tend to think that youth have rejected the values of their parents. They have created their own culture, their own politics and their own symbols for communicating with each other. We seem to forget that among us there is a great disparity between creed and deed. In many cases, it is not true that the young have rejected the values of their parents.

In 1971 there was an uprising in Ceylon and a great number of young people were slaughtered. An Anglican monk, Sevaka Yohan Devananda, wrote the following poem:

When a poor man
in desperation,
gets drunk,
picks a quarrel,
draws a knife,
kills,
that, obviously, is murder — violence,

punishable by death.
When company directors
sack workers with impunity
and so condemn whole families
to penury and want,
that is not violence,
because no knife has been used.
No knife need be used
a peremptory word suffices
labour tribunals need not be feared overmuch,
loopholes can be found, law delays, political influence.

When politicians and government officials whatever the
party in power ignore basic needs and just complaints
of the people,
on a vast scale,
daily, continuously,
that is not violence
because no blows have been dealt
visibly, materially.
No blows need be dealt
because
power, authority, influence
is on their side,
and the might of the armed services and police
stands behind them.
When religious leaders—
Church dignitaries, mahanayaka theras,
church committees, dayaka sabhas
embrace vested interests, exert various dubious moral
pressures,
enjoin passive compliance on the people,

in the name of religion and peace,
that is not violence—
only religious obligation and duty.
They talk endlessly, mouthing empty phrases
in out-dated language
on abstruse doctrines,
slaves to useless customs and superstitious ceremonies,
raising funds continuously
from the people
for buildings and institutions
and for bolstering their tottering position and prestige.
But they are silent and inactive
on the things that really matter,
the things that really concern people—
social change, land reform, employment,
human relationships, human dignity,
involvement with the people,
being alongside the people

in dialogue;
for without dialogue,
without a truly sensitive and truly human relationship,
there can be no inspiration,
no teaching—no learning
no communion.
So our religious leaders, by and large,
remain aloof, out-of-touch, clueless,
irrelevant,
unheeding and unheeded.

And what about the police and the armed forces?
Immaculate in shining uniform and belt,
they march faultlessly in step.

Supposed to be symbolic
of discipline, of controlled strength.
But their basic method, tactic, with the people—
a sound thrashing—guilty or not guilty.
Everyone knows it.
How do they keep the peace?
If a policeman's hat is filched,
the offender may have to pay for it with his life.
If a soldier is actually hurt,
a whole village may be destroyed.
Utterly disproportionate retaliation,
that is the order of the day
the cement of our society,
violence.

What the poem says is not only a reflection on Sri Lanka, it is also true for most of our Asian countries. Alongside the rising discontent and frequent social and political protests, student groups desire to reform the artificial barriers between the role of the student and that of the teacher, and to participate actively in the educational process. They demand changes in the content of education to make it more relevant to their concerns in all fields, whether social, political, cultural, or religious. In short, the unrest of the youth of today reflects a yearning of the young people for participation in solving their own problems and in changing the large society which they reject in its present form; along with such participation, the young people seek emancipation from old customs and shackles and a new sense of equality with adults in terms of rights and freedoms.

88

The Catholic Church obviously realizes this, as it has said, "To be attuned to our young people is imperative. They do not reject their religious and cultural heritage; we perceive in them an earnest search for meaning, moral rectitude, spiritual ideals, and a thirst for justice which is one of the beatitudes."

When these are denied to them, they either resort to what we term violence or to drugs or they "drop-out." The attitudes and values between young and old in the west and in Asian countries also show an interesting, pattern. In a South-East Asia Study Group on Cultural Relations for the Future, sponsored by a Quaker Foundation, of which I am a member, we drew some conclusions on youth and age. It could be best explained by a diagram

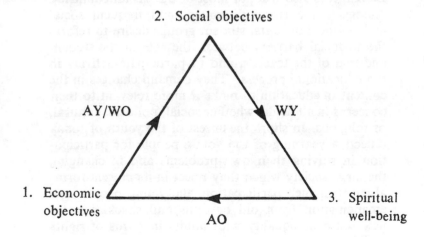

2. Social objectives

AY/WO   WY

1. Economic   3. Spiritual
   objectives   AO   well-being

Dimension 1—Economic objectives—Development in terms of GNP.

Dimension 2—Social objectives—Justice and distribution of material wealth.

Dimension 3—Personal and/or group identification and spiritual well-being.

WO = older generation in the west
WY = younger generation in the west
AO = older generation in Asia
AY = younger generation in Asia

It could be seen that the older generation in Asia is one step behind the young; and they, in turn, tend to be one step behind the youth of the west also.

This is understandable, since, as I said at the begining, our educated elites receive their value patterns from the west. While members of our Asian older generation pretend to cling to spiritual well-being or traditional religious values, in fact what they mainly desire is money and power. To confirm this opinion one only has to look at our Asian politicians, our business men and some church dignitaries, too. In the west, these people are for the most part rich enough so that they can afford to care for social justice. However, there is often a difference between what they can afford to do and what they actually do. Our youth, out of idealism and abhorring their elders, look to the goal of social justice; that is why our youngsters do not care so much for spiritual well-being and the traditional way of life. You have to achieve social objectives somewhat, before you feel that what you really need is an identification with the absolute Goodness, Truth and Beauty.

Furthermore, if we take the global context into account, in societies where change is taking place rapidly, the young or the progressive and/or radical elements in the society may strive for different goals from the establishment. For the purpose of simplication, we can classify societies generally into four categories:

1. Traditional, relatively stagnant countries, e.g. Laos or Siam until last October. The value patterns will fall between dimensions 3 and 1.

2. Industrialised countries with relatively stable and controlled values, e.g. Singapore and USSR. These will fall between dimensions 1 and 2.

3. Poor countries with changing values, e.g. Philippines before the martial law or Siam at present. The establishment, which represents the older generation, will fall between dimensions 3 and 1, while the young, progressive and/or radical elements will fall between dimensions 1 and 2.

4. Industrial countries with changing values, e.g. USA. The establishment will fall between dimensions 1 and 2, while the progressive youth will fall between dimensions 2 and 3.

However, the more the society allows freedom and toleration, the more the situation shows some possibility of compromise or accomodation, even though the compromise may be superficial. Yet, if the generation gap cannot be bridged, there will be more harmful results, as the old system of problem solving does not work any longer. To bridge the gap, both the old and the young must understand its own position and understand the attitudes and values of others fairly and clearly too. As members of the older generation, we must ask ourselves, whether we practise what we preach and is what we preach meaningful to others? Again may I quote Devananda's poem once more:

The Lord Buddha taught:
"Preach, monks, the dharma,
which is lovely in the beginning,
lovely in the middle,
and lovely in the ending.
Explain both in the spirit and in the letter
the good life
that is completely fulfilled,
wholly pure."

The Buddha and his disciples
drew the people and liberated them
by the sheer attractiveness,
in depth,
of the dharma they preached,
and lived—
a glorious past of history and culture.
But have our Buddhist bhikkhus and Buddhist laity in
the present
drawn our youth or liberated them?
How compelling, in depth,
has been the dharma they have preached,
and lived?

The Lord Christ said:
"I have come
that man may have life
and may have it in all its fullness.
I am the good shepherd;
the good shepherd lays down his life
for the sheep."
The Christ and his disciples drew the people and
liberated them
by a dharma preached in all its fullness,
and by a life lived in all its fullness,
in sacrificial care and service of others—
an inspired past.
But have our Christian ministers and Christian laity
in the present
drawn our youth or liberated them?
How full in sacrificial care and service of others
have their lives been
or the dharma they have preached?

There is now a danger that just as scientists are becoming more religious, theologians are leaving their medieval retreats to embrace materialism. Within most cultures, religion plays two roles, the priestly and the prophetic. In times of peace, most priests have traditionally sought to maintain the status quo within a stable society. The priest has been identified as conservative and abhorring change. In troubled times, however, he may become a prophet. The prophet seizes upon instability within society and uses it as an instrument to promote change and improvement. He is a visionary Utopian, looking beyond the present to the future he believes may be attainable.

As religious leaders, what role should we now play? Should the church remain a Constantinian church and side with the status quo, or should it revert to a primitive church and create Abrahamic cells for the young to achieve their ideals. A conference such as this would be a very good platform for discussion of this crucial question. Can the religious force effect a creative tension between imagination and tradition, between innovation and the status quo?

A report on Cultural Relations for the Future, which I referred to earlier, reminds us that we must recognize and encourage thoughtful young people to build more networks or relationships nationally, intra-regionally and inter-regionally. The problems of youth are our problems, and we must think of them in terms of the totality of our communities and our societies.

What we have to consider now is how to review, refine and strengthen the role of young people in the creation of a new and different world. This may mean institutional changes; making it possible for younger people to assume greater responsibility earlier in life. It may mean establishing educational methods to enable youth to learn certain essential things more quickly and to prepare them for careers more effectively than under the traditional educational system, which enslaves people. Men and women become free through their own efforts.

This may mean the development of new patterns of work and learning; as expounded by people like Paulo Friere and Ivan Illich, both of whom are members of

the Catholic Church. We also need different career
perspectives in business, government or education.
In my own society, we are now searching for a new
Buddhist pattern of life in the sphere of economics as
well as politics, which would free us from western
materialism — Communistic or capitalistic. These
changes could not be easily achieved, but they point to
the direction towards which urgent efforts must harness
and channel the creative and dynamic social energy of
youth.

Thus new concepts of the future and new patterns of
work will have to be worked out. The young must
participate and share responsibility. This will require
tremendous institutional change in all societies. But
it does not mean that the older generation should
abdicate its responsibilities. We ought never hold
back suggestions, ideas or solutions drawn from our
deeper knowledge of history and broader experience.
The older generation owes it to youth, as to itself, to
fight for its ideas and principles and in no way deprive
youth of the right and the privilege, in return, of fighting
for its ideas.

DECLARATION

The following Declaration is from a group of religious-minded people comprising both Buddhists and Christians, Catholics and Protestants, clergy and laymen, who met together on March 17th, 1976, at the headquarters of the Church of Christ in Thailand and established the Coordinating Group for Religion in Society:

1. Because the nation is presently in a state of crisis, with attempts being made to polarize people politically to either the extreme left or the extreme right, therefore this group resolves that religious people should not take sides, and they should not split religious groups into the left and the right, but should seek ways to bring about harmony for the sake of the majority of the people who are in the middle and who are being made victims of psychological warfare from both sides. Neither the left nor the right provides the real answer. The real answer is to be found in reducing injustice and narrowing the gaps between the rich and the poor and between the powerful and the powerless. This can be done by non-violent means.

2. We propose that religious leaders should denounce killing and assassination in all circumstances and should call upon the government to find ways to arrest the criminals.

3. People are fearful and apprehensive not only because of the killing of individuals and the slandering of

each other by groups, but also because of the strong rumours of a violent coup d'état to come at any moment. The National Women's Council has published a declaration opposing a coup d'état, calling for a parliamentary solution to the problems of the nation for the sake of the future. The Siamese Society is joining the Union for Civil Liberty in a meeting to be held on the 18th of this month to consider the problem of a coup d'état in Siam. They are preparing to put out a joint declaration on the subject. We encourage this initial effort, and also request The Church of Christ in Thailand, the Catholic Bishops' Conference of Thailand, the Buddhist Universities, the Young Buddhist Monks, the Ecclesiastical Council of Maha Theras and the various Buddhist Associations to join together in publishing a joint declaration warning of the dangers of a coup d'état.

4. We give to the soldiers our assurance of friendship as fellow humans. We would advise them to be friends of the people. They should not think of killing people simply because they believe those in this village or that city are terrorists. They ought not to oppress the citizens. Even though students may use some violent language, yet if the soldiers use violent means with citizens, the mass of the people will hate the soldiers. The more people are killed, the greater will the hatred grow. Even if the army were able to seize power or were able to control the situation, it would be for only a short time.

5. In regard to those who set themselves up as being anti-military, who accuse the soldiers of killing those in their group, we would call on them to be peaceful, for evil is overcome only when revenge is foregone. Killing cannot be stopped by killing. The killer may be a soldier or a civilian. In many cases he kills because he is afraid, or because he is ignorant of the real facts, or because he is a tool of a politician or of a crooked system. The killing does not correct the situation. The solution must be found through some system which all the Thai people together should be able to devise through peaceful methods without allowing foreign influences to interfere.

BUDDHISM AND NON-VIOLENCE

In July 1976 I was asked by the Buddhist Association at Thammasat University, Bangkok, to deliver a lecture on "Buddhism And the Problems Of Killing" in response to a popular Buddhist monk's astounding comment in the local newspapers dated June 30 that "to kill a communist is not sinful." Indeed, the monk, Kittivuddho Bhikkhu, later had to retract his earlier statement by saying that "to kill communism or communist ideology is not a sin." He claimed that he did not encourage people to kill people. He confessed nevertheless that he was a nationalist more than a practising Buddhist. He was willing to abandon his yellow robes in order to return to the lay life so that he could take up arms to fight against the communist invaders from across the borders, namely Laos, Cambodia, and Vietnam. He claimed that by so doing he could preserve the three national institutions — the King, the Kingdom and the Buddhist religion. In fact, this monk was accused of being instrumental in leading groups of extreme right wing reactionaries against the student movement. This resulted in an attack on the peaceful demonstration organized by undergraduates and other people at Thammasat University, the same university during the same year. The following coup d'état was the only treacherous and bloody one in recent Thai history, despite the fact that Siam had experienced more than ten coups during the past four decades.

From the above paragraph one can draw quite a number of conclusions. (1) Young people were astounded when a Buddhist monk tried to justify the act of killing. (2) Although a number of monks in the past have tried to condone "just war," they could not find a canonical source to back this opinion. That is why our contemporary monk had to retreat from his earlier statement. (3) The strength and the weakness of Buddhism seems to be tested here, i.e., what will happen when nation and religion are threatened by an enemy?

Dean Inge of St. Paul's Cathedral, London, once wrote, "If Christians had been as pacifist as Buddhists or if Western Europe had been as well suited to hordes of cavalry as Russia and Hungary, there is scarcely any doubt that the 'legacies' of Greece, Rome and Palestine would have been finally and totally extinguished." He went on about war saying that "the reproach has often been brought against Christianity that it has done so little effectively to deliver mankind from this monstrous evil. Buddhism, we are told, has really created as well as inculcated a peaceful disposition."[1]

Mr. Christmas Humphreys, founding President of the London Buddhist Society, stated that one of the reasons why he abandoned Christianity, was that during the First World War, when his brother was killed in serving his King and country, both English clergymen and German pastors invoked the same God to guide the

[1] W.R. Inge, *Christian Ethics and Modern Problem*, 1952.

soldiers in warfare and to encourage them to fight for the victory of the respective nation.

Before the end of the Vietnam War, I asked Ven. Thich Nhat Hanh, a well-known practising Vietnamese Buddhist monk in exile, whether he would rather have peace under the communist regime which would mean the end of Buddhism or rather the victory of the democratic Vietnam with the possibility of Buddhist revival. His answer was to have peace at any price. He argued that Buddhism does not mean that we should sacrifice people's lives in order to preserve the Buddhist hierarchy, the pagodas, the monasteries, the scriptures, the rituals and the tradition. When human lives are preserved and when human dignity and freedom are cultivated toward peace and loving-kindness, Buddhism can again be reborn in the hearts of men and women.

In the whole Buddhist history there was never once a holy war. Yet, surely Buddhist kings waged war against one another. They might have claimed to do so for the benefit of mankind or for the Buddhist religion, but they simply could not quote any saying of the Buddha to support them however just their war might have been. The Buddha said, "Victory creates hatred. Defeat creates suffering. The wise ones desire neither victory nor defeat... Anger creates anger... He who kills will be killed. He who wins will be defeated... Revenge can only be overcome by abandoning revenge... The wise ones desire neither victory nor defeat."

Emperor Aśoka was so moved by such sayings that he was converted to Buddhism after having waged so much war. Buddhist kings, on the whole, liked to model themselves on Aśoka. Only when Buddhism is no longer a national culture which permeates its environment and gives it spiritual depth, will killing and violence be regarded as something positive. Buddhism retreated from India, China, Vietnam, etc. rather than involve its believers in armed struggles to preserve itself in these countries. This is again the strength and the weakness of Buddhism.

On many occasions in the past history of Ceylon and Buddhist Southeast Asia, monks have been asked by kings to initiate peace treaties. Never have Buddhist monks involved themselves directly in warfare. They could not. To kill a human being or to cause a person to be killed means that a monk immediately ceases to be a monk because he would have committed a sinful act of such a magnitude that forgiveness is not possible. Personally a monk may agree or disagree with any war, he is however required to refrain from exposing his opinion in this respect.

In Siamese chronicles we find the story that a great king personally fought the crown prince of Burma, both on elephants, and the Siamese king won by slaying his opponent. He was angry with his generals for not following him close enough and thus letting him face the enemy singlehandedly. He condemned all of them to death. The Patriarch and other senior monks visited the King and asked him to pardon the generals. The monks said that on the eve of the Buddha's enlightenment, had the Blessed One been surrounded by all the deities and had the Blessed One been victorious over the hordes of Mara—the evil ones in various forms of hatred, greed and delusion — this would not have been as supreme a victory as the one when the Buddha single-handedly overcame the entire army of sensuous desires. Likewise, had His Majesty been surrounded by all his generals and had he won the battle, it would not have been as great a victory as His Majesty's single-handed victory over the Crown Prince of Burma. His victory could be regarded as a victory similar to that of the Great Buddha. With this metaphor the monks got all the generals released. But the king remarked that in this case the generals should wage war once more against the Burmese to show their courage. The monks, however, said that warfare was not their business and begged to leave for their monasteries.

Hsuan Tsang, the famous Chinese monk, was once asked by the Emperor of China to accompany him on a military campaign. The monk's reply showed his tactfulness and his adherence to Buddhist ethical codes: "Hsuan Tsang knows himself not to be of any assistance to your military campaign. I feel ashamed to be the object of unnecessary expenses and a useless burden. Moreover, the Vinaya discipline forbids (the monks) to see military battle and display of armies. As Lord Buddha gave such an admonition, I dare not, to please Your Majesty."[2]

---

[2] Bhikkhu Thich Minh Chau: *Hsuan Tsang: The Pilgrim And Scholar* (1966) p. 31.

In *The Heritage of The Bhikkhu*, Dr. Wapola Rahula mentioned that Buddhist monks were involved in the Sinhalese national freedom movement and the protection of peace. Yet, the monks could not take part directly in the killing or warfare. Even when they condoned the Kings who fought to protect the Buddhist religion, they could not quote the scriptures to support this position. Ceylon was invaded by foreign aggressors many times and Buddhist monks were so pacifist that the lineage of the Bhikkhu was discontinued. The King of Ceylon had to send a mission to Siam for a chapter of Siamese monks to ordain Sinhalese novices and laymen. Thus, the lineage could again be continued.

Buddhism is indeed known to be the religion which regards peace and non-violence as its cardinal virtues. The Buddha said, "There is no other happiness greater than peace." The ultimate goal for a Buddhist is to reach the peaceful state of *nibbāna* and the means to reach this goal must be peaceful ones. To be a Buddhist, one is required first of all to observe the precepts *(sīla)*, i.e., one must not take advantage of oneself or others. Being neutral towards all beings, one can embark on the spiritual journey of meditation and reach tranquillity of the mind *(samādhi)*, so that, eventually, one could be enlightened and gain *paññā* which means that one would have the insight wisdom of seeing things as they really are. Buddhists call this the realization of total Awakening or Enlightenment *(bodhi)*.

Of the five precepts a Buddhist lay person is expected to accept, the first one is "I take the precept to abstain from the taking of life." (A precept is not a commandment from God because the Buddha is only a teacher who helped to point out the way.) A Buddhist, therefore, promises to himself not to destroy, cause to be destroyed or sanction the destruction of a living being, which could be anything that has life, from insects up to and including man. In taking this precept, a Buddhist recognizes his relationship to all living beings, a relationship which is so close that the harming of any living creature would inevitably also constitute harm to himself. The Buddha taught how advisable it is to compare one's own life with that of other beings, "Everyone fears violence, everyone likes life; comparing oneself with others, one would never slay or cause to slay."

The precept applies to all creatures irrespective of size. It does not exclude the killing of animals to be sacrificed to God or the gods, as do the commandments of some religions. A Buddhist does not sacrifice living beings for worship or for food, but sacrifices instead his own selfish motives.

The extent of moral guilt in killing depends on the physical and mental development of the being that is killed and the circumstances under which the deed is committed. The *karmic* results of killing a man or killing an animal vary in proportion to the evolutional, physical and mental development of the two. Patricide, matricide, the slaughter of innocent people and of people with considerable spiritual or mental development are, therefore, particularly productive of evil results for the killer. The respective injunction runs, "Do not kill a living being. You should not kill or condone killing by others. Having abandoned the use of violence, you should not use force either against the strong or the feeble."

Non-violence *(ahimsā)* is the positive counterpart. One should not only abstain from injuring oneself and others but also practise loving kindness *(mettā)* toward all.

One who, observing the first precept, wishes to practise non-violence, ought to meditate on or be mindful of *mettā* — a positive loving force which can be cultivated within oneself. It is orthodox Buddhist practice to first sever the impediments inimical to one's peaceful surroundings. Then one should select a suitable time and a secluded place where, without interruption, one can devote oneself to practising meditation. One should then perceive the danger of anger arising and, at the same time, one should realize the advantage of having patience, because anger has to be abandoned and patience has to be fostered in the development of one's meditation. The danger of anger should be understood in every possible way. The most effective method, for the Buddhist, would be to understand anger in accordance with the teaching of the Buddha.

A cultivator embarks on the development of *mettā* to rid his mind of hatred which is a danger and to acquire patience which is known to be an advantage. In fact, Buddhism regards patience as a foundation stone to build up spiritual strength toward enlightenment. To meditate successfully, one should be in a peaceful situation, as free from distractions as possible. To begin meditation, the practitioner should assume a posture

which is most convenient to him or her. The proper
postures are lying, standing, walking, and sitting.
The ideal posture, if convenient, is sitting cross-legged,
with one's spine erect, one's head straight, one's eyes
half-closed, and one's hands in one's lap. For the
orthodox Theravada Buddhists who practise in Ceylon,
Burma, Siam, Laos, and Cambodia, the first step for the
beginner should be to develop oneself, so that one
would be free of enmity, ill-will, distress and would
keep oneself happy, i.e., be peaceful.

There are many sayings of the Buddha which medi-
tators can use to remind themselves of their goal, such
as:

*"In those who harbour such thoughts, 'He abused me,
he struck me, he overcame me, he robbed me,' hatred
never ceases.*

*In those who do not harbour such thoughts, hatred will
cease.*

*Hatred never ceases through hatred in this world,
through non-violence it comes to an end.*

*Some do not think that all of us here one day will die;
if they did, their dissension would cease at once.*

One should give up anger, renounce pride.

*Let a man overcome anger by loving kindness; let him
overcome evil by good; let him overcome the miser by
liberality; let him overcome the liar by truth.*

One should speak the truth, not giving way to anger.

There is none in the world who is not blamed.

One should guard oneself against misdeeds caused by speech. Let him practise restraint of speech. Let him practise virtue with his mind.

The wise who control their body, speech, and mind are indeed well controlled."[3]

Once one is content and peaceful, one then may spread one's loving kindness toward others:

"*May all beings be happy and secure;*
May their hearts be wholesome.
Whatever living beings there be,
Feeble or strong, tall, stout or medium,
Short, small or large, without exception,
Seen or unseen,
Those dwelling far or near,
Those who are born or who are to be born,
May all beings be happy."[4]

When a cultivator sits in meditation, both his body and mind can be at peace and in total relaxation which is very much needed in this day and age. A non-Buddhist can also adopt this technique and take sayings, perhaps

---

[3] These quotations are from the *Dhammapada*, a small book of verses containing short but salient sayings of the Buddha.

[4] The above is taken from the *Mettā Sutta* which most practising Buddhists recite every day in its full length.

of Christ if he were a Christian, to guide him. Non-violence, in the opinion of Buddhists, would not be possible unless one is already mindful and peaceful. But the state of peace and relaxation differs fundamentally from the lazy, semi-conscious state of mind which one is in while resting and dozing. Sitting in such lazy, semi-conscious state is far from being mindful. It is like sitting in a dark cave. In mindfulness one is not only peaceful and happy but alert and awake. Meditation is not a means of evasion, it is a serene encounter with reality. The person who practises meditation should be as awake as a driver of a car. When he is not awake, he will be distracted and forgetful and, just as the driver who is not awake and alert, he could easily cause a grave accident. One should, therefore, be as awake as a person who walks on high stilts. Any misstep could lead to one's death. One should be like a medieval knight walking weaponless in a forest of swords.

In a family, when there is one person who practises meditation, the entire family will benefit from this loving kindness. Because of the presence of one member who lives in mindfulness — full of compassion — the entire family will be reminded to live in such a spirit. When in one village, a villager practises *mettā*, the entire village will be influenced, thanks to the constant reminder given by the example of that one person. Hence, in a Buddhist monastery, there must be at least one meditation master so that a peaceful atmosphere can be created for the happiness of monks and lay people who live nearby. The presence of one who perpetually practises the mindfulness of loving kindness can be considered as the presence of a Buddha. In a cosmopolitan area or in a modern city with complex organizations, mass media, etc., Buddhism is yet to find its way to cope with such a set-up. Capitalism, materialism, and Western technology have more negative effects on Buddhism and on most religions than people tend to realize.

In any family, village or monastery, a Buddhist is expected to follow this principle. We should not worry that those around us are not doing their best toward the practice of non-violence. One should only worry about how to perfect oneself. When one does one's best, this is the surest way to remind those around to do their best. When one wants to be a worthy Buddhist, one must practise mindfulness and observe the precepts *(sīla)*, of course. Only by such practice one will not lose oneself but will be filled with bright joy and peace. Only by practising mindfulness, one will be able to look at everyone else with an open mind and eyes of love.

Buddhism enters the life of society through the presence of people who practise and bear witness to the way *(magga)* toward the ultimate goal, through thought, speech, and actions.

Anyone who looks at this world and society and sees its tremendous sufferings, injustices, and dangers, will agree on the necessity to do something, to act in order to change, in order to liberate people. But how many people are already active? How many organizations, political parties, fronts and strategies are there already? Our world has no lack of volunteers to help. Save us ´rom programs and groups who promise to redeem others. In all likelihood, we have far too many saviours. They seem only to intensify the chaos and the confusion. Is it because we have placed too much faith in the power of action, especially political action? We are caught in a tornado of action in which the individual is no longer in control but the machine of society controls all. How many of our "saviours" are mindful of themselves? They may be intellectually clever, but do they act out of real understanding of the world, do they act with loving care or do they act out of selfish motives hidden somewhere? Perhaps they never have the time to ask themselves, let alone to investigate closer the so-called "self." Hardly any of them close their eyes while they are awake. They only close their eyes to sleep, often with the help of sleeping pills! For those who practise *mettā*, even during sleep, they sleep in comfort, do not have bad dreams, awake in comfort and are dear to human and other beings.

The presence of Buddhist sages — or, indeed, any humanist leaders who have obtained the Way *(Magga or Tao)* — means the presence of wisdom, love and peace. In most societies, the so - called leaders are themselves confused, engrossed in hatred, greed or delusion, so they become the blind who lead the blind. When they do not have peace of mind, how could they lead others without love or compassion? In Buddhism, we believe that such a presence is very important. Such a presence could have an influence on society. In Buddhist terminology, we use the word emptiness of action or non-action. To act in a way that arises from non-action is to act in a way to truly influence the situation in a non-violent way. Naturally, humanists and masters of the Way contribute to the ends to save life, but their most valued contribution is their *presence*, not their actions.

When they act, their actions are filled with the spirit of love, wisdom and peace. Their actions are their presence, their mindfulness, their own personality. This means that the presence of their non-action is their most fundamental contribution. This leads us to recognize that the important thing in an individual who acts is not his action but his personality. In the Thai context, a monk like Bhikkhu Buddhadasa is so important, although he hardly does anything to the outside community, except preaching and writing, and lives far away from anywhere. Whereas the other monk whose name I mentioned earlier in this article, Kittivuddho, is more harmful than good, because the actions of a person who is not yet a true and whole person creates only more confusion. The more such a person controls the mass media, the more his image will have a popular appeal and the more destructive he will be to his society. Correct action is characterized by kindness, broadness and unselfishness. The presence of virtuous people is the foundation of world peace. This belief is found not only in Buddhist tradition but in almost all of Asian civilization. A Chinese sage said, "Whenever an enlightened person appears, the water in the rivers turns clearer and the plants grow greener." Cultivators of Zen would say that we need "A True Man With No Title."

The presence of individuals who have attained "awakening" is not a passive presence or one that lacks zeal. People who have attained the Way are living individuals and because they are living their language is a living language. Their thoughts, their speech and actions express their attitudes and views towards life—in fact, toward the problems of life. In any religious set-up, when the high priests and leading monks use only clichés and worn out words which have no meaning for the modern world, it indicates that the religious tradition is dying. There may be many churches, temples, pagodas, rituals, etc., but these are only outward forms of religious practices without spiritual depth or spiritual presence. With masters who live their religion, however, their awareness is the awareness born from their own experience and not just knowledge derived from books. Their awareness is not of the intellect nor is it based on the views of some partisan groups or ideologies. They live according to their own true self and not according to the rule of the public opinion or the authorities in power. This means that they stand on the side of those who protect freedom and truth. They may be theologians, scientists, artists or literary men. Their friends in the domains of religion, science, art and literature are gladly influenced by them. They do not accept their thoughts, art and science being used to serve partisan struggles. They have a Great Action in mind, the Right Action *(sammākammanta)*, one which unites all people in resisting the threats and perils to mankind. Their thoughts, art and science are permeated with the character of love, wisdom, and humanism, and they reject the path of war and ideological conflict. They envision a society that unites humanity. They work toward the steady healing of borders and schisms that divide countries, peoples, and religions. They heal the painful divisions.

Awakened Buddhists in the past have often been philosophers, poets or artists. In the cultural and artistic spheres of India, Ceylon, Southeast Asia, China and Japan, the role played by enlightened masters of the Way is well worth mentioning. The influence of compassion and serenity can be seen in folk tales, in poetry, in architecture, sculpture, painting, etc. Through thought and art, the source of Buddhist wisdom has reached teachers, scientists and politicians. Apart from the nature of Buddhism, there is nothing precious about Buddhism. It is the way of mindfulness and peace.

Buddhism being present does not mean having a lot of schools, hospitals, cultural institutions or political parties run by Buddhists. The presence of Buddhism means that the schools, hospitals, cultural institutions and political parties are permeated with and administered with humanism, love, tolerance, and enlightenment, characteristics which Buddhism attributes to an opening up, development and formation of human nature. To us this is the true spirit of non-violence.

To be present, for Buddhism, does not mean that the Buddhist hierarchy is aligned with political power. A Buddhist monk does not have to preach for or against any individual or ideology. Buddhism is present when the Buddhist leadership is known for its spiritual value. We bow our heads before a senior Buddhist monk—indeed we prostrate ourselves before him—not out of fear, but because we deeply respect him. A master can help us attain awakening. He will not imprison or excommunicate us.

Having grasped the spirit of Buddhism, we must face the world in full awareness of its condition. In Buddhist terminology, the world is full of *dukkha*, i.e., the dangers of impending world destruction through nuclear weapons, atomic fall-out, air, land and sea pollution, population explosion, exploitation of fellow human beings, denial of basic human rights, and devasting famine. We ought to realize that when we wish to avoid these catastrophies, humanity must cease at once all partisan brawls to concentrate all its abilities and energy in the urgent effort to save ourselves,

World *dukkha* is too immense for any country, people or religion to solve. We can only save ourselves when all humanity recognizes that every problem on earth is our own personal problem and our own personal responsibility. Such a realization, however, can only take place when the divisions and the strife between religions, peoples, and nations cease. We can only serve ourselves when, for example, the rich feel that they should contribute toward alleviating the famine of the world. Unless they change their life-style seriously, there is no hope of solving this problem. Those in the northern hemisphere ought to see the difficulties in Indochina as their own problems. They ought to see the denial of basic human rights in Siam and Chile as their own problems and the famine in Calcutta as their own agony. The United Nations must become a true world government which represents all people and cultures and which is not just controlled by a few of the big powers as it has been up to now.

Extreme nationalism must be abandoned. The small countries are placed in a difficult position. For a long time, their sole weapon to struggle for freedom and equality has been nationalism. The last Thai coup was in a way an expression of extreme nationalism at the expense of love and non-violence and of Buddhism itself (although the people who staged the coup did so in the name of Buddhism, among other things), because they felt that without a strong dictatorship the nation would be overrun by Communists. To abandon nationalism, especially extreme nationalism, means to them to be without the strength needed for defence and for the anticipated struggle. An individual who struggles, struggles for a flag, for the sacred nation or for the sacred monarchy or for the sacred religion. Would not telling such people to drop the chains of nationalism be the same as telling them to cease struggling for preserving national identity?

We can easily see that the struggle of the peoples of the Third World could go on for many more dozens of years and that, because of war, resources are wasted and economies cannot be built up. In the Thai case, the government wants to spend more and more money to buy weapons from rich countries — mostly

from the USA—to fight a civil war. Thus all countries
at war are placed farther and farther behind on the
path of development. But how can they cease to
struggle on the basis of love for their country? The
situation grows more and more complex. The fate of
humanity is too great a burden. The dead end ahead
looms each day closer. What must we do? How does
Buddhism answer this question?

The narrow concepts of nationalism such as "my
country right or wrong" must first be rejected by the
powerful nations. Leading politicians of great powers
have in tough circumstances appealed to their people
to love their country, but their appeals did not attain
the desired results. During how many world wars
have people sacrificed their lives and, see, what has
happened to the world? Through the guidance of
several prominent and progressive humanists, intellectuals, and religious leaders, many people in the
developed countries have come to recognize the
unjust actions their countries commit in the less powerful countries. They stand up to oppose the policy
of their governments and, in many instances, receive
backlashes from their governments. The peace
movements in the USA, U.K. and Japan and in a
number of other nations allied to the United
States represent a real danger to the interests of
their governments which profit from any war — be it
in Korea or Vietnam. Not only powerful nations but
also powerful multinational firms create many
problems for developing countries. Again, progressive
people have realized this and begin to react against

such exploitation. But however progressive people are, when they live in developing countries where basic rights are denied to them, they are not in a position to do anything openly against their governments or against superpowers or multinational firms in which leaders of their governments have vested interests.

For those of us who are travelling through developing countries, what we can do is to urge humanists, intellectual and religious leaders that when your countries are fortunate to be relatively free from slavery and poverty, and when you have the conditions and resources to transcend nationalism, work toward a family of man. Whereas we, who are in a situation of great hardship, still need to cling to some form of nationalism just in order to survive. You, however, must use your position to help us all progress. You must try to stop your government from sending arms to our part of the world. Stop your government and multinational firms located in your part of the world from exploiting us. Use your influence that we too may enjoy basic human rights. Only when we can build a united world in which every problem is perceived to be a collective responsibility, will we then be able to be liberated together.

The thoughts and the spirit of Buddhism are well suited to the needs of a united world and to the removal of dividing, painful boundaries. Reputable historians, sociologists, psychologists and even, of late, economists have talked about this and have expressed their hope that Buddhists will contribute to the building of a new world culture.

The wisdom of Buddhism must provide a shining and illuminating outlook. The language of Buddhism must offer answers which fit our situation. Only then Buddhism will survive, today and tomorrow, as it did in the past and it will influence mankind positively and generate love, peace, and non-violence.

IV

FUTURE GOALS

RELIGION AND NATIONAL DEVELOPMENT

Editor's Introduction

It is possible to be a critic of society by pleading special causes, such as preservation of the cultural past, protection of the environment, or advocacy of a private religious vision. While Sulak Sivaraksa embraces these concerns, he has paid special attention to the problem of social and economic development — which is the major preoccupation of the leaders of Third World nations. By teaching philosophy in the School of Economics at Thammasat University, Sulak has integrated his concerns for the well-being of his people with his Buddhist values and with the economic realities of the modern world.

This appeared in his *Religion and Development* delivered at a Christian College in Chiang Mai in February 1976. Immediately afterward, Sulak returned to Bangkok to take part in a panel discussion with leading Buddhists from many countries to remind them of "Tasks for Modern Buddhists."

The following month, Sulak addressed Thai Buddhists and Christians, both Protestants and Catholics, who were concerned about the rumours of *coup d'état*. The text of his talk has been translated as it now appears in the second article in this section. What followed from his pleas, one could see in the Declaration of the CGRS in Part III # 7. Unfortunately the *coup d'état* took place as predicted but 6 months later—on 6th October 1976.

The last article on the future goal of Buddhism, however, was delivered in Canada two years later in a colloquium "Multiple Loyalties: Buddhism and Christianity in Crisis" under the chairmanship of Willard G. Oxtoby. Those taking part were Wilfred Cartwell Smith, Roger Hutchinson and Abe Masao.

In June 1980 Sulak agian took yet another leading role in a Buddhist—Christian Renewal for the Future of Humanity, at the University of Hawaii in Honolulu, where we first met in June 1977. Despite his harsh criticism of the present state of affairs, Sulak indeed has a vision for renewing society beyond the horizons.

TASKS FOR MODERN BUDDHISTS

If I am allowed to be honest, Mr. Chairman, I must say that I am very disappointed with the performance of this panel discussion. When I was invited to take part in it, I thought it was great. The WFB must have now grown to maturity, since it dares to allow an outspoken person like me to be among its distinguished delegates. Perhaps it would now like to hear constructive criticism and would do something down to earth, instead of being on a lofty cloud, passing beautiful resolutions without seeing whether they are implemented. It might now perhaps be tired of listening to eulogistical messages with empty contents.

I came down especially from Chiang Mai to attend this meeting, and to find out that the same old clichés are still being said "We Buddhists are the best people in the world. We are full of tolerance. Our teaching is very scientific. Our way is the only way" etc. What do delegates do at home? Do they fight against poverty and social injustice? Do they stand for freedom or do they go along with any autocratic regime? What is the Buddhist way versus modern materialism—be it capitalism, neo-colonialism in the form of multinational firms, or Communism? Once they come to attend such Buddhist organizations as this, do they have the chance to visit poverty stricken areas, to visit some places where Buddhist methods are being applied to cure social as well as spiritual illness? Or do delegates only stay in big hotels, see beautiful development projects, visit gigantic Buddhist establishments, and be invited to dinner at Government House? The Prime Minister in fact came to this grand opening. Indeed it is the Thai Government's financial assistance that made the WFB meeting and organization possible. Hence you have to be polite to the Government, to say nice things about it, and yet you say that as a religious institution you are non-political. In fact, by so doing are you not political already? Or does non-politics only mean that we can do anything, provided that that action is not contrary to the wishes of the Government and the Establishment?

The irony is that most governments in the region, nay in the world, do not represent the people—despite democratic systems and all that. So religious people who try to be close to any government are bound to be political one way or the other.

What is wrong with politics, may I ask? It is only wrong—when dealing with politics, economics, or indeed with any profession—if we who claim to be practising Buddhists are not aware of what we are doing. Without sati—mindfulness—we could easily become tools of politicians, businessmen or those tycoons who control the mass media and hence create social norms and values. By giving us so called religious people a little, we are easily bought and we close our eyes to the wickedness and oppression that these people do to other human beings, animals and nature in general. These people tend to stick to forms but not to the substance of Buddhasāsanā. We like them when they perform Buddhist ceremonies, we do not like the young because they rebel against the traditional mode of behaviour, although in many instances the young are much more sincere and try hard to solve social as well as spiritual problems.

The practice of mindfulness—if we do practise it at all—means that loving-kindness(mettā)and compassion (karunā) must be real. We must be willing to share the suffering of our fellow beings—be they human, animal or natural. The practice of meditation does not only mean to close one's eyes to the world problems and say "we are all right Jack."

In traditional Asian society, it is possible for people to withdraw from the world, to go to the forest, to contemplate deeply into one's nature and the law of the universe in order to find enlightenment. Indeed those of us who are men and women of the world must try to preserve this tradition and this atmosphere, so that this practice will still be possible in the years to come. For without an enlightened community, Buddhism would be a much poorer way of life. Without the spring of pure water, the stream will indeed be soon dry.

So, fighting against environmental destruction (twenty-five percent of our forestry in this country has been destroyed during the last decade alone), against social injustice (since a small handful of rich people who associate themselves very closely with the politicians destroy our natural environment and create as well as widen the social, political and economic gaps between people) must be the task of modern Buddhists. We can only do so by understanding social reality(vijjā)and by applying loving-kindness and compassion to solving the problems. Hence we cannot agree with the Communists or any violent means. Yet from what happens in Laos, Cambodia and Vietnam—all of which were supposed to be Buddhist lands once—we must learn the lessons and watch the situation mindfully. It is no use making any propaganda efforts against the new regime in those countries. We ought to learn from the failure of our Buddhist brethren there, extend our equanimity (upekkhā) to them and try to do our best so that we could strive to bring about social revolution and political reform peacefully and justly—in the Buddhist manner.

At the same time, we must learn of efforts being applied in other countries to utilise Buddhist teaching as a means to develop them — political, economic, social, cultural and of course spiritual. The Sarvodaya movement in Sri Lanka, the fighting illiteracy programme in Burma and the School of Youth for Social Service in South Vietnam could be very good examples. Our monks' training efforts as well as the curing of drug addicts by Bhikkhus in this country should also be studied carefully. We should see the strengths as well as the weaknesses of these movements and organizations.

If we Buddhists understand what is happening in Vietnam and in this country at this moment, we will have to think hard. The example of Vietnam is a good one. We should know the difficulties Vietnam is encountering in both North and South. We need not mention the People's Republic of China, Laos or Cambodia. In South Vietnam itself, thousands of Buddhist orphanages, dispensaries, elementary and high schools and the Buddhist University have been taken over by the new regime. The School of Youth for Social Service with its experimental farms and campus has also been confiscated and the monk-director placed under house arrest. Recently the Komol Keemthong Foundation was asked by the Vietnamese Buddhist Peace Delegation in Paris to send some rice to the Buddhist orphans at An Quang Pagoda in Saigon. With all our efforts through the Asian Cultural Forum On Development, the UN High Commission for Refugees as well as the Thai and the Vietnamese Red Cross, we managed to send the rice over; the Thai Government being kind enough to exempt all taxes and premiums. We had a guarantee that at least some of the rice would reach those poor orphans at the Pagoda but in fact they received very little.

If Buddhists do not take action, Buddhism in our lands, especially those lands which happen to be adjacent to the Communist countries, will suffer a similar kind of treatment. Capitalism exploits religion one way, Communism another. We must fight against both.

One action which we Buddhists could do, i.e. if we are aware of the problems, is to appeal to our Government to follow the policy that will make it possible for the people to avoid a war like those in Vietnam, Cambodia and Laos. Such a policy is to take measures to abolish all forms of social injustice. People with goodwill, especially the young, once disappointed because of the government's policy, can turn easily to support violent revolution.

Now if a non-violent way for social justice is prescribed with the support of Buddhist organizations like the Sangha, the WFB, the Buddhist Associations, and the Young Buddhist Federations, people will have an alternative to choose and the movement will quickly take shape. Yet these organizations so far, in this country at least, seem to be inactive. They say they do not want to play politics, while in fact they support the *status quo* all the time. Thus the rich become richer and the poor poorer. Polarisation must in fact be abolished and reconciliation put in its place.

Is it too much for us Buddhists to appeal for :

1) The return to the traditional culture and spiritual values, for the elimination of those foreign elements which can cause discord and hatred among the people and can destroy the beauty of our traditions and customs.

2) An educational system that provides equal opportunities to every citizen, rich and poor, city dwellers and country people.

3) An economic policy that does not create gaps between people. There should be a policy which prevents the minority becoming richer and richer, while taking away the chances for a decent living from the majority. The Government should refrain from importing luxurious items for the sake of the consumption of the rich minority,

forbid the transferring of money by the rich to deposit in foreign banks outside the country—not to mention the rich buying real property abroad!

4) The re-organisation of the armed forces, to educate soldiers to become friends of the villagers, not to oppress and terrorize them. The ignorance and ill-behaviour of the soldiers can lead to more opposition that is violent from among the population.

5) The reform of life in the countryside. Efforts should be made to help farmers, small merchants and others to exercise their professions and organize themselves in order to produce better and to sell their products, and to encourage and protect people who are working to help in the work of rural development.

6) Attention to miserable conditions in the slum areas. Land should be distributed to those in the slums who would like to go and settle in the rural areas in order to have a better life. Food and transportation should be provided to those who wish to participate in such a programme.

7) A neutral and independent policy towards the conflicting powers to maintain a truly independent stand, non-aligned, trying to avoid involvement in any international conflicts in order to preserve peace.

8) A sensible and intelligent policy towards the armed opposition movement. Violent confront-

ation should be avoided. Sincere and direct contact with the leaders of the movement should be made immediately. Try to listen to every point of criticism and prove to the people by action that the points being made by them can be realized in more peaceful ways and in cooperation with them.

Let me ask once again, whether such an appeal could be launched. If we cannot say this and cannot act accordingly, can we still call ourselves Buddhists? How can we be followers of the Compassionate One, while we let our Buddhist way go astray, by playing safe, i.e. by not doing anything for fear of upsetting the estabilshed social order, which becomes more and more polarized. Such is indeed a cowardly way of living. It does not contribute towards the preservation of the Sāsana, especially in a critical period like this.

Our Bhikkhus and rich lay supporters, on the whole, are not aware of what is happening in the country, of the existing social unrest and injustice. They only believe in propaganda and accusation through the gossips and the mass media. Even a person like me is often accused of being a Communist! They must engage themselves in the work to help the poor people with education and social reform, while not neglecting their duties to learn and practise Buddhism.

To me this is an essential task for modern Buddhists. If we do not take this seriously at this very moment, there will not be much chance to preserve Buddhism as a noble way of life in the near future.

"RELIGION AND DEVELOPMENT"
THE NEXT STEPS

Introduction

I think we come to this meeting today because we have in common three main aims which are: 1) wanting to think together, 2) wanting to speak together and 3) wanting to find the way to work together—in applying religious Dharma to develop society so that it will become genuinely and justly peaceful.

1) We come to join hands and to think . If each one thinks and considers only one's own opinion and judgement, that may make him speak and act so differently from others, that this conflict may arise unnecessarily. Especially among religious leaders, the more they avoid conflict and turn to help each other in presenting and using useful religious teachings or religious principles for everyone's sake, the more advantageous will it be for this society. At this moment, it is quite necessary that those who have good wishes for the people at large should firmly unify their intellectual power even more than before.

2) If we can think together, even though we do not agree completely in every respect, but are honest and have sincere regard for each other, we can certainly discuss and take council trustingly with each other. Every religion teaches people to behave well, think well and speak well; will then it be right if we use

ideologies, sects, religious denominations or other small differences to arouse conflicts and cause suspicion and mistrust? At the same time, we have to admit the fact that many religious leaders in the past were prone to suspect, to distrust and to be jealous of one another.

As this is the first time that we have held a meeting at which various religions in this country have conferred together, I would like to ask for forgiveness, and urge that at this meeting we shall not ignore what one and the other say, even if there are those who speak too strongly or too frankly. I would like to ask each of you to be firm, to restrain your own temper, to forgive one another, and try to listen carefully and respectfully to others' opinions, other religions, based on a real sympathy with each other.

In discussing and conferring today, it would be admirable if we can agree to issue a statement, or to widen the sphere of ideas in the form of written articles to remind ourselves, other religious friends who share the same ideologies, and other people who share the same circumstances with us, by pointing them to some facts and pulling them from the flood of slandering which happen almost everywhere in every circle—in order that they will have a better understanding and be able to see the real situations, and then do something without being in confusion. Anyway, all this depends on the meeting's judgement.

3) If we can think together and reach agreement on any subject, then, we should join hands to do some-

thing together. Even the things that we have done separately, we could make known among ourselves. It is a good sign that now there is co-operation in many circles; both Buddhists and Christians, Catholics and Protestants, try to come to work together more and more. But, there are many people who do not yet know about this co-operation. There are still even those among fellow Buddhists and among fellow Christians who don't want to join hands, who distrust each other, and try to create discord.

Although we, who come to join each other today are not the most important ones who can effect everything, if we start from such points, agreeing about, what we shall do together according to the order of importance as we see it, and considering present and near-future situations as the main factors, we might be able to find ways to improve our society.

Religion and Development

As the person who arranged this meeting told me to begin to speak, by summarizing the Sinclair Thompson Memorial Lectures which I gave at Chiang Mai at the end of last month, and as he also asked everybody to read *Religion and Development* in advance, I need not say more; for I amplified it when I talked about "The Future of Siam" in the documents for a panel discussion at Dr. Puey Ungphakorn's birthday on the 9th of this month.

Here, I would like to repeat only that for religious leaders or those who want to apply religion for the use of stimulating the development of society, we have to face ideologies : capitalism and communism. Both have their roots in western civilization. The more these two ideologies develop the weaker religion in the western world becomes. Both ideologies object to religion, and are dangerous to religion. Both lack an in-depth understanding of man, but still claim that they do everything for the sake of mankind. Each attaches great importance to materialism and secular develop-ment. Capitalism kills religion slowly with a neat trick without letting the religious leaders realize what is happening, while communism tries to uproot religions as if they were drugs or to force them to support it. But in this country now these two systems have become important principles that create discord among religious people in almost every denomination, and every religion. That is: when the monks or priests or religious leaders assume the role of capitalists, whether consciously or not, (for example, if they have to take care of temporalities of the temple or church, or take part in activities involving big amounts of money so often), they become attached to the value of living and eating luxuriously, to comfort, wealth, honour and fame. Then they conceive a dislike for change, and don't want to be concerned with the poor. They feel afraid of the youth and consider them violent and radical persons. The help for social welfare is just amusement; here is no real intention to do good. Christians especially, being a minority and having a background based in powerful western countries, sometimes even abandon basic religious principles in order to get along very well with the society. I once mentioned this matter to the Christians in Chiang Mai in mid-1973, saying : 'Those who are Christians in this country, are in a minority. Therefore, I wish you to consider your deeds whether they support the government and principal institutions or whether they support the welfare and unity of the majority of the people. When a Christian becomes a dean, a rector or a minister of state, you get very excited, don't you? But do you go on to ask whether they got those positions because of their own abilities, or because of their glib tongue, which might even be contradicting the teachings of Jesus? When your association or yourself go to see an important, famous, powerful person, you think it's an honour, it's fame, don't you? But do you go on to ask whether that person is a good person; if he is Christian, does he behave as Jesus taught? Or if he says that he has a different religion from you, can you use your religious standards to praise him sincerely? If not, that means you prefer to associate yourself with the rotten characteristics of Thai society rather than to want to uphold your Christian characteristics. Your prophet teaches you to love truth and your fellow human beings; in the circle of power in Thai society, do they love truth? Do they love their fellow human beings? If not, why don't you remonstrate? Each time they carried out a revolution, for whom did they do it? For themselves, or for the people? As Christians, have you ever demonstrated against American bases in this country? Have you

ever protested against sending soldiers to fight in
Vietnam, Cambodia and Laos? How did you react
where they imprisoned without trial the three members
of the House of Representatives? Moreover, what
about the increasing number of bawdy houses, night
clubs and massage locales? Don't you think these
things are damaging; or are they the responsibility of
the government only, about which religious persons
need not be concerned? Even demonstrations are
an expression of violence which is not characteristic of
Thai people! When Dr. Bradley first came to teach
Christianity, he did not conform to Thai characteristics,
but acted only on Christian ones, so that he dared to
remonstrate with King Mongkut even in the matter of
having so many minor wives. Did he do wrongly or
rightly? And in the many cases I mentioned, how do
the Christians today react, wrongly or rightly? Please
look for the answer in yourselves. Moral value is not
easy to judge. I would like only to remind you sincerely that if we dare not face moral or ethical value, we
will retreat from the essence or essential characteristics of human beings more and more. If we dare not
protest to the Thai government and the American
government on political matters which are matters
of ethical and religious principles, we may become an
instrument of the other side, who conceal themselves
in the form of Christianity and who, in fact, are more
American than Christians, capitalists who prefer to
have war rather than love, peace and fellow human
feeling. Thus Cardinal Spellman could readily exhort
American soldiers to kill the Vietnamese, and Billy
Graham could maintain that Mr. Nixon is a good

Christian. In the same way many Thai monks are ready to make a stand on the side of the powerful and rich. These powerful and wealthy persons may give funds to support you; they may send missionaries to help you, money to build huge churches or modern hospitals, but please do ask yourselves whether they are buying you or do they just want to remind you about humanity and human worth? Social justice and the quality of life are what Jesus taught; and these are characteristics the Buddhists and Christians have in common.' (from *Periods of Revolutions*, S. Sivaraksa: Klett Thai, 1974, pp. 108-110).

My opinion about Communism has already been presented in the lectures *Religion and Development* (pp 71-90); and in the documents entitled "The Future of Siam." I have already stated that Communism is not an ideology up to the point where we would destroy the person we don't like or don't understand by accusing him of being a communist, for so doing is not a good method at all. It might even serve the cause of Communism. Young people who consider Communism as a success, a miracle, or who like to use violent words from the Red Book of Mao Tse Tung, have to be understood generously. Try to find the cause and reason why they become like that. Don't assume easily that they are Communists. Don't find adherents for Communism unnecessarily.

For Communism, whether we consider its pure teaching, philosophical ideal, or even the guerilla movements, cannot destroy the power of the state by itself, unless we who regard ourselves as its opponent help it, either directly or indirectly. We can see clearly from the history of our neighbouring countries that important friends of Communism are the American government and fraudulent governments supported by the Americans, no matter whether it be the governments of Kao Min Tang, Tieu, Lon Nol; or Suvanaphuma. We must admit that these governments didn't do anything to benefit the people, but made use of the principal institutions of the country and also the process of law and justice for the profit of a minority. If the religious leaders pay attention to communicating only with these kinds of people and then just talk and talk about wanting to help the poor; if they suspect those who work devotedly for poor people and try to destroy them; praise only immoral and insincere persons; and if at the same time the religious institutions still squeeze and bleed people and construct marvellous luxurious structures and pay attention to small ceremonial things which are able to deceive only silly people; the more they do and behave like that, the quicker will they—religious leaders and institutions,—stimulate the country to have a Communist government.

Even the Dalai Lama said to Thomas Merton that Tibetan monks made mistakes in ignoring the problem of the poverty of people. They concentrated on maintaining the temple grounds and practising Dharma without thinking of the changing society. Moreover, the fraud and luxurious lives that occur in religious institutions, commercializing merit and sin, heaven and hell, earning a living by creating magic talismans or interfering politically to maintain their own selfish interests, all these are the best means to open the way for the Communist Party.

In Vietnam, Christianity and Buddhism had diverged widely and use to take advantage of each other; and so on. Buddhism itself lacked devoted leaders and became the instrument of politicians. But in the last decade, the religions there began to realize their own weak point and began to join hands. They tried to work together in social service and even to practise meditation together while being imprisoned. Anyway, it seems that they came to realize all this rather too late! As for Siam, I think it is also quite late; but not too late yet.

Religions should perform two duties. One is to always maintain a pure, just and peaceful order in society. When we talk about Country, Religion and Kingship, we mean that these three main institutions are the principles on which justice with peace is based. But if those who talk about these three institutions are dishonest and unjust and commit crude crimes against labourers' leaders, student leaders or anyone who obstructs their interests, how can we believe in their words, how can we associate with them, unless we ourselves are also insincere and dishonest? Or we are too 'naive' to be aware of their political tricks and we believe them because we don't want change, isn't that so? Do we forget the second duty of religions which is to call for the better, more just and calmer society? Even though that demand means losing something of ours—even our lives—we must comply. If we don't believe and don't do so, how can we call ourselves 'religious'? How can we be absorbed only in maintaining churches, temples, position, status and wealth, while cruelty and violence grow more and more serious, poverty and malaise spread wider and wider, and the value of righteousness is challenged? Only by performing devotedly, flawlessly and justly with love, compassion and friendliness, can religions conquer the other side. We must conquer anger with love, greed with generosity, ignorance with wisdom and an awareness of the situation in the world and the universe. The answer for those who practise religion is to follow modestly, detachedly, the Master's steps with profound consideration.

Being human beings, we might commit errors. In many cases, we are weak and defeated by lust, pride and stubbornness. We have to look at ourselves and our relationships with fellow beings : human and other living beings. We should try to decrease the desire to stand out, to be famous, to have better living standards; we should try to live simply for then we will not take advantage of others. If we are to do so, we have to be persistent in practising meditation and examining our faults. Buddhists have to use the doctrine of Wise Consideration, Christians have to ask for Grace from the Lord—the Omniscient One. With this power of conscience which is always available, the religious man will establish the value of Wisdom and will be able to face unhappiness and danger in society with awareness, and smile even at his enemies. For the religious people, this is the only way; the way to develop society is to develop the individual. In this way, despite different religious ideals, different denominations should be able to meditate together as is beginning to happen in various countries. This fact, Thai religious people should learn, examine and apply so as to be able to work together. Don't think that my religion is more wonderful, greater than yours; I am better than you. Though we have different characteristics, we also have in common some which could unite us. For the religious man nothing is more important than meditation and contemplation. Nowadays, we may meditate and contemplate even while working in society. If we work in society, but miss out on practising mindfully or meditation at the level of wisdom, failure, frustration and destruction may happen very easily. (See *The Miracle of Being Awake* by Thich Nhat Hanh, Sathirakases-Nagapradipa Foundation, Bangkok 1976.)

If we can see clearly this point concerning Religion and Development we must abandon small and unimportant things. Men of religion have to study other religions, other ideologies, even Communism, in order to see the good point in their teachings, while at the same time taking one's own religion as centre. What we can accept from other ideologies and religions, we should do; where we cannot accept, we need not blame or attack. We also have to study modern knowledge in the same way. We do not have to appreciate science and technologies to such an extent that we evaluate them more than religious principles. At the same time we need not reject and fear them so much that we become reactionary. Modern knowledge also is useful; we should know that and know how to make use of it by mastering it, and not be mastered by it. We should also adapt it in a religious way such as Schaumacher does for example, in "Buddhist Economics." (See *Seeds of Peace* Vol. I Māgha Pūjā Number 1976 p. 108.)

If we don't come to terms with this matter, we may fall into one of these traps, e.g. 1) if we blindly accept modern knowledge, science and technologies, so that we see the answer in the ideology of Marxism or Capitalism, we will fall into materialism and misguidedly develop in a secular way until we treat religious principles as of subordinate importance. Most leading religionists and politicians seem to do so, even though they always say they are 'religious', or 2) we will obstruct secular development at every point, until religions have to turn away from secularity, and oppose every kind of scientific knowledge. Only when the religious leaders are aware of both these traps, will they be able to apply religious principle as the supreme one, with other areas of knowledge and ideologies as subordinates or followers, in order to lead the path of human development toward purity and justice by non-violence.

When the Buddhist Association of Thailand and the Siam Society arranged the seminar on "Buddhism and Modern Thai Society" in 1969, Phra Maha Prayudh Payutto (Phra Rajavaramuni) said that the religious leaders could have a role in society, if they have three qualities, namely, purity, sacrifice, and wisdom. Nowadays, we lack leaders in almost every area of life including the religious one, therefore we should emphasise these three qualities. If religious institutions can produce leaders who have 'moral courage' (Prince Siddhiporn Kriddakara's word)i.e., people who do not blame anyone easily, do not believe or spread rumour, but dare to do the right thing even though what they do may go against those who have political power, grandeur and influence in society, or even go against public opinion, much can be done. If we ignore those things, or only want people to praise us, do not want to be enemies of anyone, and always flatter each other, religions and the country and the other main institutions will not survive.

All I have said summarizes and supplements what I said in *Religion and Development*. Henceforth, I will make some suggestions for your consideration.

Propositions for Consideration

(1) In the past, Buddhism and Christianity consisted of the leaders who showed the people the way of release and enlighthenment, with profound principles which the Masters and their followers lived devotedly. Now, can religions still have this role? Can religious people live according to the principles that they unremittingly teach others? How can religionists stop behaving as capitalists in a capitalist society? Can they dare to face the 'Communists' without fear, but with wisdom, with moral courage, with sacrifice and with love?

(2) Some people put moral behaviour and duty at the centre of life; for others it is only peripheral. Is it right

that while going to church on Sundays, religious people still squeeze others and take advantage of other people, other nations, the other sex, and other beings? For the Buddhists, the first Sīla doesn't mean only to stop killing with weapons. It also means not to live luxuriously, not to consume wastefully, while a lot of people lack and starve to death. Will not acting like this be counted to be against morality, too? Letting foreigners use the bases in our country to make aggressive war with our neighbours and pretending to ignore this, isn't that also against the first rule? Can those who are religious and moral still ignore the assassination of our fellow-countrymen especially during this time, and be able to live happily? Even worse is the investment in armaments companies, and the factories that cause pollution problems which do harm to lives. Not only religious people but also religious institutions seem to put money in such companies, whether knowingly or unknowingly. This first Sīla is like the fifth commandment of Christianity. Rev. Fr. John Collins S.J. pointed out that Christians should apply the Ten Commandments in present society. "Do not have other Gods beside Me" means "Men of religions should consider whether they observe this, for example; do we treat wealth and our own progress as our Gods, without thinking of others' rights and happiness?" So with the third commandment: 'You shall not take the name of your God in vain.' We should also think over whether we use the priesthood or religious privileges selfishly or to avoid responsibility for our fellow human beings. If we think and consider in such a way, the ten commandments and the five Sīla can complement each other pretty well.

Besides, the Tiep Hien Order of Mahayana tradition goes as far as to recite the adaptation of the Patimoksa as follows:

1. One should not be idolatrous about or bound to any doctrine, any theory, any ideology, including the Buddhist one. Buddhist systems of thought must be considered as guiding means and not as absolute truth.

2. Do not think the knowledge you presently possess is changeless, absolute truth. Avoid being narrow minded and bound to present views. One has to learn and practise the open way of non-attachment from views in order to be open to receive the view points of others. Truth is to be found only in life and not in conceptual knowledge. One should be ready to learn during one's whole life and to observe life in oneself and in the world at all times.

3. Do not force others, including children, by any means whatsoever to adopt your view, whether by authority, threat, money, propaganda or even education. However, one should, through compassionate dialogue, help others to renounce fanaticism and narrowness.

4. One should not avoid contact with suffering or close one's eyes before suffering. One should not lose awareness of the existence of suffering in the life of the world. Find ways to come to those who are suffering by all means, such as personal contact and visits. By such means one should wake oneself and others to the reality of suffering in the world.

5. Do not accumulate wealth while millions are hungry. Do not take as the aim of your life fame, profit, wealth or sensual pleasure. One should live simply and share one's time, energy and material resources with those who are in need.

6. Do not maintain anger or hatred. As soon as anger and hatred arise, practise the meditation on compassion in order to encompass with love the persons who have caused anger and hatred. Learn to look at other beings with the eyes of compassion.

7. One should not lose oneself in dispersion and in one's surroundings. Learn to practise breathing in order to regain control of body and mind, to practise mindfulness and to develop concentration and wisdom.

8. Do not utter words that can create discord and cause the community to break. All efforts should be made to reconcile and resolve all conflicts however small they may be.

9. Do not say untruthful things for the sake of personal interest or to impress people. Do not utter words that cause division and hatred. Do not spread news that you do not know to be certain. Do not criticize or condemn things that you are unsure of. Always speak truthfully and constructively. Have the courage to speak out about situations of injustice, even when it may threaten your own safety.

10. One should not use the Buddhist community for personal gain or profit, or transform one's community into a political party. One's religious community, however, should take a clean stand against oppression and injustice and should strive to change the situation without engaging in partisan conflicts.

11. Do not live with the vocation that is harmful to humans and nature. Do not invest in companies that deprive others of their chance to life. Select a vocation which helps to realize your ideal of compassion.

12. Do not kill. Do not let others kill. Find whatever means possible to protect life and to prevent war.

13. Possess nothing that should belong to others. Respect the property of others but prevent others from enriching themselves from human suffering.

14. Sexual expression should not happen without love and commitment. In sexual relationships one must be aware of future sufferings it may cause to others. To preserve the happiness of others, respect the rights and commitments of others.

If religious people do not forthwith apply and use the essence of religious teachings in order to bring the society towards a clean, enlightened and calm way, the society will be violent and confused as it is nowadays.

Men of religion can help to decrease pride, unreliability, deceit and violence only when they themselves possess calmness inside. Resentment, desire or darkness must occure some times, because we are human, but we must extinguish them with compassion, we must decrease our own comfort and join people's sufferings and sorrow in order to find peace for the masses.

Anger, hatred, fear, greed, ignorance do not help to create peace; whenever these 'Mara' happen, one has to practise contemplation with wisdom, being aware of the situations, finding enough resource, acting with non-attachment to things and persons. Whether one is accused of being a Communist or not is not important. To declare country, religion, and king or not is not important. The important thing is whether we speak truthfully, and do rightly.

If our minds are calm, we will have peace inside. The power of mindfulness will be mighty to give us wisdom and to see everything in its reality. It will help us be modest and to be concerned with the lives of all creatures. We love our lives, they also love their lives. Therefore, we should not do harm to others, neither with thought nor words, which sometimes are more cruel than real killing!

From such beginnings, religious people may conquer the sufferings of each individual and of society. The relationships between ourself and others will be for helping each other, not to take advantage of them, nor because of the fear of losing wealth and power. The rich will help the poor, the poor will not hate the rich. More and more, the gap between the social classes will decrease; working for justice will be easier. The goal of living for society and the individual will be peace, attained by peaceful means.

(3) The situation of the country nowadays is a crisis one. If we don't think clearly, we won't be able to find the way out wisely. If the religious leaders do not warn us, who is going to do so? At the same time, if we let the situation become worse and worse by taking sides with or without knowledge, we will become stimulators of the quicker end of the religion. In fact, religious institutions should not support either the extreme left or the extreme right. They should not cause divisions into left, right, red or blue. In religious circles, one should try to unite in friendship and care for the sake of the majority who are neither left nor right, but who have been falling under the impact of a psychological war to enlist supporters. Neither left nor right is the answer. The answer is to decrease injustice, and the gaps between the rich and the poor, between the powerful and the powerless, and to decrease it in a non-violent way.

Religious leaders have to condemn killing and assassination in every case, and to call on the government to arrest the murderers. How many persons have been killed, but not even one person arrested? There is only confusion and a growing defamation, aggravated by the state mass media which is in the hands of the rich. Are the religious leaders still quiet? Only when these problems cannot be solved will the Communists come to power.

(4) It is not only assassinations, one by one, and the blackening of group after group, that makes people

afraid at this moment, but also the rumour that there will be a violent and bloody revolution very soon. Many groups, many associations and unions, together or separately, bring out statements to the effect that this bad and cruel event will happen. Will the religious leader still sit by? Whether we associate ourselves with them or not, should the Church of Christ, the Catholic hierarchy, the Patriarch's Council, the Monks' Universities, Buddhist clubs and other various religious groups join hands to open conversations with the government, politicians, militarists and also the youth, or not? I would like to leave this matter for discussion.

(5) Is there any way by which religious leaders could call for a return to the essence of Thai culture, with its religious and moral base, in order to wipe out the danger from modern imperialism whatever guise it comes in, Capitalist or Communist, and in order to decrease the lust for power and prestige, anger and hatred, and to a return to helping each other instead, for the sake of freedom, liberty, truth, virtue and beauty? This is the real way to honour the nation, religion and the king.

(6) In education, can we find the way to get rid of this bad system which produces men to serve the system in which the rich become richer and the poor poorer until they have almost no hope of earning their living? What can we do in order to teach a person to be, a 'real human being', one who has an elevated spirit to be free, to be generous, to be devoted and to have moral courage by going out to serve the people more than earning only for their own profit, by considering

human beings more important than wealth or fame?
If we can call for these things now, we should do so.
If we are not ready to do so, we should think seriously
about the consequences.

(7) The religious leaders should also be interested
in economic policy. They should call for protective
laws which would hold back the rich from becoming
richer *more easily*. The constitution stipulates that
ministers and members of Parliament are to announce their economic situation, but there is no law
issued to enforce that stipulation, no forbidding the
importation of luxuries from foreign countries, no
strictures about the money sent out of the country.
Opium and heroin are in the hands of those who have
political and commercial power and who run business
with a modern imperialism in the form of multinational firms. Progressive Christians have begun to
study and research on this matter. They also study the
ways the trading companies and the owners of industrial factories take advantage of the workers, by
spreading rumours, creating discord and distrust and
dividing the community. Shouldn't we take hold of
this point and encourage the religious leaders to
study it together, in order to serve poor and suffering
people?

(8) Concerning the soldiers, religious leaders should
not behave as sluggish chaplains, but should expand
compassion to them as fellow human beings, and
should explain to them that they should be friends
with the people. Most of them come from poor families. They should not kill merely on the presumption

that the villagers or the city-dwellers are Communists. They should not suppress and persecute people. Though the students may utter rather strong words, they never kill, never do harm to soldiers. If the soldiers behave violently, they will be hated by people. The more they kill, the more they will be hated. Although they have power in their hands and can control the situation, this state of affairs will last only a short time. Then there will be civil wars, guerilla wars and finally the Communists will come to power. Soldiers should be disciplined; even if the country is in chaos, and even if they feel that they are insulted, they should restrain anger and be patient for the sake of all. Soldiers should learn to prepare to be good citizens, should not seek for or believe untruthful news, should not think that they know everything. Good soldiers should find a way to deal with, correct or even to get rid of anyone or any group which behaves wrongly, uses power in a wrong way, or uses influence over students negatively, using gangsters, against civilians in order that soldiers will be friends and loved by the people. Soldiers have a duty only to protect the country, to fight with the country's enemies. Therefore they should not live more comfortably than ordinary people. They should not expect to rely on other powerful countries, they should not think in a dishonest way, nor concern themselves with political matters by being adherents of anyone or any party.

Religious leaders should speak openly on this subject. They should discuss it with individuals and they should join hands with leaders of other groups in bringing out a statement. Anyone who knows any military officers should say this to them and not only listen to the viewpoint of soldiers or politicians. Talking, communicating, should not merely be a one-way traffic; we should encounter each other, we should respect, and honour each other, believing in the good intentions of all, and persuading everyone to have a love for peace as we do ourselves.

(9) Those who treat the soldiers as their enemies, as their killers, should be urged by religious leaders to think of peace, to remind them that killing cannot be ended with killing, otherwise they will engage in endless retribution. In many cases, they killed because they feared, they killed because they didn't know, they killed because they were agents of politicians and a fraudulent system. To kill back cannot solve the problems; one must correct the system itself—which is not easy. Neither can it be done by following Marxism or Communism. As for countering killing by killing or by spreading the same kind of false reports, that will not solve the problems at all.

To fight with the killer, one must not only use compassion and non-violence, but also one has to learn the techniques of non-violence, the art of releasing one own self from ignorance, the way to avoid becoming the agent of the tempter. One must be aware of oneself and of the system, namely, one has to always keep a clear mind, even though our friends, our relatives and we ourselves may be killed. Killing one good person may lead hundreds, or thousands, of good people to join a movement for non-violence. If someone is killed, we must not then flee into the forest and take weapons to kill back. That is the method of ignorance, of cruelty which will lead to extremes, namely dictatorship, and cause ever-increasing ruin and death; and finally, no one will gain. There will be only losers.

Religious people have to warn both themselves and others. They have to bring forward a common statement. They have to study and to act together in this serious matter.

(10) The countryside is the heart of the nation. We have to seek ways to help and serve the farmers, small merchants and small people. Religious people should pay more attention to Co-operative movements like the Credit Union. We should try to urge that the relationship among the agriculturalists to be closer and firm. Students who go out to work and stay in the countryside should be cared for and accepted by the religious leaders. Religious people should not be afraid of them or dislike them. Though they sometimes use too strong words, we who are older, have more experience, must be patient. We must join hands with them, let them learn folk cultures. Through our sacrifice, our sincerity and our awareness, we will not be reactionary, we will not obstruct social change, but will be promoters of reformation in a non-violent way.

(11) The problems in the city are also so important that the religious leaders should not neglect these either. High ranking churchmen and senior monks

should go to visit the slums as often as they go to eat and preach in the houses of the rich. They should seek ways to help the poor, the pauperized patients, the prisoners, and make them realize human values, let them taste compassion. They should try to seek ways to reform the medical system and the processes of justice; they should study the labour union movement by a detailed study of all the issues. There must not only be talk with big words, but we must, little by little, seek ways to improve the lot of our fellow human beings step by step.

(12) Nor can religion remain unconcerned with foreign affairs. We would call for a neutral policy and at the same time, try to keep our liberty and integrity. Though our country is poor, it's better than receiving financial aid from foreign countries which often involves the recipient in tricky conditions and commitments.

Here, I would like to issue a warning about financial aid that comes through various religious organizations. This should not be too hastily accepted, for many governments deceive by using religions as a blind. If we are not careful, we will become agents of those powerful countries without knowing it. But this does not mean that we will refuse totally the relationship with other countries and their assistance. We, at first, have to be sure what we will do first, what later; what will serve our country and our countrymen; we should discuss and come to an agreement before asking for aid. Otherwise, financial power may confuse us; it may corrupt and break our unity. Or we may merely think up schemes in order to get money, which will be a very dangerous thing.

(13) All I have said will be achieved only when religious leaders know enough facts: that injustice spreads wider and wider; that almost all political and commercial leaders use religion as a blind for their own profit; that poverty increases, especially in the countryside; that the number of monks decreases; that the young generation despise and insult religion as lacking morality and leadership of any kind, except only ceremonial leaders who maintain the status quo of an unjust society.

a) To solve this problem, religious organizations ought to join hands with each other to set up a research institute of their own, seek information, seek truth for themselves, and not believe too readily the government or the mass media. In this matter the Society of Friends (Quakers) and other religious organizations, both Catholic and Protestant, are acting progressively. Should those in this country co-operate to act too? If we cannot act by ourselves, we can join with neutral technical institutes. It should be able to start in the near future. Then, if we can use the available data, and the fruit of our research for serving the masses—at present, it serves only the powerful and the rich—the religious organization will be of great assistance in disseminating the truth. If this is not the new way of propagating religions, what will it be? It is already unfashionable for religions to propagandize for followers by attacking and blacking each other, or by 'advertising' that my heaven is better than yours.

b) When we have facts, have truth, we must spread that truth. Each religion has its own magazine or newspaper already. Whom do those mass media serve? Do we have them for making known the facts which affect the fateful affairs of the country and people? Other kinds of mass media, such as radio, television, cinemas, slides, speeches, debates, should be thought about deeply and seriously rather than being used as medium for earning a living or creating personal prestige as they are now. A good sign is that there is a tendency in this direction, like the magazine of the Centre for Social Development of the Conference of Thai Catholic Bishops and *Voice of Dharma* of Maha Chulalongkorn Buddhist University, for example. Senior monks and high priests must be generous, patient and support these new ventures, and not accuse them of being Communist.

c) Finally men of religion should act together—those of the same religion, of different ones, and among the unorthodox, too. Though they have different views and different opinions from ours, if they act for the masses and for justice, we must join them in a spirit of non-violence.

At this moment, we are in the midst of crisis which goes implicitly with materialism, both right and left. Religion must be the third way out, it must fight against these values. Even though many religious leaders have been already defeated by this new evil, and see us who fight against this evil as evil ourselves, we ought to be patient and not to give up, while we call everybody one by one to think together, discuss together and act together.

You who are Christians, you trust in the power and providence of your God. We who are Buddhists believe in the enlightened mind of each human-being; though the Evil One may possess human minds, it cannot possess them forever. With our firm trust and faith in our Master we should apply Dharma in order that mankind will develop under the guidance of religion and morals forever.

The crisis in the present time cannot last forever. But the better situation depends on the wisdom, ability and sacrifice of every one of us who will join our strength to help each other in thinking, talking and acting together, and become a movement, in order to clear the way to a better future.

BUDDHISM AND SOCIETY:
BEYOND THE PRESENT HORIZONS

I

When I was teaching at the University of California at Berkeley last spring, a colleague who taught Mahayana Buddhism there remarked that Buddhism in East Asia has little future: Japanese Buddhism, for instance, too, is dying, though gracefully. Although there are Buddhists who pursue the Noble Eightfold Path seriously in Japan, Korea and Taiwan, their number is limited, and their impact on the wider society is very slight. Admittedly, there are numerous Buddhist scholars, especially in Japan. Buddhist temples and ceremonies are very much available, but are used mostly for funerals. These countries are no longer Buddhist lands as they once were. As to the People's Republic of China, it is even more difficult for the Buddhist sages to exist. He said some enlightened and concerned Buddhists of the Far East are aware of this state of affairs. They feel that in the future Buddhism may have to take root in Europe and North America. The labor of Daizetz Taitaro Suzuki since the end of the last century is now beginning to bear its fruit in the west. Following the Chinese invasion of Tibet, the Tibetans now are seriously propagating Buddhism abroad, and are even establishing Buddhist training centers in many non-Buddhist countries. It may take some generations to see the impact in western society. Yet, their efforts seem to me•to be more successful than those of the Theravada Bhikkhus, who started missionary work in the west with the foundation of the Maha Bodhi Society by the Venerable Dhammapala in 1926.

However, this colleague of mine went on to say that Theravada Buddhism in South and Southeast Asia is very much alive. It has a great impact on the way of life of the people in the wider society. The Thai, Burmese and Sinhalese are, on the whole, proud to be Buddhists, and Buddhism permeates their cultures. He said that if he were younger, or if he were starting his career in Buddhist studies now, he would rather concentrate his efforts on Theravada Buddhism, the Southern School, rather than Mahayana, the Northern School.

I am not in a position to offer an opinion on Buddhism in China, Japan and Korea. But before I comment on Theravada Buddhism in Southeast Asia, I would venture to make some remarks about western Buddhists. In a way, it is gratifying to notice the increase in interest in Buddhism, both qualitatively and quantitatively. When Rhys Davids founded the Pali Text Society in London in 1881, only a handful of scholars were interested in Theravada Buddhism, and only a few of those admitted that they were Buddhists. When Christmas Humphreys founded the Buddhist Society in England in 1924, non-scholars were included, but still they were only a handful.

Many members regarded Buddhism as no different from Mme. Blavatsky's Theosophy.

When I went to the United Kingdom as a student in 1953, the Buddhist Society was still the only organization available in that country, and it was a very small organization indeed. At that time I could afford to buy all of the books on Buddhism that were being published. Today, in Britain alone, there are many Buddhist institutions in various parts of the country, and there are many books and magazines on Buddhism being published. In the United States, Buddhism is becoming one of the many organized "religions." While still recognizably Buddhist, it is beginning to take on forms of organization and congregational services modelled on the western pattern. One characteristic which this kind of Buddhism shares with conventional middle class suburban Christian organizations is an extreme reluctance to become involved in, or even to allow discussion of, matters of a political nature.

A few years ago, when I edited *Seeds of Peace*, a Buddhist periodical of social concerns, I wrote to various Buddhist organizations in Europe and America asking their members to subscribe to the magazine and to contribute articles to it. On the whole, the reply was negative: The Venerable Saddhatissa, head of the London Buddhist Vihara, wrote to me that most western Buddhists embrace Buddhism out of private spiritual need, and not for social responsibility. He advised me to contact western Christians who are sympathetic to Buddhism and to social justice. He was

not wrong: The encouragement the magazine received
in the west was from the Quakers. An American under-
graduate at Swarthmore College who happened to
practise Buddhist mindfulness ordered 20 copies of
the magazine. A Catholic lady who worked with a
Protestant Aid Giving Organization in Germany
bought quite a number of copies to be distributed
among her friends. She felt that cultivating peace and
non-violence for social justice should not be left only
to Buddhists. The Buddhist Association of Thailand,
however, ceased publishing the magazine as soon as
I was no longer the editor.

So perhaps, some eastern Buddhists, as well as
western Buddhists, regard Buddhism as an asset or
an ornament only. And as long as they do not test
Buddhism's strength in society, they cannot really
grasp the essential meaning of Buddhism.

Max Weber said of Buddhism, "Salvation is an
absolutely personal performance of the self-reliant
individual. No one, and particularly no social community, can help him. The specific asocial character of
genuine mysticism is here carried to its maximum."[1]
This misunderstanding has been repeated by scholars
in the west, and even by reputable Indian scholars:
"The Arahat (Theravada 'Enlightened Noble Disciple') rests satisfied with achieving his own private
salvation; he is not necessarily interested in the
welfare of others. The ideal of the Arahat is made of

---

[1] M. Weber: *Religion of India*, New York, 1958, p. 213.

selfishness; there is even a lurking fear that the world would take hold of him if he stayed here too long."[2]

To speak of Buddhism as something concerned with the private salvation of the individual is to ignore entirely the basic Buddhist repudiation of the notion of the individual soul. The teaching of the Buddha is not concerned with the private destiny of the individual, but with something much wider: the whole realm of sentient being, the whole consciousness. This inevitably entails a concern with social and political matters, and these receive a large share of attention in the teaching of the Buddha as it is represented in the Pali Canon, the basic scripture of Theravada Buddhism. To attempt to understand Buddhism apart from its social dimension is mistaken. Preoccupation with the individual places limits on love, and Buddhism is an attempt to deal with what it sees as the disease of individualism. Buddhism is primarily a method of overcoming the limits of the individual self; consequently, it will entail a concern with the social and political dimensions. Unless and until western Buddhists are aware of this very fact, the embrace of Buddhism will not help them get rid of their ego. Ego seems to play a predominant role in the development of modern western civilization. Yet I am sure that once Buddhism takes root in the western world, western Buddhists will go beyond the present horizon

---

2 T. R. V. Murti: *The Central Philosophy of Buddhism*, London, 1955, p. 263. The author is a Hindu, not a Buddhist.

and will contribute meaningfully and positively to their society and to the world at large. The west will become more humble, will treat the rest of the world, especially economically poorer nations, as equal partners or friends, and will have less aggressive attitudes toward non-human beings and the whole atmospheric environment.

II

I agree with Trevor Ling when he says that Buddhism can be regarded as a prescription, both for the restructuring of human consciousness, and for the restructuring of human society.[3] Without the former, the latter will be ineffective. Indeed religions at various times in human history have expressed a concern both for the attainment of personal salvation and for the establishment and maintenance of proper order in the world.

In Buddhist countries in South and Southeast Asia, Buddhism has been concerned with both all along. The wheel of righteousness *(dhammacakka* or *buddhacakka)* must have influence on the wheel of power *(ānācakka)*. In order for Buddhism to survive, it must

---

[3] T. O. Ling: *The Buddha*, London, 1976, p. 183.

be supported by a righteous ruler—*dhammarājā*—
the king who rolls the wheel of state in the name of
righteousness. The ruler is envisaged as necessary
for the implementing of the Buddhist scheme for
society; the king rules in subordination to one power
only—that of the eternal universal law, the law of
dhamma. It is this subordination which gives his rule
a unique quality. Buddhist kings in Theravada countries since the time of Emperor Asoka have sought
to achieve this ideal. It is the ruler's duty to restrain
the violent elements in society, discourage crime by
the alleviation of poverty, and provide the material
necessities to enable the citizens of the state to pursue
the Buddhist life unhindered.[4]

If this ideal is not carried out, at the worst, the
tension between the two wheels of righteousness and
of power causes the wheel of power to collapse, and
a new ruler takes over. The wheel of righteousness
is represented by the *sangha*, the Buddhist community

---

4 For a full treatment on this subject, see the following:
   Bardwell L. Smith (Ed.): *The Two Wheels of Dhamma*,
   American Academy of Religion, No. 3, 1972; R. S.
   Sharma: *Aspects of Politics and Institutions in
   Ancient India*, Delhi, 1968, pp. 64-77 (a good brief
   account of the Buddhist concept of monarchy), and B.G.
   Gokhale: "Early Buddhist Kingship," *Journal of Asian
   Studies*, XXVI, No. 1, November 1966, pp. 33-36, and
   his "The Early Buddhist View of the State," *American
   Oriental Society*, LXXXIX, No. 4, Oct.-Dec. 1969, pp.
   731-8.

of holy brothers *(bhikkhu)*. (The *bhikkhu sangha* would not get involved directly with the wheel of power, the *sangha* could affirm or deny the government's legitimacy.) Indeed, support of the state from the *sangha* is a necessity for the political, social and economic well-being of the community.

In situations where the Buddhist ideal has been most nearly approximated, there has been a triangular relationship of a close and intimate kind between the *sangha*, a king, and the people. The *sangha* advises the king, guides him in the *dhamma*, and supports him in his administration of the state. In return, the king provides protection for the *sangha*, ensuring optimum conditions for their pursuit of the Buddhist way. For the *sangha* is its vanguard, so to speak. They are expected to be the growing point of the restructured consciousness and the reconstructed society.

Between the king and his subjects, there is expected to be a reciprocal relationship of respect and support. Without an efficient ruler, society reverts to barbarism, where large devour small, strong oppress weak and clever people take advantage of foolish ones. On the other hand, without loyalty from the people and due observance of laws made for the benefit of all, the ruler cannot function efficiently or humanly, and must necessarily become either a tyrant or a puppet.

In the Pali Canon, there are many descriptions of the ideal king and exhortations concerning good government. The realm of the wise king is one which is free from all oppression, not ruled arbitrarily but with equity, where good men are honoured and where the king and his officials exhibit qualities of selflessness, rectitude, mercy, political wisdom and a sense of equal respect for all beings, including different classes of society, townsmen, countrymen, religious teachers of other faiths, and even birds and beasts. The importance of the personal righteousness of the king is strongly emphasized. For instance, it is the tradition in Siam up to now that on the king's birthday a *bhikkhu* is always invited to remind the king of the importance of righteousness.

Kingly virtues and the duties of the king are spelt out in detail in the Pali Canon.[5] They are (1) generosity, (2) high moral character, (3) self-sacrifice, (4) honesty and integrity, (5) gentleness, (6) self control, (7) nonanger, (8) non-oppression, (9) forbearance, (10) conformity to the law.[6] If things go wrong in the kingdom, for instance too much robbery, famine or drought, the king's lack of virtues is usually blamed.

> *. . . And in those days all men and beasts*
> *Shall surely be in mortal danger*

---

[5] Phra Rajavaramuni: *A Dictionary of Buddhism*, Bangkok, 1975, p. 207. See also, Prince Dhaninivat, "The Old Siamese Conception of the Monarchy," *Journal of the Siam Society*, XXXVI 2, 1947, p. 91.

[6] King Prajadhipok of Siam said this in 1931. See Benjamin Batson: *Siam's Political Future*, Cornell Data Paper (revised edition), 1977.

For when the Monarch shall betray
The Ten Virtues of the Throne
Calamity will strike, the omens
Sixteen monstrous apparitions:
Moon, stars, earth, sky shall lose their course
Misfortune shall spread everywhere
Pitch-black the thundercloud shall blaze
With Kali's fatal conflagration
Strange signs shall be observed throughout
The land, the Chao Phraya River shall boil
Red as the heart's blood of a bird
Madness shall seize the Earth's wide breast
Yellow the colour of the leading sky
The forest spirits race to haunt
The city, while to the forest flee
The city spirits seeking refuge . . .
The enamel tile shall rise and float
The light gourd sink down to the depths.[7]

So lamented a Thai poet of the seventeenth century.

However, the royal duties are not interpreted as a strict code of conduct in a puritanical sense. The same is true for the Buddhist layman's behavior; the more he strives toward enlightenment and for the welfare of all, the better it is. But if he fails here and there, it is only human. For instance, one king of Siam had practised the celibacy of the *bhikkhu* for 26 years. Yet when he left the *sangha* and became king, he was remembered

---

7 Quoted by B. Anderson in *Bulletin of Concerned Asian Scholars*, Vol. 9, No. 3, July 1977.

by his subjects with gratitude for producing almost a hundred princes and princesses of the blood. He did much for the reform of the *sangha* as well as for the benefit of his country and his people. Indeed, it is largely due to this king that Siam survived colonialism. There is a limit to this tolerance, however, although the limit is very flexible.[8]

"When kings are righteous," says the Pali Texts, "the ministers of kings are righteous. When ministers are righteous, brahmans and householders also are righteous. The townsfolk and villagers are righteous. This being so, moon and sun go right in their course. This being so, constellations and stars do likewise; days and nights, months and fortnights, seasons and years go on their courses regularly; winds blow regularly and in due season ... Rains falling seasonably, the crops ripen in due season ... when crops ripen in due season, men who live on these crops are long-lived, well favoured, strong and free from sickness."[9]

In such a state, the people would be in a position to put the teaching of the Buddha into serious practice. There would be a similar reciprocal relationship of respect and support between the *sangha* and the people.

---

[8] This same king is ridiculed in *The King and I* film and stage play versions of Margaret Landon's fictionalized biography *Anna and the King of Siam*.

[9] *The Book of Gradual Sayings*, Vol. II, p. 85.

Until colonial expansion in the nineteenth century, the *ārāma* (the dwelling place for the *sangha*) was not only a spiritual center, it was also the social, cultural, educational and artistic center of every town and village. The *bhikkhu* would be regarded as the leader, who bridged the gap between the king and the people. He would set the Buddhist values above all others. Yet Buddhism would not deny non-Buddhist elements, whether they came from other religious traditions, local culture or any other sphere of the arts or sciences, provided that the Triple Gem of the Buddha, the *Dhamma*, and the *Sangha* are regarded as supremely valuable. The Triple Gem could help people to understand themselves, the society to which they belong and the universal law of righteousness. If other arts and sciences, indeed, even if other leaders and gods could help them in one way or another, Buddhism would not object to it. Indeed those elements could well be incorporated into popular Buddhist beliefs and practices. Once the Buddhists are awake, or aware, they would be "mindful" about themselves and others. They would discard impure elements, one after the other. Eventually, they would not even need the Triple Gem. They would be able to tackle all problems of spiritual and social life confronting mankind, and could offer guidance to others as much as the degree of their enlightenment would allow.

There is a Buddhist story that one day a leader of a religious sect came to visit and asked the Buddha, "If I follow your Way, what will I do day by day?" The Buddha said, "Walk, stand, lie down, sit, eat, drink . . . " The man asked, "Then what is so special about your Way ?" The Buddha answered, "It is indeed special. The ordinary man, though he walks, stands, lies down, sits, eats and drinks, does not know he is walking, standing, lying, sitting, eating and drinking. But when we walk, we know that we are walking, when we stand, we know that we are standing, . . ." This is a simple story, but it points to a practice which is most effective. To be able to see one's own self, to be "mindful" of every act and movement of one's heart and mind, leads one to begin to realize concentration power.

Once the heart is mastered, wisdom is born. Although self-restraint and wisdom are but first small building-blocks, they are infinitely precious material. Our heart and mind, under the guidance of self-restraint and wisdom, will know which path we need to take, and we would act with loving kindness, compassion, sympathetic joy and equanimity. Without proper mindfulness, an ordinary man is addicted to pleasure and is at the mercy of his senses. He is enthralled by the eye, with objects that charm, by the tongue, with flavors that charm, etc. He follows his natural desires, and eats his fill with ravenous delight. He welcomes personal fame and praise and resents obscurity and blame. He is easily provoked to evil deeds. He is greedy and lustful. He resents any ill fortune : when afflicted with pain, he is distressed and overcome with bewilderment. He finds that those things on which he sets his hopes frequently turn out to be a disappointment. He dislikes the sight of disease, or old age or death. When old age comes upon him, he mourns and pines and is tormented by sorrow. All this is because he is lacking in wisdom and in knowledge of the truth. Not only does he adhere to popular superstition, but he does not see things as they really are. Hence he needs teachers and friends.

In Buddhism, teachers and friends *(Kalyāṇamitta)* are very important. After all, the Buddha is regarded as the best teacher as well as the best friend Buddhists have. He said, "As at dawn light is shining forth, this is the first mark of sunrise. Likewise, a good friend is the first mark of the dawn of the Noble Eightfold Path."[10] Having good friends, one would have good company, one would have friendship with the lovely, which will lead to a favourable social environment.

Especially in Theravada Buddhism, the Noble Disciples are regarded as the best friends and teachers apart from the Buddha himself. In Buddhist terminology, *sangha* refers not only to the holy brotherhood of *bhikkhu* who leave home for the homeless life to strive for enlightenment, but also to any disciple who has reached the state of sainthood or has become "awake." Such a disciple could be a Stream Winner right up to an arahat.

The *sangha* community in fact provides the environment in which awakened consciousness becomes

---

[10] Phra Rajavaramuni, *op. cit.*, p. 1.

possible as a result of the denial of the idea of absolute and permanent individuality. Some members of the *sangha* wander about without fixed abode, but most have their normal dwelling in an *ārāma*, a kind of open monastery, which has become the center of Buddhist society.

At its best, the Buddhist *sangha* has the special characteristics of (1) constant cultivation of mindfulness concerning human existence, and (2) complete accessibility to the people. Both are equally important. Social contact and intercourse are essential if the ethical and spiritual values of Buddhism are to be transmitted to the surrounding society. Equally essential is the faithful practice of the contemplative life, if what is transmitted is to be worth transmitting and is to have ennobling effect.

For instance, there is a large *ārāma* in Bangkok where the head of the Thai *sangha* used to reside. It is called Wat Mahadhatu (Monastery of the Great Relic). This *ārāma* was well-known for its scholarship and involvement in the arts, including music and the art of kite fighting. It is said that whatever the royal page department in the Grand Palace could provide, *bhikkhus* and lay people of the *ārāma* could do just as well, or better, since at the *ārāma* they were more "mindful" of their activities and there was more collaboration and less competition.[11]

---

11 Prince Damrong Rajanubhab : *History of Wat Maha-dahatu* (in Thai).

In the nineteenth century, a Roman Catholic bishop remarked, "When we speak of the great influence possessed by the religious Order of Buddhist monks, we do not intend to speak of political influence. It does not appear that in Burma they have ever aimed at any share in the management or direction of the affairs of the country ... But from a religious point of view alone, their influence is a mighty one. Upon that very Order hinges the whole fabric of Buddhism. From it, as from a source, flows the life that maintains and invigorates religious belief in the masses that profess the creed. We may view the members of the Buddhist Order as religious, and as instructors of the people at large, and principally of youth. In that double capacity, they exercise a great control and retain a strong hold over the mind of the people."[12] Other Western observers of Burma seem to be of the same opinion.

In 1928, an American professor wrote, "The influence of Buddhism on the Siamese people is generally admitted to be, from the moral point of view, excellent. This is the chief reason, many missionaries will tell you, why Christian missions have made such slow and slight progress, especially in those parts of Siam, like Bangkok, where Buddhism is at its best and at its strongest. The Buddhists are so satisfied with their own religion that it is difficult to make them see they need another. So the missionaires tell me.

---

[12] P. Bigandet: *The Life, or Legend of Gaudama The Buddha of the Burmese*, Rangoon, 1866, p. 523.

Buddhism is, moreover, probably the greatest force for democracy in Siam. The poorest peasant may become a monk, and once a monk, he is spiritually on the level of the King. For the happiness of its adherents, Buddhism also does much ... It teaches its followers that this is an ideal world, that the forces which ultimately control it are moral forces, that what a man sows he inevitably shall reap, and that death is not the end."[13]

It seems clear to me that the Buddhist *sangha* illustrates that a radical, contemplative form of religion is not necessarily insular or individualistic in form or socially ineffective. But if it is to endure amid surrounding popular beliefs with which it is not in harmony, it must be embodied in a community within which its own special insights are accepted criteria of thought and action. In the continuing life of such a community, those insights will be preserved and transmitted to the larger society within which it exists. But if the community is to continue to exert a beneficial influence on the larger society, the members of the community must have as their primary concern the maintaining of these special insights which are the essence of their faith.

---

[13]   J.B. Pratt: *The Pilgrimage of Buddhism*, New York, 1928, p. 184.

III

What I have said so far refers to traditional Buddhist societies in South and Southeast Asia from the time of Emperor Asoka. In most villages, the impact of the *sangha* on the community is still prevalent today. But it is no longer so in cosmopolitan cities like Bangkok, where the impact of western technology and materialism is so strong. In fact, the decline of Buddhist influence began with the British conquest of Sri Lanka and Burma. Although the French kept the kings of Laos and of Cambodia, they became only puppets. Hence the triangular relationship between the *sangha*, the rulers and the people was undermined. Although Siam remained independent, her new political elites, at least since the end of absolute monarchy in 1932 (or at least since the name of the country was changed to Thailand in 1939) came willy-nilly under western intellectual imperialism. Although the new rulers paid lip service to Buddhism, their lifestyles and goals in developing their countries were contrary to the teaching of the Buddha. One source of challenge is the "radical youth," who question the king's adherence to the royal virtues.

In Sri Lanka, and especially in Burma, members of the *sangha* identified themselves with popular anti-colonial movements in order to achieve independence. Although they realized it was not possible to reinstate the Buddhist monarch ousted by imperialism, they felt it would be possible to have a righteous ruler if he was one of their own nationals who put the Buddha's teaching into practice. As Siam had no foreign colonial powers to fight against, the *sangha* remained close to the royal government. Unfortunately, the government became more and more corrupt, and in recent years, even oppressed its own people. The *sangha* hierarchy in Bangkok, unaware of political complexity, yet praised by high officials, tended to support the government. With materialism and commercialism creeping into a Buddhist state, life for *bhikkhus* becomes more comfortable. Too often they are invited to bless rich householders, and perform the many ceremonies needed for the cosmopolitan city of Bangkok, which two decades ago was an agglomeration of villages. The *bhikkhus* are so handsomely rewarded for the services that they tend to practise less mindfulness and become unaware of the people's poverty, oppression and other forms of grievances. Without righteous rulers to support them, they are supported by the so-called Buddhists who care for their own gain, fame, praise and worldly happiness rather than for the sake of the true teaching and the welfare of the majority. The political and economic elites, despite their Western education, still cling to superstition, magic and astrology, so *bhikkhus* who like to be in close contact with the new rulers tend to go for these pseudo-scientific subjects or any study which tends to be an obstacle to the Noble Eightfold Path. While in former days, *bhikkhus* practised these arts too, they did so in order to help the lay people to be in the frame of mind to strive for higher spiritual pursuits. Of the more progressive *bhikkhus* who go to Buddhist universities to study Western social sciences and the humanities, their object on the whole was for social mobility. With such degrees or diplomas they would be recognized or promoted in the hierarchy or else they would disrobe to join the lay life. In Burma and Siam, the disrobing monks are not being looked down upon by society as in the case of Sri Lanka.

A Thai political scientist who studied the *bhikkhus'* involvement with the Government's national development program has this to say:

As the progress of the society and the Sangha seem to be closely inter-related, and are inter-dependent, because of its prestige and connections the Sangha may be used in nation-building programmes; nevertheless, it needs to be so used with great caution if the programmes are not to defeat their own purposes. Through the Sangha, Buddhism could provide an aura of sanctity for secular activities. Rather than being a mechanism which could be manipulated by the government in achieving politically secular goals, the monks' freedom of action will become severely limited even in the realm of religious affairs. If it is to manipulate traditional values for political ends, the government needs all the more to remember that government should not be capricious; that is, politicians should not misuse public power, and they should remain deferential to their trust. If the manipulation of primary traditional rules for political ends becomes too obvious, Buddhism and the Sangha may cease to provide a major source of legitimacy.[14]

Unfortunately, politicians have not heeded warnings such as this. While the Thai *bhikkhus* claim that they are non-political, in fact, those in the Buddhist hierarchy support the political parties in power. Thus, the Buddhist hierarchy become more and more alienated from the majority of the people, who remain poor or become even poorer. At least two of the three parts of the triangular relationship still exist fairly strongly, although the *sangha's* leadership has been much more challenged intellectually by the new lay educated. Yet in the country, it is only members of the *sangha* who still provide leadership to the villagers.

Unfortunately, in countries where members of the *sangha* worked closely with the masses to gain independence from foreign rulers, they became so involved with politics that they neglected the constant cultivation of mindfulness. After independence was achieved, quite a number of *bhikkhus* remained involved in political matters, so they lost the spiritual life.

Indeed in all Buddhist countries, there are still living masters, who shine and illuminate. But without truly Buddhist rulers to support them, and with the expansion everywhere of modern development on capitalist models, would not South and Southeast Asia end up like Taiwan, Japan, and Korea?

[14] Somboon Suksamran: *Political Buddhism in Southeast Asia,* London, 1977, p. 121.

An anthropologist observed :

Tainted by implication with the profane, monks who engaged in political action and other forms of worldly behaviour are no longer revered. If, then, the common veneration for the symbolic ego ideal is weakened, one of the few bases for mutual identification is simply weakened, and with it the primary basis for social integration in Burma.[15]

A Sinhalese writer put it even stronger. He wrote:

The Ceylon Sangha, as a whole, have degenerated and no longer are they leading the selfless lives the Master exhorted them to do. The main reasons for the deterioration are the selfish motives and considerations of the bhikkhus themselves, their self-interest, greed and ignorance, and their failure to adhere to the principles of the teaching of the Master. The Siam Nikāya, the principal sect of the Sangha of Ceylon, is not only caste-ridden but also class conscious. They grant the Upasampadā or higher Ordination to one particular caste only, and the Malwatta Chapter, which controls the largest number of bhikkhus, has always been dominated by Kandyan monks, although the largest number and the most learned bhikkhus of this sect are of the low country. Nayakaships, or High Priesthoods, are sold for considerations, and in some of these Chapters, the bhikkhus are simple folk without any learning and not a few of them of a very low standard of morality.

---

[15] M. Spiro : *Buddhism and Society*, New York, 1970, p. 477.

180

> *During the times of the Sinhalese kings, they, as Protectors of the Faith, purged the Order of the undesirables who had crept into the ranks of the Sangha. The* Mahavamsa *mentions several instances when this was done; but now, without royal patronage and the guidance and supervision of a universally accepted leader, the Sangha is daily deteriorated, and one shudders to think of the fate of the Sangha Order in the coming generations.*[16]

With these strong words, there is some optimism, however. The author provided possible solutions for the future, and the book was published to commemorate the 2500th anniversary of the Buddhist Era, with a magnificent title *Triumph of Righteousness*. Besides, the foreward to the book was written by no less a person than the "High Priest" of the Malwatta Chapter himself !

IV

When the Sinhalese and the Burmese think of the declining state of Buddhism in their societies, they seem to look back to their kings of olden times.

[16] D. C. Wijeyewardane: *Revolt in the Temple*, Colombo, 1956, p. 585.

Despite the fact that Mindon lost lower Burma to the British, he is still remembered for his patronage of the *sangha*, especially during their reformation effort, as well as in the organization of the fifth Great Council of the *bhikkhus* — in order to settle questions of doctrine and to correct the text of the Scripture. Once Burma's independence was achieved, U Nu tried to imitate the *dhammarājā* concept, but, unfortunately, his efforts failed.[17] No other Buddhist leader has tried to imitate him. People only want to imitate success.

It is sad but true that contemporary political leaders in Buddhist countries all could be regarded as failures. In Buddhist countries of the so-called free world in particular, political and economic elites were born of a colonial past. Despite the fact that some of them fought their colonial masters, all of them are now collaborators with foreign interests. The life of the privileged elites and the life of the commoners are incomparably different. In the pre-colonial period, the gap was not great, due to Buddhist influence to avoid the extremes, non-sophisticated technology of exploitation for economic gain, and smaller populations.

---

[17] For full treatment on this subject, see E. M. Mendelson: *Sangha and State in Burma*, Ithaca, New York, 1975, and Trevor Ling: "Buddhist Values and the Burmese Economy," in L. Cousin, et. al., (eds.) *Essays in Honour of I. B.Horner*, Boston, 1974.

The worst aspect of colonialism which still has a strong imprint in Buddhist countries (even in countries which were not colonized politically) is Western intellectual imperialism. Although the political elites, claiming to be Buddhists (and some of them even wear their national costume to look like 80-90% of their subjects), their lifestyles are imitations of their former Western master, and they blindly want their countries to develop on the Western development model. They want to make Bangkok, for instance, be like London, Tokyo or New York, rather than to preserve it as a center of Buddhist culture and civilization. If some aspects of Buddhist Bangkok could bring in tourism, hence money, that will be fine. If there is a conflict between Buddhist values and modern progress or Western materialism, those elites are ready for the former to give way. This is harmful indeed to the essential teaching of the Buddha, which warns people against hatred, greed and delusion, whereas Western materialistic development encourages this triad of Buddhist evils as great virtues of commerce and the power base. Politicians and economists work closely, hand in glove, for selfish materialistic ends, thus fostering ignorance. Modern development encourages competition and success whereas Buddhism encourages collaboration and contentedness. In former days, most people were poor together, and they shared common technology. Medicine and childbirth for queens and commoners were the same. Education was entirely in the hands of the *bhikkhus*. Anyone could go to any *ārama* for instruction. But that state of affairs is considered unfavorable to progress. Today, spiritual advisors to the so-called Buddhist leaders are no longer members of the *sangha*. The *bhikkhu sangha* are still invited to perform state ceremonies and to preach sermons in the traditional manner, which have no relevance to modern society, and they confine their sermon subjects at state ceremonies to those which provide spiritual comfort to politicians.[18]

The new "spiritual" advisors are usually from Harvard Business School, Fletcher School of Law and Diplomacy, or the London School of Economics and Political Science. Many of these advisors, some of them natives of these Buddhist lands, are well meaning, but most of them no longer understand the message of Buddha. It is worse in the case of the natives who usually claim that they understand *Dhamma*, although they do not practise it. One Burmese expert even claims that economic stagnation of his country was due to Buddhism. A Thai psychiatrist made a statement that mental illness in Bangkok was largely due to the practice of Buddhist mindfulness. Had not these so-called experts been educated abroad, no one would take them seriously.

Materialism, either in the form of capitalism or communism, is harmful to Buddhism. Indeed it is harmful to anyone who wishes to restructure his consciousness for spiritual liberation, and who at the same time wishes to restructure his society for social justice, freedom and human dignity. This restructuring

---

[18] S. Sivaraksa: "Buddhism and Development: Is Small Beautiful?" See pp. 52 to 78.

activity is liable to be seen by the authorities as in conflict with the state. But if he does not continue this activity, he could very easily sell out to an establishment — be it religious hierarchy, commercialism, or even academia's ivory tower.

It is not possible to hope for a righteous ruler in any Buddhist country right now. Those of us who live in the so-called free world realize that we could not overthrow capitalism overnight. As a Thai university president once remarked, "Man is born free, but everywhere in Southeast Asia, he is in chains."[19] What can be done in such a situation?

First of all, one must practise the teachings of the Buddha. One must not grasp at self-importance. Yet with inner strength, from the practice of mindfulness, one would want to have good friends to work together for the benefit of society, mankind and all beings. Buddhists' friends and teachers nowadays need not be confined to the *bhikkhu sangha* only. Living masters of any faith who are selfless and compassionate could well be regarded as *Kalyāṇamitta*. Indeed, those of other religions, including those who claim no religion at all, could have some moral or spiritual strength to help us. And we in turn could, perhaps, help them. Together, we can work for ourselves and for others,

---

19 Puey Ungphakorn: *The Scope and the Promise of Non-Governmental Cultural Interchange Within Southeast Asia.* Paper prepared for a Williamsburg, IV Conference, Nov. 15-18, 1976.

especially in opposing human oppression and exploitation, in combatting disease, hunger and ignorance, which confront the majority of humanity. Members of the *sangha*, too, must be brought to this awareness, so that the *sangha* will still be relevant, bringing enlightened openness, love, and selflessness to the multitudes. For instance, urbanization is new for Buddhist Asia, where the *sangha* is used to working with the social problems of villages; those of us who know something about urban problems ought to share our knowledge with members of the *sangha*. Every effort should also be spent in bringing the message of the Buddha to the rulers, although nowadays it is easier to have dialogues with advisors to political leaders, rather than the leaders themselves. Most important of all is to be equal partners with the people. Learn from them, especially in the field of Buddhist practice. However poor they are, on the whole, they still practise simplicity and generosity. Do not look down upon their popular beliefs. But try to understand the social implications of such beliefs before attempting to use "skilful means" to uplift them. Yet we must let them know that they are being exploited, and warn them of the glittering message of modern materialism.

One must work within one's own religious and cultural background. However, in this day and age, one must work also with *kalyāṇamitta* who share one's aspirations and concern outside one's country. Some Westerners too are aware of the danger of Western materialism and technology. The efforts of some concerned Christians in the capitalist West should be studied with care. These people can work with us, as friends and teachers. We must learn from each other and must collaborate for peace, social justice and freedom of mankind.

With this kind of Buddhist philosophy at the back of our minds, a group of us has worked closely with non-Buddhists in Asia, in organizations such as the Asian Religious and Cultural Forum in Development (ARCFOD), which was funded initially by the World Council of Churches and the Papal Commission on Peace and Justice.

ARCFOD is a provisional organization of individuals and groups belonging to principal religious groups in Asia: Buddhists, Hindus, Muslims, Protestants and Catholics unified in a common moral concern for development.

Recognizing the limitations and inadequate relevance of social service, educational and "spiritual" roles that the religions of the Asian region have hitherto played, ARCFOD strives for a common regional initiative that will be sustained by innovative Action Projects and well-documented research projects.

ARCFOD views Development as a process in which traditional values are adapted or transformed to meet the needs of modernized societies. It views Development as a normative concept, whose norms and values are no more than the interests of people, and objectivity no other than agreement in community through free and informed participation in the determination of their own advancement.

ARCFOD recognizes that the most fundamental problems of development are moral in nature, viz. unjust international and intranational economic structures that systematically worsen the poverty of Asian peoples. Development has increasingly become the development of the rich countries and the anti-development, or under-development of the poor countries, particularly the broad agrarian populations of the latter.

Consequently, ARCFOD accepts as its foremost task and responsibility the promotion and strengthening of efforts to stimulate among the vast Asian populace an awareness of their condition, and the strength to strive towards meaningful participation in, and direction of, their own processes of change.

In this respect, ARCFOD hopes that the member-governments of the United Nations in Asia will adhere in more practical ways to their common agreement and official resolution to develop and outreach to the growing sector of international non-governmental organizations, national non-governmental organizations, voluntary agencies and voluntary programmes.[20]

---

[20] ARCFOD is now called ACFOD, with the word "religion" dropped off. It published *Asian Action*, a bi-monthly newsletter, with special issues on "Health in Asia," "Asian Rural Drama," "A Dialogue on People's Action," "Development," etc. Subscriptions are available through: Asian Cultural Forum on Development, GPO Box 2930 Bangkok. See also, Kathleen Bagen: "Religions in a Changing World, *Visakha Puja 2518*, annual publication of the Buddhist Association of Thailand, Bangkok, 1975, pp. 92-93.

Within my country, a group of university teachers and students, weary of the polarized conflicts, resort to the ancient Buddhist practice of meeting in public parks to eat together one meal a day, sharing it with *bhikkhus* and to discuss our problems and how to solve them in a Buddhist way. This was successful for a short while: participants went home with more peace in their minds. But this did not prevent assassinations or violence of various kinds.

Another group in Siam started meeting on the subject, "Peaceful Means." They discussed more concrete topics such as economic and social development, social justice and democracy. They soon were branded communists. After the change of regimes in Vietnam, Laos and Cambodia in 1975, the Thai political and military elites became even more insecure in their adherence to capitalism. Hence in 1976 they made the first bloody coup d'état in modern Thai history. Anyone branded as communist or "a danger to society" could be put in jail without trial. Some were even assassinated.

As a result of this 1976 coup, intellectuals who are concerned for the political and social well-being of the country can be divided roughly into three categories. Those who happened to be abroad or could be employed temporarily in the West, are no longer in the country; these are mainly professors. Younger people, mostly university students, apart from the 3,000 to 4,000 who were arrested and about 400 killed by the police, went into hiding or joined the "liberation movement" in the jungle. The third kind of concerned intellectuals are those who stay on at the universities or in government service and remain quiet. Yet there is a fourth category, who formed themselves openly and legally as the Coordinating Group for Religion in Society (CGRS). The first chairman was a Thai Protestant, and the present chairman is a Thai Roman Catholic bishop. They bravely visit political prisoners, and look after their families. They visit the slums and go into the countryside to investigate reports of official abuse of power. They work in collaboration with various national councils of churches, with Quakers and with Amnesty International. Only recently, three of their members were arrested as "communists." Other members of CGRS, including *bhikkhus*, have been interrogated by the police, followed by intelligence operatives, who spread all kinds of foul rumors about them.[21]

I do not know how long efforts such as those by the CGRS can continue. But to be a Buddhist, one must be willing to share the suffering of others. Vietnamese Buddhists used to suffer much more than the Thai, especially those in the School of Youth for Social Service. Gain or loss, dignity or obscurity, praise or

---

[21] "Human Rights in Thailand and Implications for U.S. Policy," testimony by Stewart Meecham before the Sub-Committee on International Organization of the International Relations Committee, House of Representatives of the United States, Washington, D.C., June 23, 1977, and David W. Chappel: "Thailand Churches Fear New Oppression," *Toronto Star*, March 12, 1978.

blame, happiness or pain are worldly conditions, taught the Buddha.[22] A common man only seeks the positive and wants to avoid the negative at any expense, where the noble disciple takes them as they come. He does not grasp after one or the other. The practising Buddhist should bear this in mind and keep on testing his inner spiritual strength against worldly conditions.

All these efforts, however, may fail to preserve Buddhism or Buddhist society — but they may succeed. But even so, we can build up human beings, with inner spiritual strength, with moral courage, with enlightenment. With enough quality and quantity, there may be enough of a community to be the growing point of the restructured consciousness for the reconstructed society.

The modern *sangha* need not be confined only to *bhikkhus*. It should embrace, as well, lay followers who practise Buddhism seriously. In the Pali Canon, the Buddha refers to the Four Assemblies which comprise Buddhist society as: monks, nuns, laymen and laywomen. And *sangha* includes anyone who is of good conduct, worthy of respect; he or she may be a Stream-Winner (who need not be a *bhikkhu*).[23]

The Sarvodaya Movement in Sri Lanka is an effort to reconstruct society in a Buddhist and interreligious

22 *Aṅguttaranikāya*, Vol. IV, p. 157.
23 *Majjhimanikāya*, Vol. I, p. 37.

manner.[24] Yet as a Thai Buddhist, I feel that one should learn from such an effort, although it is not yet a story of success. We ought to learn from each other in success and failure. And it is better to learn from a similar culture as in the case of the Sri Lanka movement, or from those who have similar concerns — like the Movement for the New Society in Philadelphia,[25] than from the usual establishment of well-known western institutions, although these institutions could be useful too. (The paper by Roger Hutchinson on *Christian Socialism: A Religious Minority in Canada* should also be studied seriously by Buddhists in Asia.)

In Vietnam, the Venerable Thich Nhat Hanh founded Van Hanh University and the School of Youth for Social Service. Both institutions are unique each in its own way. Members of both institutions have shown much courage and compassion, and both are still operating in his country, although the founder is not allowed to return home. About ten years ago, he proposed that modern Buddhists need retreat monasteries and spiritual centers or *ashramas*, which would be places of serenity and retreat. He feels, as I do, that for those of us who work constantly in the city, daily practice of mindfulness alone may not build

---

24 D. L. Wickremesingha: "Religion and the Ideology of Development," in *Religion and Development in Asian Societies*, ed. by N. Jayaveera, Colombo, 1973.

25 S. Gowan, et. alia (eds.) *Moving Towards a New Society*, Philadelphia, 1975.

sufficient spiritual strength. *Ārāmas* for *bhikkhus* too become so involved with mundane life, especially in times of crisis, that they lose their tranquillity — not to mention those establishments which have become altogether commercialized. So he proposed that both monks and laypeople who care for the social welfare of others should retreat regularly to such meditation centers, in a forest, where people can come to practise mindfulness seriously. Without such inner strength, one could not endure in the turmoil-filled world outside.

In fact, an Anglican monk who works closely with Buddhists, Hindus, and atheists in Sri Lanka attempted to make a religious center for spiritual retreat also a headquarters for land reform, and to make the people there aware of social ills.[26]

Nhat Hanh also proposed the establishment of an Institute for Buddhist Studies. He does not want it to be a place for degrees and diplomas as a means for getting jobs. But he does not want Buddhism to be studied "in vitro" either. He wants the Institute to be built and maintained in order to provide a living community for people who truly seek to understand a spiritual way of thought and explore the artistic life of the Buddhist tradition. Unfortunately, neither of his proposals materialized. Nor was his proposal *The Future of Buddhism* ever published.[27]

---

[26] *Living Dialogue*, World Student Christian Federation of Asia, Book No. 2, Hong Kong, 1977.

[27] A Thai version was published in Bangkok by the Komol Keemthong Foundation in 1977.

In the case of Burma, the present political leaders do not proclaim Buddhism as the state religion, as did U Nu. They are corrupt and the bureaucracy is inefficient, and in some cases, even arrogant. Yet the Buddhist values and way of life seem to be more nearly approximated in that country than in any other Buddhist country. To an outside observer addicted to the Western materialism development model, Burma is certainly a decadent and stagnant country. Yet, the Burmese, the Shans and the Mons are not obliged to accept the presupposition of the Westerner that industrialization is good because it brings increased consumption of material goods, and thus a so-called higher standard of living. Burmese culture is geared to a more modest economic goal than the Western one of exploitation of every possible material substance which man can lay his hands on. The Burmese economy is geared to low consumption rather than high, especially of such goods as fuel, cloth, housing material and even, to some extent, food. The *less* that is consumed annually the better. Siam of old was like this, too. A Westerner once complained that the Siamese would rather have "a coconut and a few bananas and a long nap, than all the comforts of civilization, with no leisure to enjoy them. We are doing our best to convert them from their heathen point of view and to bring them to a realizing sense of a thousand artificial needs."[28] As Schumacher put it, the Burmese Buddhist aim is "to obtain the maximum of well being with the minimum of consumption. Thus,

---

[28] Pratt, *op. cit.*, p. 146.

if the purpose of clothing is a certain amount of temperature, comfort and attractive appearance, the task is to attain this purpose with the smallest annual destruction of cloth and with the help of designs that involve the smallest possible input of toil. The less toil there is, the more time and strength are left for artistic creativity. It would be highly uneconomic, for instance, to go in for complicated tailoring, like the modern West, when much beautiful effect can be achieved by the skilful draping of uncut material. It would be the height of folly to make material so that it would wear out quickly and the height of barbarity to make anything ugly, shabby or mean. What has just been said about clothing applies equally to all human requirements."[29] One needs a British Roman Catholic like Schumacher to understand and appreciate the Buddhist economics of Burma.

Added to the Buddhist emphasis on simplicity in everyday living standards is the emphasis on non-violence. These two emphases have been central to the lifestyle of the Buddhist layman since the time of Asoka. The Burmese seem to have been able to preserve these emphases more than others, due, perhaps, to the fact that they closed their country to outside intruders in 1965. Although the rulers are not in close touch with the *sangha*, they are not hostile to Buddhism either. And although the *sangha* receives little state support, the traditional practice of mindfulness is still strong.

---

[29] E. F. Schumacher: "Buddhist Economics" in *Small Is Beautiful*, London, 1974.

Without material goods pouring in from abroad, (except in the black market from Siam) and without the affluence of capitalism, Buddhist values survive in Burma even more than in Sri Lanka.

The average Burmese, like those who practise Buddhism seriously in Siam, feel that to use any material resources heedlessly or wastefully would be morally wrong. Renewable goods, like wood and water, should be used with care. Non-renewable goods should be used only if they are indispensable, and then only with the greatest of care and the most meticulous concern for conservation. To use them heedlessly or extravagantly is an act of violence.

Thai Buddhists ought to learn from present day Burma in order to better understand their own society and compare the present generation with that of their forefathers.

Both Burma and Sri Lanka regard themselves as socialist states and belong to the non-aligned camp, which holds the West at a distance. Yet political leaders of Sri Lanka are much more capitalistic. Ne Win of Burma and his close associates may be corrupt, but those who run his administration are serious Marxists of the Soviet persuasion. Although the aims and methods of communism have been rejected, since 1965 the Burmese government has espoused a socialist theory of the state. The goal seems to be a national culture, combining the tenets of both Buddhism and socialism, for socialist theory is seen to be in accord with Buddhist principles, and without any need for subtle exegesis.

The egalitarian nature of Burmese society is one result of Burma's Buddhist culture. Another is the rejection of the private-profit motive. This is explained in the government's 'philosophy' by the use of the Buddhist concepts of *lobha* or greed, and deviation from ethical conduct *(sīla)*. But such exposition is hardly necessary. Buddhist Burma is traditionally a non-acquisitive society. Burmese culture discourages the accumulation of capital. Burmese society is essentially non-capitalistic in nature. In the long-term view, U Nu's government and Ne Win's are pursuing the same ends, although U Nu seemed to be more traditional and spiritual, while Ne Win is more secular and authoritarian. Yet they start from the same premises in Burmese Buddhism. It is this, more than any single factor, which explains how Burma became socialist. And it is equally Buddhism which is responsible for Burma's refusal to travel that other road, which for a number of reasons might have seemed attractive — the road to totalitarian communism.

Traditionally, the Thai and the Burmese were very similar socially and culturally. The Burmese let the Indian Chattias run their commerce, as the Thai let the Chinese run theirs. With Ne Win's drastic nationalization, Burma, for better or for worse, was rid of the foreign entrepreneur class. In Siam, the Chinese and Thai assimilation was so great that the Thai themselves are now running the country's business. The Thai hierarchy seems to be more Khmer and Hinduistic than Thai, at the expense of Buddhist equality. Economic and political elites are so united in opposition to fundamental Buddhist values, that the Fabian road to Buddhist socialism now seems impossible.

Pridi Panomyong, who staged the first successful coup against the absolute monarchy in 1932, did try, unsuccessfully, to implement a kind of Buddhist socialism before and immediately after the Second World War. He might be one of the few members of the Thai political elite who studied Marxism seriously.[30] Some leading Buddhist thinkers like Buddhadasa Bhikkhu also talk about Buddhist socialism, but purely from the Thai Buddhist point of view — without any awareness of Marxism whatever.

But to look beyond the present horizon of Buddhism and society in South and Southeast Asia, is it possible not to look at Marxism seriously?[31]

---

[30] Pierre Fistie: *L'Evolution de la Thailande contemporaine*, Paris, 1967. (Pridi was the first Thai statesman to be accused of being a Communist.) See also Peter F. Bell: "Marxist Scholarship in Thailand: The Work of E. Thadeus Flood (1932-77)" mimeographed. Pridi wrote an article in Thai *The Impermanency of Society*, which was translated into English but has not yet been published in full.

[31] T. O. Ling: *Buddha, Marx and God*, New York, 1966, provides a good background information on this topic.

V

At the end of the colonial period, countries in Asia were divided into two camps: the "free world" and the "communists." Both seem to be under the influence of Western intellectual imperialism. The former take capitalism and free trade seriously, hence the rich become richer, the poor poorer and natural environment gets much worse. The latter take Marxist-Leninism so seriously that they do not allow any dissent from the Party's line. On the whole, there seems to be in Asia much more totalitarianism than democracy, despite the fact that democratic terms appear here and there. To me, personally, the situation in both camps is quite deplorable. Yet one must say one thing about the communist camp. Their political leaders are, on the whole, honest and work for the social and economic welfare of the masses, although freedom of dissent from the government is denied to the masses. Whereas in the so-called "free world," political leaders are often corrupt. They work for their own self-interest and collaborate closely with superpowers and multinational firms in the West rather than for the benefit of the common people, who are in fact being exploited more and more.

In the "free world," Buddhism is allowed to exist; Buddhist ceremonies and dignitaries are even honored with great rituals, as long as Buddhist leaders do not challenge political leaders and economic elites. At the same time, intellectual, cultural and social activities of the Buddhist establishment gradually are being replaced. Such activities are allowed and indeed encouraged if they are being carried out with support or approval of the state. The *sangha* gets itself involved with capitalistic ventures. Abbots become landlords. Monasteries operate as tourist attractions and religious trust funds act as private banks. Meditation masters can hardly exist in the city, but forests and jungles are being cleared away in the name of progress. So forest *bhikkhus* too find it difficult to practise mindfulness in remote areas. *Bhikkhus* can, however, offer help to the faithful in the realm of personal comfort and salvation. Thus, Buddhism is being killed by capitalism—slowly, to be sure.

In communist countries, China for example, Buddhism was killed more instantly. Yet old people are still allowed to participate, as individuals. In affluent capitalistic societies of Asia, most of the young do not seek personal salvation from Buddhism either.

So capitalism or communism are no friends of Buddhism. But these two ideologies are the facts of life at present. Buddhists ought to be aware of this. With awareness, we ought to be able to cope with them.

We could not praise the Chinese communists for what they are doing to Buddhism, but we ought to praise them for uplifting the Chinese people to have enough of the four Buddhist requisites—namely; food, clothing, shelter and medicine. This we could not say for the majority of the Buddhist "free world" countries in South and Southeast Asia, which were in much better condition than China a few decades ago.

If one wants to find out more about the sad state of Buddhism in China, one ought to look at the Buddhists themselves. Had not they been in the state of decline long before the Chinese communists took over the reins of power? If we have enough awakened Buddhists, it does not matter what the government will do to the Buddhist establishment, Buddhism will survive. After all, Buddhism does not mean the number of people who go to the monasteries, the number of Buddhist books published, the number of ceremonies performed, etc. Buddhism means the number of enlightened people who could influence the society positively and effectively for less greed, less hatred and less delusion.

Buddhism had disappeared from India long before it did in China. We could not blame the Muslims for that either, although they were not friends to Buddhism. After all, Hinduism survived the Muslim conquest and persecution.

To me, the lesson to learn is that Buddhism's strength and weakness, its survival and disappearance, is due to its syncretism with other "isms." Theravada Buddhism's strength and survival for so long is due to the fact that it embraced Hinduism, and animism as well as other arts and sciences, while it keeps the pristine teaching of the Buddha — as expressed in the Pali Canon — as pure as possible. The *sangha*, through the *bhikkhus*, were pure in their strictness of observing the *vinaya* rules and regulations laid down by the Buddha himself. They studied the teaching thoroughly and they practised mindfulness seriously. Whenever there was serious lapse in any of these, they were reformed, usually with support of righteous rulers, and they looked back to their ancient lineage of Noble Disciples to measure their standard of purity, so that they could have enough wisdom and compassion to be useful to the society. With this as a base, they used other deities, systems of beliefs, and various other methods to be helpful to the masses. Hence they have always been looked up to as spiritual, as well as intellectual and cultural leaders in the society. Once this leadership role is lost and with no sympathetic righteous rulers to support them, the *sangha* will disintegrate. The Buddha no longer has witnesses to propagate his *dhamma* in a real and meaningful way to the society.

In India, before the disappearance of Buddhism, the *sangha* and the laity syncretized Buddhism so much with Hinduism that it could be a form of Hinduism. The *bhikkhus* compromised so much of their ascetic life, that the people could no longer regard them as being pure. To be sure there were some enlightened masters, but most people just would not practise mindfulness. Hence their selfishness overtook Buddhism and, consequently, Buddhism disappeared. Could not a similar analogy be drawn in the case of China? In fact, the Dalai Lama once told Thomas Merton that he had warned the monks of Tibet to spend more time on spiritual matters, and to think more seriously of not involving themselves with landlordism.[32]

In the case of Vietnam, we do not know much yet. But since Thich Nhat Hanh's proposal to have three meditation centers established was ignored even by the *sangha* hierarchy, the state of mindfulness could not be that great in that country before the communists took over. Whether Vietnam would follow the practice of China on this matter of Buddhism we do not know. But when a Thai friend of mine visited Hanoi before the change of the regime in Saigon, he was told that the Vietnamese official view was that it regards Buddhism as the base of Vietnamese culture, Confucianism as the fabric, crowned by Marxism. If this could be taken seriously, Vietnam may not wish to attack Confucianism as the Chinese did. So far, they have not done so, and they may wish to make use of Buddhist contributions to remold their country too.

One must realize that when Saigon was defeated, Buddhist students at Van Hanh University acted as mediators between the two opposing parties, and the University is still run by the *bhikkhus*. One must not be too optimistic or too naive about this; at the same time, one must not be too harsh or cynical about the communists, either.

In Cambodia, we hear much about violence, aggressiveness and atrocities, which is contrary to Buddhism.

An appendix on "Marxism and Monastic Perspectives" in Thomas Merton: *Asian Journal*, New York, 1973.

Atrocities take place in Thailand too. Therefore, I should not like to pass any judgment on Cambodia. But I would like to mention that an American journalist friend of mine who was captured by the Khmer Rouge in 1970 was well treated by them, and he said that the cadres propagating Marxism to the people used Buddhist terminology.[33]

In Laos, at present there seems to be a clear and genuine effort to synthesize Buddhism and Marxism at the practical level. *Bhikkhus* who propagate the *dhamma*, who are strict on the observation of the *vinaya* rules, and who practise mindfulness are still respected. The government proposed a new system of making offerings to *bhikkhus* in a more socialistic and economic manner, since the country is now much poorer economically, but they seem to care for the welfare of the monks. Those who claim magical power and seek fame and money at the expense of the masses were exposed and sometimes even executed — in a respectful Laotian manner.

I have already mentioned Burma, which does not claim to be a communist state, but there Marxism seems to work side by side with Buddhism — not perfectly or harmoniously by any means, but anyone who wishes to see Buddhism and society beyond the present horizon ought to study Burma much more seriously.

---

[33] R. Dudman: *Forty Days with the Enemy*, New York, 1971.

Like Burma, Buddhists of Sri Lanka have had bitter experience with Marxists in the past. Yet, Sinhalese scholars, more than Buddhists elsewhere, have attempted to compare Buddhism and Marxism for a number of decades. Jayewardene's lecture on *Buddhism and Marxism*[34] delivered to the Ceylon University Brotherhood in 1950 is political and anti-marxist. Yet a Burmese political leader about the same time said that the acceptance of Marxism does not necessarily make one a communist; in his view, Marxism is complimentary to Buddhism. Marxist theory deals with mundane affairs and seeks to satisfy material needs in life. Buddhist philosophy, however, deals with the solution of spiritual matters. He ended by claiming that his study of Marxism had only strengthened his Buddhist convictions, and that the two systems were ultimately in harmony.[35]

Padmasiri de Silva's "The Image of Man and Human Nature in Marxism and Buddhism" compares and contrasts the two ways of thinking succinctly:

In the course of our discussions, some points of similarity between the humanistic outlook of Marxism and Buddhism were discussed: our analysis was focused on human greed and acquisitiveness, the exploitation of man by man, the basic claim that a man should lead

---

34 J. R. Jayewardene: *Buddhism and Marxism*, London, 1957.

35 U Ba Swe: *The Burmese Revolution*, Rangoon, 1952, p. 6.

a full life rather than end up as a crippled, fragmented and sick human being. It was also seen that in the analysis of social change, while Marxism emphasized the economic factors rather than ideas, Buddhism considers both the ideological and economic factors as important. The Buddha has quite clearly shown that a mere change of the economic and social structures is no guarantee of the psychological transformation of the individual.

In planning and directing social change, Buddhism has a wider framework for creative thinking, whereas Marxism is tied to social midwifery. Regarding the techniques used for effecting social change, Marxism advocates violence if peaceful techniques fail. While the idea that the "end justifies the means" is the guideline of the Marxist, the Buddhist finds it difficult to justify the use of violence. The fact of change and flux, the presence of an inner dynamism of change within social phenomena are clearly accepted by the Buddha. But the Buddhist causal analysis of social phenomena does not imply any theory of historical determinism or economic determinism.

In discussing these points of convergence and divergence between Buddhism and Marxism, we have deliberately not discussed the Marxist materialist metaphysics (Theory of Reality). Now that we have completed our analysis of man and social change, it would be necessary to remind ourselves that at the basis of some of the fundamental differences between Buddhism and Marxism lie the claim that Marxism is essentially a variety of materialism. The basic

206

reality for Marx is matter in motion. The organic world, the world of animals and men are all a product of the combination of subtle material particles and has taken their present form by a gradual process of evolution. Buddhism accepts both the reality of material as well as ideational phenomena. Buddhism is not a kind of materialism. This means that while Buddhism accepts survival, Marxism does not. It accepts economic determinism; there is no viable concept of free will in Marxism. Finally, regarding the means of knowledge, both Buddhism and Marxism accept reason and experience, while extrasensory perception as a valid means of knowledge is accepted in Buddhism alone. Thus we see some clear differences in the metaphysics, ethics and the theory of knowledge. In the light of our analysis, it may be said that while the humanism of Marxism brings it closer to Buddhism, the materialism in Marx throws into relief some lines of divergence between Buddhism and Marxism."[36]

Until recently, we thought of communism as a rigid monolithic ideology. But now it becomes clearer that there are quite a number of schools or denominations in this new communist church. The Italian and French Communist Parties in particular are willing to synthesize Marxism with other forms of socialism, and believe in liberal and democratic approaches too. If

---

[36] P. de Silva: *Value Orientations and Nation Building*, Colombo, 1976, p. 28.

they could come to power by parliamentary means, they do not want violent revolutions either. Modern critical Marxists like Tonnies, Lukacs, Gramsci, Goldman, and Marcuse should be taken into serious consideration. Even Chinese Communism in the future may become more liberal and synthesize other elements of Chinese society. But in China, Buddhism was so weak already before the Communist victory that its revival as a major factor in Chinese society would be difficult to conceive at present.

But in countries where Buddhism is still fairly strong, even if much weaker than formerly, cooperation between Buddhism and Marxism is certainly possible. So far, only the Buddhists are talking about the possibility. It would be interesting to see a Marxist viewpoint of Buddhism.

A Thai youth leader of the popular and peaceful demonstrations which were largely responsible for the overthrow of the military regime in 1973 saw the possibility of Buddhist socialism for his country.[37] Since then, he has fled to join the "liberation movement," which is being supported by the Communist Party of Thailand, and which believes in using violent means to overthrow the present regime. If such a man had a chance to write about the relationship between Buddhism and Marxism, I wonder what it would be like.

---

[37] Saeksan Prasertkul: *Siding With the People*, Bangkok, 1974 (in Thai).

If Buddhist Asia were to become Marxist, the Buddhist elements would certainly retain some of their influence. Even at the worst, Buddhism will have its effects here and there, as Mao Tse Tung admitted that the kindness and saintly character of his Buddhist mother had had much influence on him. Or in the case of secular India today, one sees the Wheel of Righteousness and Asoka Singha as national emblems. Nehru stated that if he belong to any religion, he would choose Buddhism, because of its humanity and castelessness.

But as long as Buddhists in Buddhist societies practise their mindfulness and are aware of their responsibility in the society, Buddhism will have much more effect than that. Even if new Marxist rulers were to be so rigid as to prosecute Buddhists openly, Buddhism will still survive — shining and illuminating through darkness and suffering — compassionate to all, including those who persecute them. If the Marxists are more tolerant and are willing to tolerate Buddhism in their system, they will learn a great deal, and Marxism may become less aggressive, but more tolerant and humble. Marxism's courage, vision and struggle may combine with the gentleness, vitality, joy, and peaceful non-violence of Buddhism.

SOURCES

1) "The Role of the Siamese Intellectuals" first published in *Solidarity*, Manila, September 1971 and reprinted in *Siam through the Looking Glass* Bangkok 1973. It was adapted for delivering at the Institute of Southeast Asian Studies on 5th May 1973 and was later published by the ISEAS, Singapore in *Trends in Thailand* 1973.

2) "Cultural Freedom in Thai Society" was delivered in Bali in January 1971 before the governing board of the International Association for Cultural Freedom under the chairmanship of Lord Bullock of St Catherine's College, Oxford. It was published in the *Bangkok World* 28th March 1971, *Solidarity* September 1971 and *Siam through the Looking Glass* 1973.

3) "Thai – US Relations" first published in *Common Ground*, journal of the American Universities Field Staff, New Hampshire, July 1976. It was reprinted in the *Nation*, Bangkok on 14th July 1976. After the October *coup* of the same year the American Friends Service Committee in Philadelphia had this reprinted widely all over the USA. It was also quoted in the hearing of the Subcommittee of the US Congress on Human Rights in Thailand in 1977.

4) "A Thai Image of Japan" was delivered at the 106th Foreign Relations Dinner Address Meeting held on 2nd June 1970 at the International House of Japan, and was first published in the *Bulletin of the International House*

of Japan No. 25 April 1971, and reprinted in *Siam through the Looking Glass* 1973. It was translated into Japanese in Bangkok and in Japan. The Japanese version was widely reprinted in magazines as well as in a book.

5) "Buddhism and Development : Is Small Beautiful?" was first delivered as a Berry Lecture on the 70th anniversary of the University of Hawaii in May 1977. It was first published as an occasional paper by the Asian Studies Center, Michigan State University, East Lansing Michigan in 1978, a portion of which appeared in *Visakha Puja*, Bangkok, May 1978 and *Info on Human Development*, Manila, October 1978. The full text was published in the *Nation*, Bangkok 10 and 17 December 1978, *Gandhi Marg*, New Delhi, March 1980 and *Impact*, Manila July 1980. An abridged version appeared in *Asian Action*, Newsletter of the Asian Cultural Forum on Development No. 21 Bangkok, April 1980. The article was later expanded and delivered at the UN University workshop on Goals, Indicators and Processes of Development Project at Bariloche, Argentina in December 1980. An abridged version of this appeared in *Ideas and Actions* FAO publications, Rome, No. 138 (1980/6).

6) "Some Aspects of Youth in Asia" was delivered at the Asian Bishops' Conference at the Sacred Heart Noviciate, Novaliche, the Philippines, 3rd March 1974. It was first published in *Solidarity* March 1974 and *Visakha Puja*, May 1974.

7) "Declaration by CGRS" *Visakha Puja* 13 May 1976.

8) "Buddhism and Non-violence" was delivered at the University of Hawaii, Honolulu, May 1977. It was first published in *KALAVINKA : Voice of Dharma* Hawaii Buddhist Information Center, 15th February 1978, a portion of which was published in *Visakha Puja*, May 1978. It also appeared in *Gandhi Marg*, Journal of the Gandhi Peace Foundation, New Delhi, September 1980.

9) "Tasks for Modern Buddhists" was first delivered on a panel discussion at the World Fellowship of Buddhists Headquarters in Bangkok, when delegates of the WFB attended their 25th anniversary meeting in February 1976. It was first published in *Visakha Puja*, May 1976.

10) "Religion and Development—The Next Steps" was delivered at an Inter-religious Conference, at the Christian Women's Building, Church of Christ in Thailand, Bangkok 17th March 1976. It was first published in *Seeds of Peace* 2, The Buddhist Association of Thailand, 11th July 1976.

11) "Buddhism and Society: Beyond the Present Horizons" was first delivered at the Combination Room, Trinity College, University of Toronto, on 28th March 1978. It was first published by Asian Studies Center, Michigan State University in 1979. An abridged version appeared in *Visakha Puja*, May 1979. It was later revised and presented at the International Conference on Thai Studies at New Delhi, 25-28 February 1981.

V

APPENDICES

Samples of Buddhist writing
by learned Thai Bhikkhus
translated by S. Sivaraksa

FROM THE HORSES' MOUTHS

Editor's Introduction

So far in the text the reader has the chance to know Sulak's views on a Buddhist vision for renewing society. The following is his translation of three renowned Thai Buddhist monks' writing or preaching on different occasions so that the reader would have it from the hierarchy, as it were, apart from what he has already got from a mere Buddhist layman.

One monk, the Prince-Patriarch, is no longer alive. He was a great-grandson of H. M. King Mongkut, Rama IV, and was preceptor of the present King. He was highly regarded spiritually as well as intellectually.

Another monk, Somdej Pra Ñāṇasaṃvara, was ordained a Mahānikāya and was later reordained by the late Prince Patriarch into the Reformed Sect. He is the second highest ranking monk of the realm, next only to the Supreme Patriarch. He is regarded as the spiritual mentor of the King. Among the many people he ordained was Field Marshal Thanom Kittikhajorn, former Prime Minister and Supreme Commander of the Thai Armed Forces, who sought higher ordination in 1976, which was a cause of the October *coup* of that year.

Last but not least is the very well-known Bhikkhu Buddhadasa, who remains outside the hierarchy. He is perhaps the most outspoken and controversial Thai monk, who is also much admired for his spiritual depth and scholarly contributions. Quite a number of books and Ph.D. theses were written about him.

NB S.P. Ñāṇasamvara was appointed Supreme Patriarch on 21 April 2532(1989). Bhikkhu Buddhadasa passed away on 8 July 2536(1993).

THE RIGHT APPROACH TO DHAMMA

Fellow Buddhists, both members and non-members of the WFB, Bhikkhus and lay people.

I have been invited by the President of the WFB to address this distinguished assembly. What I am about to say to you will be said as a fellow sufferer in birth, old age, sickness and death. Please forgive me, and allow me the opportunity to speak to you frankly. Truth, dedication, and the love of our fellow beings is the true spirit of us Buddhists.

What I am going to say within a short time is the result of my observations over the last 30 years, and I feel that it is the most important aspect of our great efforts, particularly when our world-wide activities have reached this stage. Yet we have not paid enough attention to this most important endeavour.

Firstly, in the modern Buddhist world there are many Buddhist societies dedicated to propagating Buddha Dhamma. However, they are more interested in the method of propagation than in the actual teaching itself—which is the heart and core of Buddhism. Nor have they paid enough attention to the practice of that Dhamma. People are preoccupied with ceremony and ritual. This kind of Buddhism, I am afraid, will result in:

1. Less people truly and directly are understanding Dhamma through their own efforts and practice. In such a case there will be no one working toward the essence of Dhamma, for they will be pursuing secondary interests instead. Hence, the real meaning of the WFB will become more limited and consequently unable to fulfil the goals to which it should aspire.

2. True Buddhists interested in the practice of Dhamma will pay less attention and respect to the WFB. Or perhaps they will lose confidence in it. If such is the case, the WFB will find it difficult to carry on or expand its activities according to its proposed objectives. Its work will be confined to routine tasks and social affairs. Buddhists will necessarily be accused of fun-making, and sight-seeing on international missions. If this is true, most members and committee members will be engaged in their own enjoyment at someone else's expense. Under these circumstances, our organization must perish. Please, therefore, pay particular attention to the true goals a Buddhist should have in mind. We must be wary of a devious approach to Dhamma, and try to improve and re-direct ourselves to the work at hand.

What we need to do is to create interest in what is known as the heart of Buddhism; this is, working directly toward the elimination of each individual's defilements. We must work towards extinguishing the suffering of mankind. Once interest has been stimulated people will investigate, consider and seek to understand the essence of Buddhism. Preaching morality for the benefit of society and the state, or interest in Buddhism as a philosophy, or a source of literary enjoyments is less meaningful than self-practice and individual endeavour.

Man's defilements are the direct cause of his suffering. The unpleasantness of life does not emanate from ignorance of social morality, literary appreciation, or intense philosophical interests. Those who are well versed in these academic disciplines are still unable to deliver themselves from the unsatisfactoriness of the human condition. The only way to rid oneself of defilements is through the control and subservience of our sense organs. Once attaining this stage, social morality is no longer a problem, and peace and everlasting happiness will ensue. But this will not occur, I assure you, by treating Buddhism as a philosophic or aesthetic interest. Studying Buddhism through the medium of worldly interests has the inevitable effect of dividing Buddhism according to the differences among various schools of thought and speculation. Hence, Buddhism can become a subject of theoretical interest, mere verbosity, and less practice.

In order for Buddhist organizations, like the WFB, to be able to fulfil its intended purpose, according to the heart of Buddhism, we must first abolish the concepts of "we" and "they." Once personal and organizational differences and divisions are removed, the concept "World Fellowship" will become meaningful. The word Dhamma itself means the true nature of things and recognizes no divisions, nationalities, or separation according to creed or faith.

Misinterpretation of the Dhamma usually stems from those who pursue Buddhism from a worldly point of view. Many Western books concerned with Kamma and re-birth present unintelligent evaluations of Buddhism and are far from the essence and importance of the teachings. Even those who profess Buddhism often misunderstand the Buddha's teachings and consequently promote an impracticable approach to Buddhism. To use a concrete example, the Pali word *jāti* can be interpreted as meaning actual birth or the concept of "I" or "I-ness." If these two meanings are misunderstood or confused, one cannot grasp the true teaching of the Buddha. "Rebirth" in Buddhism has nothing to do with *avatāra* or reincarnation as understood in Hinduism or the *Upanishads*. Most Westerners tend to explain Buddhism from this attitude. "Rebirth" in Buddhism should be comprehended as a repetition and continuation of the "I-ness" concept. Understanding rebirth as an element and phenomena of the present life (continuous belief in "I", and an attachment to "I") is indeed more important than the rebirth that follows death.

This becomes quite clear when we examine the Law of Dependent Origination *(Paṭiccasamuppāda)*. Here the word '*jāti*' obviously means egoism. It has nothing to do with physical birth. The twelve elements of Dependent Origination are, in fact, aspects of dukkha as the Buddha pointed out in the Four Noble Truths. The reality of the theory of Dependent Origination does not present itself as an object for far flung philosophical speculation, as seems to be fashionable today.

Rather, its significance should be appreciated and used as an approach to daily practice, i.e., control of the sense organs, in order to prevent the occurrence of mental formations through ignorance. Without this constant process there is no dukkha.

Now regarding kamma, people are usually only concerned with good and bad kamma, black and white kamma, and the results that follow. This, in fact, is not an essential teaching of Buddhism, for this explanation of kamma was known and taught by other religions long before the Buddha. What the Buddha added to this theory was a kind of kamma that was neither black nor white. The principal teaching was, instead, the cessation of all kammas. This teaching can be found in the Pali Canon *(Anguttaranikāya Catukkanipāta Kammavagga)*. Practising the Noble Eightfold Path is, in fact, a kind of kamma that is neither black nor white, for it leads to Nibbāna which is the end of all kinds of kamma. This latter kind of kamma is unique to Buddhism, yet most Buddhist authorities persist in ignoring it. It is therefore the responsibility of Buddhist organizations like the WFB to correct this misconception. If we accept "Dhamma" as the basis and core of Buddhism, we can really grasp the significance of anattā. Once we understand anattā, we are prepared to understand kamma as the force that puts an end to all other kinds of kamma. Therefore, both kamma and anattā are aspects of the same principle. Once there is no self, there is no concept of "I" or "I-ness"; hence, there can be a real world fellowship. There will be no divisions between different creeds such

as Buddhism, Christianity and Islam. What the Buddha
has discovered and taught us is the way toward the
destruction of self. Selflessness is, indeed, the true
essence of nature. Once we label Buddhism "ours,"
it implies a division between "we" and "they." Those
who call themselves Buddhists can no longer grasp
the real teaching as discovered and defined by Lord
Buddha. To them, Buddhism has become a collage of
secondary and inferior additions obscuring the true
teachings. This makes Buddhism an instrument encouraging division and sects, and robs it of its universal
quality and application.

The word "Dhamma" may be interpreted in many
ways. Each of the various definitions of Dhamma will be
examined here. Ultimately, we hope to arrive at the
Dhamma, or kind of Dhamma that is most descriptive
of the essence of Buddhism.

The definition of *Dhamma* in Pali and *Dharma* in
Sanskrit has an all encompassing meaning. It includes
all that is both known and unknown to human beings.
Hence, it is impossible to accurately translate this
term into other languages. In order to convey the
meaning of this word in the short time allotted to
me, I propose the following definition: Dhamma is
1) nature *(sabhāvadhamma)* 2) the law of nature
(saccadhamma) 3) man's duty to conform to the law of
nature, *(patipattidhamma)* and 4) the results of action
performed in accordance with the laws of nature
(Pativedhadhamma or vipākadhamma). This concept of
Dhamma is fully explained in the Pali Canon and all
the commentaries. Each one of these factors is directly

related to nature. So, if we fail to understand Dhamma as related and conforming to nature, we cannot possibly avoid the suffering and unsatisfactoriness that inevitably must follow action opposed or contrary to the law of nature.

The problems and complexities of life, which man considers unsolvable, are the result of man's failure to understand what is referred to as the essence of Buddhism.

Of the four aspects of Dhamma that we have defined, which one of the four amounts to the essence of Buddhism? To answer this question, we must return to the Pali Canon. In the Samyuttanikāya, the Buddha reveals that the knowledge he attained through Enlightenment can be compared to the quantity of leaves in the forest, while what he has taught compares only to the number of leaves held in one hand. From such a metaphor, one deduces that the Buddha discov ered every aspect of Dhamma, but that he taught only the Four Noble Truths. In the Alagaddūpamasutta Majjhimanikāya, the Buddha's explanation is more explicit. He emphasizes that the Tathagata's teachings are concerned only with "dukkha" and the cessation of dukkha. In the Cuḷataṇhāsamkheyyasutta Majjhimanikāya, the Buddha succinctly reduces all his primary teaching to one sentence: *sabbe dhammā nālam abhinivesāya* which translates as "Nothing can be taken as self or as belonging to self."

From the above references, we can see that Dhamma, as the essence of Buddhism, means all aspects of nature, both changeable and unchangeable, and which are not to be regarded as self or belonging to self. If things are accepted as self or belonging to self, it is contrary to the law of nature and suffering will arise, either directly or imperceptibly. Man must therefore conform to the law of nature by acting unselfishly and in harmony with the realization that both self and an attachment to self are contrary to natural law.

Once we all recognize "self" as a delusion, it will, at last, be possible for man to exist in a common world free from the quest of personal advantage. Detachment must be thoroughly understood and put into practice bodily, verbally, and mentally. This concept of detachment does not lend itself to theoretical speculation, philosophical enquiry, or lengthy and unproductive discourse as seems to be in vogue today. Consider the time of the Buddha when his followers delved immediately into the essence of his teachings and became Arahants. They did not linger over complicated philosophical questions or become distracted by psychological or literary reflections. The teachings were at once put into practice and from this spiritual training and inspiration, they reached Enlightenment. There are, in the Tipiṭaka, psychological references, literary allusions, historical facts, anthropological resources, and philosophical theories. But none of these is the essence of the teaching; they are mere adornments that have become attached to the main teaching. The core of this teaching can be succinctly stated as dedication to our duties and tasks in a selfless manner.

I maintain that the principal teaching of Buddhism is identical to the main tenets of other religions; for all true religions seek to reduce and minimize man's self importance. Theistic religions teach the faithful to submit themselves to God or be united with God. This obviously coincides with decreasing the significance of self and removing the causes that give rise to belief in egoism. Even those religions that place faith in the permanence of soul or *atman* teach that the real soul or *atman* will ultimately be united with God. In this context, the soul is not the source or cause of selfishness or egotism. Even those atheistic religions that emphasize the principle of personal action teach their followers to regard life as self-sacrifice for the collective benefit of humanity. And those religions, during the Buddha's time, that represented the theory of anattā incorrectly, because they did not agree with the Buddha's own principles, still taught their adherents to reject absolute faith in self and the pursuit of selfishness. From the examples offered, it is not difficult to discern that all religions encourage the destruction of personal attachments. Disagreement over minor details, practices and approaches does not obscure the fact that the central teachings generally concur.

The Buddha's teaching that "All things should not be grasped," therefore applies to the principles of all true religions. Members of the World Fellowship should not limit themselves to the confines of one particular religion; for if they do, they are not acting in conformity to the laws of nature, since nature recognizes no boundaries and no divisions. Buddhism is a religion in harmony with nature. Buddhists should therefore expand their world fellowship to include all spheres and interests that are in concord with nature. If we cannot accomplish this goal, it indicates that we are failing in the primary task of understanding our fellow human beings. We must realize that there are numerous Buddhists whom we have not yet recognized, while they, themselves, have not yet acknowledged the fact that they are Buddhists.

In my opinion, a Buddhist is someone who devotes his life to the control and final destruction of egoism. Various labels and classifications are unimportant. The terms Theravāda and Mahāyāna, as a case in point, have no more significance other than assigning people to different herds like cattle. Buddhism knows no differentiation according to sect. While the Buddha was alive, he taught the Discourses *(Dhamma)* and established the Discipline *(Vinaya)*. Neither of these two original elements of Buddhism should be misunderstood as encouraging or influencing division. Sects or *Yānas* developed as the result of people emphasizing some parts of *Dhamma* and *Vinaya*, while ignoring or neglecting others. Their divergent approaches were determined by inclination or circumstance rather than the practice of personal detachment. Within the Mahāyāna and Theravāda Schools themselves, there are further divisions and differences in which controversy sometimes becomes more acute than between the two major branches of Buddhism. Even the devout and faithful often work towards their own or secular benefit. One who works for or pursues self interest can, in no way, be considered a true Buddhist. On the contrary, those who do not consider themselves Buddhists (or are not recognized as Buddhists by other Buddhists), but strive to develop selflessness, are, by all means, to be regarded as true Buddhists.

Because these true Buddhists have long been ignored or, in most cases, not even considered, an enormous task confronts the WFB. Is it possible that we, who call ourselves Buddhists, are withdrawing and separating ourselves from the majority of true Buddhists? If so, we are working against the law of nature. To re-align our efforts and establish a harmonious relationship between man and natural law *(Dhamma)*, we must first extinguish the personal prejudices and greed that are the principal causes of division and self interest. The solution lies not in the exclusiveness of doctrine, but only in the universality of the correct approach to Dhamma.

Ven. Bhikkhu Buddhadāsa

First published by the World Fellowship of Buddhists at their meeting in Kuala Lumpur 1967.
Visakha Puja 2510/1967.

DHAMMA - DESANA
BAHUSACCADIKATHA

At the royal merit-making ceremony at 5 p.m. on Tuesday, September 14th, commemorating the seventh day rite after the passing away of His Highness Prince Dhaninivat, Krommamun Bidyalaph Bridiyakara, the Dhammadesanā sermon was delivered by His Eminence Somdej Phra Nanasamvara (Suvaddhano), Lord Abbot of Wat Pavaranivesa, at the Royal Pavilion for Dhamma, Wat Pencamapavitra, Bangkok.

NAMO TASSA BHAGAVATO ARAHATO
SAMMĀSAMBUDDHASSA
Bahussutam dammadharam
Sappaññam buddhasavakam
Nekkham jambonadasseva
Ko tam ninditumarahatīti

I will now offer to Your Majesty a discourse on *Bāhusaccādikatha*, in order to further adorn Your Majesty's quality of Wisdom on this solemn occasion when Your Majesty graciously performs the Buddhist Service of Charity in front of the royal urn, which contains the body of His Highness Prince Krommamun Bidyalaph, late President of the Privy Council, on this seventh day since his passing away.

His Highness Prince Bidyalaph, member of the order of the Royal House of Chakkri and a Knight Grand Cross of the Order of Chulachomklao and late President

of the Privy Council, passed away as a result óf heart
failure on Sunday, 8th September 1974. Accordingly,
Your Majesty ordered Court mourning for 15 days,
royally sponsored the bathing ceremony with lustral
water, and ordered that the royal Tong Noi urn appropriate for a Prince Regent be used to contain his body,
together with all his royal insignia and that the urn be
placed at the Royal Pavilion for listening to Dhamma
at Wat Pencamapavitra near Dusit Palace. Your
Majesty also ordered the Royal Household to carry
out all the official and religious ceremonies befitting
his princely rank in every respect.

His Highness, the late President of the Privy Council,
had all the three distinctions *(vuddhi)* : birth, virtue
and long life. He started his official career during the
Fifth Reign, holding various positions and undertaking
duties and responsibilities, all of which were beneficial
to the nation and the people, in accordance with the
wishes of Your Majesty's royal predecessors. His
last post was President of the Privy Council, which he
held until the end of his life. He was able to carry out
his responsibilities and his good deeds for so many
years because he was a learned man who had much
experience and ability, and he always behaved in accordance with the Buddha's teaching. His knowledge
was deep, detailed and subtle and yet he was careful
in all he did. He never did anything which would be
harmful to anyone. He was highly regarded by all for
his intellectual and moral worth, whether they were
inside or outside this realm.

His upbringing and his career have been clearly stated in his own *Memoirs* and in the Royal Proclamations promoting him to higher ranks. One learns that Her late Majesty Queen Saovabha, the Queen Mother of Kings Rama VI and VII, allowed him to enter the Raja Kumara School in the Grand Palace at an early age. Then His late Majesty King Chulalongkorn sent him abroad to be educated in England. He was successfully admitted into Rugby and later Oxford. He chose to read Oriental Studies in which Sanskrit Language and Literature were the major subjects, together with Pali and Eastern History. He also knew some German. His B.A. was in Oriental Studies, which was also known as Archeology. He explained his studies in this way: "The study of ancient literature and culture did not mean to read and understand all the texts fully in every respect, because there were so many books, all of which could not be perused. The usefulness in learning classical languages was to get to know sources of ancient culture, which were the foundations of our modern culture. It also taught us to understand causes and effects on the development of literature and culture, and also to see the trends started from ancient times, and the ways which they were gradually developed into new forms that form the basis of our modern culture. This meant that, although the modern period was not in our curriculum, we had to learn about it too."

After his graduation from abroad, the Prince returned to start his official career during the Fifth Reign, first as an assistant head of a division in the Ministry of the Interior. He was later sent out to serve as the Ministry's representative in the Ayutthaya Circle. During the Sixth Reign, he became private secretary to the Queen Mother, and later became assistant to the King's Secretary General, Secretary to the Cabinet and Secretary to the Privy Council. In addition he was Foreign Secretary to King Rama VI. When the King raised him from a Serene Highness to a Highness Prince, the royal proclamation read: "In all the positions which Mom Chao Dhaninivat served His Majesty, they were of great importance which required absolute integrity and ability, and he had to be fully trusted by the King." During the Seventh Reign, he became Acting Minister and then Minister of Public Instruction. In addition to that, he was also a member of the Royal Institute of Arts and Letters and Vice President of the Central Committee of the Boy Scout Association of Siam. During the present reign, he was appointed a Supreme Counsellor, who acted as Regent, President of the Privy Council, Privy Councilor and National Chairman of the International Committee on Museums. Later he became for a period the sole regent and afterward he became President of the Privy Council—a position he held to the end of his life. When he was raised to a Krom, the royal proclamation stated: "It is widely known that His Highness Prince Dhaninivat is a well-read and learned man in many academic subjects; his knowledge of language is profound as are his researches in the arts and the field of archeology. His name is highly respected among the academic communities, both at home and abroad. Whoever has had the occasion to meet him would appreciate his advice and counsel on various subjects, which proved beneficial to all concerned."

Regarding his association with clubs and societies, while a student in England, he served the Samaggi Samagom as Honorary Secretary for two years and Honorary Treasurer for one year. He was a life member of the Royal Asiatic Society of Great Britain. In Thailand, he was member of the Siam Society, was elected a Council Member and eventually became Vice President and President for 23 years. As a Rotarian, he was elected President of Rotary Bangkok and was once Governor of the whole District. In these capacities, he did much useful work in a spirit of service and sacrifice, especially in spreading knowledge and understanding of the concept "service above self."

As a Buddhist, he was ordained a- Sāmaṇera and studied under the tutelege of His late Holiness Prince Vajirananvarorasa, at Wat Pavaranivesa. This was before going to England for his education. He recollected that during his novitiate, he studied Siamese at Wat School together with other Sāmaṇeras and temple boys. He stayed in the Holy Order for several months longer than the usual Rain's Retreat. After his return from abroad, before starting his public career, again, he took Higher Ordination as a Bhikkhu and studied under the supervision of his Royal Uncle at the same monastery.

Due to his good upbringing and continuous studies, both inside and outside the country as well as in the monastery, it is no wonder the Prince had only good qualities, among them a thirst for knowledge.

The Buddha's saying quoted at the beginning of the
sermon *Bahussutaṃ Dhammadhara ṇ* etc. means one
who has listened well, i.e. ably endowed with good
knowledge, is righteous, wise, and a disciple of
enlightened teachers, can be regarded as pure gold,
beyond reproach.

The saying in this stanza praises a learned man, who
is righteous, wise, and who is a disciple of enlightened
teachers. Such a person is beyond reproach, since he
has nothing for which to be blamed. One could of course
criticize him unjustly. Purity, in its essence, however
much people may criticize it as impurity, is not lessened
by such criticism.

Bahūsūta or *Bahussuta* or *Bāhulasruta* means one has
much *suta*. The state of one who has much *suta* is
technically known as *Bāhusacca*. *Suta* literally means
"listening" and is regarded as the main source of
learning. It refers to all kinds of education, and all
models of transferring knowledge in various fields into
wise action. In olden days listening was the chief mode
of gaining knowledge. Hence *suta*. Apart from listening
with one's ears, one must also use the eyes, nose,
tongue, body and mind, in order to acquire knowledge
in all subjects. In the way of the world, one depends
on one's education to achieve worldly knowledge, so
that one can utilize such knowledge in one's profession,
and lead one's life wisely in the world. This is known
as the worldly *suta*. But in reality, one needs *suta* in
Dhamma, that is, not only to live well in the world
at present and in the future, but to be able to find
real and true happiness too. Those who have much

suta are those who are learned in the sciences and arts. A *Bahusūta* is a well-educated man. He is able to speak and instruct in the subjects he knows very well. He is able to use his knowledge to effectively and efficiently implement his work. But he must be righteous.

Dhammadhara, Righteousness, i.e. doing what is good and right, which is beneficial and brings happiness to all concerned, e.g. to be honest, just and kind. There are many sayings of the Buddha which praise honesty, such as

Dhammañcare sucaritaṃ

Let a man do good for the sake of goodness.

Na taṃ duccaritaṃ care

Let no one do bad for the sake of badness.

Dhammacārī sukhaṃ seti

Those who follow Righteousness live a happy life,

Asmiṃ loke parramhi ca

both in this world and in the next.

One can be just by not committing any of the four prejudices due to love *(chandāgati)*, hatred *(dosāgati)*, delusion *(mohāgati)*, and fear *(bhayāgati)*. On the contrary, one should be impartial. Kindness can be carried out by following the four qualities making for amicable association, which will help men to support each other, love and respect one another: *dāna*—giving and sharing one's own things with other people with whom it is proper that one should share things; *piyavācā* —talking together and discussing things with pleasant and mild speech; *atthacariyā*—doing things which are useful to others; and *samānattatā*—being even-minded and without pride. Apart from these, one should be humane: one should behave according to the dignity of a human being. If one can practise thus, one can be regarded as a righteous man, but one should also be wise.

Sappañña, being wise, means that one knows causes and effects according to their real nature, or knows the root of reality. One who is wise (having paññā) is in a higher plane than the one who is learned (having suta). *Suta* only means to be learned by rote, or to understand things which are engraved in one's memory. But if one possesses knowledge through wisdom *(paññā)*, one's knowledge can penetrate right to the essence of things and can grasp reality, and thus be able to determine whether such learning is proper or not. There is a saying of the Buddha confirming this: *Paññā sutavinicchayī*, "Wisdom passes judgement on learning."

A way to acquire wisdom is to act as a worthy man or a calm man, in accordance with seven guidelines, namely: 1. *Dhammaññutā*—knowing causes or Dhamma; 2. *Atthaññutā*—knowing effects or the meaning of Dhamma; 3. *Attaññutā*—knowing oneself, e.g. knowing that the so-called ego or self is morally composed of faith, moral conduct, learning, charity, wisdom and intelligence; 4. *Mattaññutā*—knowing moderation, e.g. what is judged to be sufficient;

5. *Kālaññutā*—knowing the proper time, e.g. this is the time for study, this is the time to earn a living, this is the time to be in solitude, etc.; 6. *Parisaññutā*—knowing the proper assembly or company, e.g. this group of people are such and such, to get to know them, one should behave in such and such manner; 7. *Puggalaparoparaññutā*—knowing that each individual is different in such and such a way.

To summarise all these, wisdom means knowing in three ways, namely, 1) knowing the way to prosperity *(āyakosala)*, 2) knowing the way to ruin *(apāyakosala)*, and 3) knowing how to find and follow the prosperous path *(upāyakosala)*.

Buddhist wisdom starts by pointing out what is good, what is bad, what is useful, what is useless. Gradually it leads one to understand the Four Noble Truths: That there is suffering; this is the cause of suffering; the cessation of suffering and the practical path that leads to the cessation of suffering. One with wisdom can see the light leading him to walk on the right path, extricating himself from all the snares that entangle him causing suffering. He will eventually free himself. He can do this, if he is a disciple of the Enlightened Teacher.

Sāvaka means one who listens, or is a disciple; *buddha sāvaka* is therefore 'a disciple of those who know.' The word *buddha* often refers to those with knowledge, who need not be the Buddha Himself. But ordinarily people use this word to refer solely to our Great Teacher, as we usually refer to Him by the word Lord Buddha. In any event, such a meaning should be confined among Buddhists only. If one makes use of the word generally, it may refer to one with knowledge. Whoever has knowledge can be regarded as a buddha. Whoever is a disciple of those teachers who know the truth can be regarded as having learnt from excellent teachers. And one who is learned, righteous and wise, must obviously have wise teachers, i.e. teachers who know the truth and who have qualities benefitting good teachers. Buddhists regard the Lord Buddha as their Great Teacher because He was truly Enlightened. His qualities can be summarised into three categories, namely: His *Paññāguṇa*, which means that He truly knows; His *Visuddhiguṇa*, which means that He is truly pure; and His *Karuṇāguṇa*, which means that he is truly full of compassion. That is why he is the first and foremost of all the Teachers in the world. His three cardinal virtues can be examples for all teachers. Whoever is a disciple of such teachers, having received instruction from such wise ones, who have qualities to some degree like those with which the Blessed Buddha, the greatest of all Teachers, was endowed, such a disciple would be prosperous in all other qualities, beginning with being learned.

Who then should reproach one who is learned, righteous, and wise and who is a disciple of those who know ? Such a one is indeed comparable to pure gold.

His late Highness Prince Krommamun Bidyalaph was known to be a learned man, a righteous man and a wise man, who was a disciple of great teachers, famous in the world of learning, and in the sphere of Dhamma. His Highness was also a disciple of the Lord Buddha, the Greatest Teacher among those who know the truth. It is for this reason that the late Prince should be praised. Indeed, Your Majesty has continuously honoured him, even now after his departure from this world, on this Seventh Day since his passing away.

May all the merit which Your Majesty has performed devolve to the benefit of His late Highness Prince Krommamun Bidyalaph accordingly.

At the end of this sermon, four members of the Holy Order will recite Memorial stanzas in order that Earnestness in the Dhamma will be clearly established among the royal audience.

The discourse which is delivered to adorn Your Majesty's quality of wisdom is thus ended.

May all blessings be accorded Your Majesty.

Evam

Thus may it be so.

ORDINATION

His Holiness Prince Vajirañānavaṃsa
The late Supreme Patriarch of Siam
wrote this treatise in 1946 for His late
Majesty King Ananda Mahidol, Rama
VIII, who wished to be ordained.

The word Ordination in Siamese comes from the Pali word *Pabbajjā* which means "going forth" or "giving up association with the home life." It also means "giving up bad deeds." To be ordained originally meant that one should go away from home to seek a quiet place such as the jungle or forest, where one made oneself a dwelling, sometimes consisting only of the leaves of trees.

People could seek this solitude for a short time, or permanently, and it was regarded as a good action of great merit. This was practised in India, long before the Buddha found enlightenment.

History tells us that when the Aryan people came to settle in India, they were polytheists, for they worshipped all sorts of deities. Later, they directed their attention to Brahma the Creator. They prayed to him so that they would get what they wanted.

Then after some time, they came to realise that this life was not the only existence, for this existence was the result of past actions.

But it was too complicated for them to solve this problem. The most significant of their beliefs was that man was born with happiness as well as with suffering, and they tried various methods to overcome this undesirable suffering. *Pabbajjā* (ordination) was one of the many ways to achieve a happy end.

There are accounts of rulers and Brahmins who left home in order to become ascetics.

In the *Ramayana* (the great epic of India) we are told that King Janaka of Mathila left his kingdom and took up the life of a recluse.

Some men who were connected with the Buddha's life, were already ordained as mendicants of one sort or another when the Master became enlightened. These were such as, Alāra, Uddaka, the thousand Jatilas, Sanjaya and his followers, and the First Five Monks who were in the company of the Lord Buddha.

Those who keep the eight precepts just for a day and a night, and those who keep the five precepts regularly, ought also to be regarded as having been ordained; but at a lower level. The Lord Buddha himself said that the teaching for the laity included, generosity *(dāna)*, ordination *(pabbajjā)*, and supporting one's parents *(mātāpitupatthāna)*.

These principles were laid down by wise men before the time of the Buddha, but he also confirmed them.

Those who are certain to become enlightened are known as *Bodhisattva*. Our Lord, when still a Bodhisattva, lived with an abundance of servants, dwellings, honour and power. But despite this, he reflected on old age, illness and death, and he saw that these would befall him as well as others. He was so distressed that the wish arose in him to cure himself and others, and so he went forth from home to the homeless life. Having found the remedy for suffering; in other words, having become enlightened, the Buddha was full of compassion and wanted to spread his teaching to others. Yet he realised that what he had to teach was very deep and very difficult to follow for those who had been attached to the world. However, the Compassionate One did not give up. He came to see that some people who were wise and had few defilements would listen to him, and would be able to realise the teaching for themselves, and they too could become enlightened. For this reason, the Buddha gave his teaching to the world.

In the beginning he tried to find those who would listen and would quickly understand. He first went to teach the company of five monks who had been with him earlier.

Then he taught the thousand Jatilas who had already left the home life. Later on he taught Kshatriyas, Brahmins, nobles, rich men and house holders; all of whom had already had some higher education and were dissatisfied with the world. When these people listened to him, they easily came to understanding. Those who had a lot of faith in the teaching and wanted to put it into practice, asked the Lord for permission to follow his path. He then admitted them to the order of monks in the following words, "Come Bhikkhu, you should practise the Dhamma well taught by me so that you may come to the end of suffering." Those who were accepted in this way were regarded as Buddhist monks, and this type of ordination is called "*ehibhikkhu upasampadā*" (lit: the "come Bhikkhu ordination"), and such a monk was known as an *Ehibhikkhu*.

When there were several Buddhist monks, the Buddha sent them wandering about in different directions to teach Dhamma. When others followed the teaching and wanted to join the Order, the monks had to take them to the Buddha so that they could receive ordination from him. Sometimes both the teachers and the candidates had to suffer much in travelling to see the Buddha. This led the Master to allow monks the right to ordain others who came to them, provided that they had their heads, beards and moustaches shaved, and they were dressed in saffron robes.

They should pay respect to the monk concerned and repeat after him that they took the Buddha, the Dhamma and the Sangha as their refuge.

Repeating these three times was sufficient to qualify them as members of the Buddhist Order. Such an ordination is technically known as *tisaraṇagamanā upasampadā*, meaning ordination by means of taking refuge in The Triple Gem.

When the number of monks increased and the Sangha was well established, the Buddha handed his authority to ordain others to the Order. The rule now is that in the middle part of India there must be at least ten monks assembled. Outside that area, five monks are sufficient. The president who introduces the newcomer into the Order is known as the Upajjhāya. There must also be another monk who declares the name and intention of the candidate, together with the name of the Upajjhāya.

His first declaration to members of the assembly is called *ñatti*. He then announces three more times, known as the first, second and third *anusāvana*. When the assembled monks do not object to the proposal, the candidate is accepted as a new member of the Order. Such a method of ordination is called *ñatticatutthakammaupasampadā*, which means, "ordination by means of the four declarations."

When this kinds of ordination came into use, the ordination by means of taking refuge was discontinued.

In the earliest period of Buddhism, the Buddha did not fix the age of candidates, and there were instances of children who joined the Order as Bhikkhus, who still behaved in a childish way and who could not practise properly. The Buddha then decreed that candidates for Upasampadā (higher ordination) must be at least twenty years old. As for those who were younger, but who desired to join the Order, they could do so as a *Sāmaṇera* (novice) by taking refuge in the Three-Gems *(Buddha, Dhamma, Sangha)* which had been the method of higher ordination, until it was discontinued. The distinction was thus drawn between the lower ordination as a Sāmaṇera *(Pabbajjā)* and a higher ordination as a Bhikkhu *(Upasampadā)*.

When women of twenty years or more wanted to join the Order, the Buddha allowed them to become *Bhikkhunī* (nun), and if younger than twenty years, they could become *Sikkhamānā* or *Sāmaṇerī* (novice).

The Order of Nuns is now extinct, mainly due to the fact that at one time there were not enough Bhikkhunī to perform the necessary function for ordination.

In the beginning there were no rules or regulations for monks. The Buddha only taught Dhamma, and recommended that monks should practise it. Those who were then ordained, did so with full faith and in earnest desire to seek the truth. Having joined the Order, they put the teaching into practice and modelled their lives on those of the Master and the Elders then living. But when ordination into the Buddhist Order became a frequent occurrence, some of these who became monks did not do so with sufficient earnestness. This led them to behave badly and they were blamed by others. The Buddha then had to establish certain modes of behaviour for monks, and should any monk act contrary to the major rules, he would be expelled from the Order.

Breaking minor rules meant that they had to ask for pardon and promise to their fellow monks that they would not break the rules again. Thus the teaching now consists of the Discourses *(Sutta)* which are intended to show the way of developing the practice of Buddhism, and the Disciplines *(Vinaya)* which are the rules of behaviour for monks.

Neither the Buddha nor the teachings of Buddhism say that people must leave their homes to become monks. Only those who have a full conviction in the homeless life should go forth to be ordained. If they are unable to lead the Holy Life, the Buddha permits them to leave the Order, and they can freely return to their normal modes of living.

There is no rule to force people to remain in the Order, and having left the Order, if they wish to return again to tread the path, they are again welcome. This liberal approach to admission into and resignation from the Sangha is to avoid bad behaviour in those who tread the Noble Path, so that those who remain within the Order have no excuse for doing anything but that which is good.

Sangha, monthly Buddhist Journal of the English Sangha Association, London 1961.

The World Fellowship of Buddhists News Bulletin Vol. 1 No. 1. January 1964.

Visakha Puja, the Buddhist Association of Thailand, 2508/1965.

ADDENDA

The Naropa Institute

presents

THE FOUNDER'S AWARD

to

Sulak Sivaraksa

for

OUTSTANDING SERVICE
IN THE
CREATION OF ENLIGHTENED SOCIETY

September 10, 1993

I
TOLERANCE FOR DIVERSITY OF RELIGION OR BELIEF: ITS IMPORTANCE FOR SOCIAL AND ECONOMIC DEVELOPMENT

I am greatly honoured to be invited to give a dinner address to such a distinguished audience. Indeed it seems most appropriate to hold such a unique conference in this wonderful city, now, at a time when tolerance of religions and beliefs is blooming. All eyes are on Poland these days and many people, myself included, applaud the new changes that have been made and hold out great hope that the country will further develop, nonviolently, towards social justice with renewed awareness of human rights and human dignity.

At the risk of over simplification, I would like to propose that each of the world's great religions consists of two main aspects, namely that of universal love, which is altruistic and selfless, on the one hand, and a tribal, institutionalized or egocentric factor on the other. If we are not careful, our religion can become very fundamentalistic and intolerant, and we will find ourselves believing that we are the only ones on the true and righteous path to salvation, while all others are merely misguided souls. It is a great temptation to compete with other religions and rationalize that ours is better rather than to work towards peaceful co-existance and cooperation.

Unfortunately, some religions are still hunting for converts using crass and destructive ideologies. I'd like to quote to you from the *Overseas Missionary Fellowship* (August-September 1987). The article is called 'Finding True Freedom in Thailand' and it says that "For 99 percent of the Thais, bondage to demons brings the greatest fear and complete deliverance an anxious hope. This is true for animistic tribesmen, prosperous merchants, enlightened graduates or stolid farmers ... revealed in conversation, TV soap operas, adornments to people's person or property ... nothing and no one has been able to remove permanently the inner anxiety that man, in manipulating the spiritual forces, can also become their victim." The conclusion you are led to, if you read the article, is that the Thais must be saved by Christian missionaries, or that as a tribe, they must be saved by U.S. Aid! I feel that people who stick with religions or ideologies such as these, who are unable to respect other people, especially the poor, may be so proud of their religion that they are no more advanced spiritually than these would be evangelists.

Indeed tribalism in itself should not be a derogatory term, but when a world religion or super power becomes tribal, it can easily degenerate to hypocrisy and arrogance and can even lead to racism, as one can see clearly in South Africa and elsewhere.

However, if we concentrate on the religious aspects of universal love, we shall all become more humble, tolerant and truly respectful of other beings — not only human, but animals, and all natural phenomena as well. As a result of this way of thinking, our social and economic development will be nonviolent. We will not be cruel to fellow human beings or to mother earth. Nor will we plunder our natural resources in the name of progress. Forests will be saved, rivers will be free of pollution. And we will realize that development can only occur at a pace at which humans and other beings matter.

In order to get rid of tribalism in religious institutions, nationalism and even consumerism and capitalism, the faithful have to practise their religion with universal love. While we act individually and locally, we must think globally. So that selfishness can slowly become selflessness. Only then can one respect other religions and ideologies whole-heartedly. Although you may not agree entirely with those of different views and beliefs, you can certainly respect them. Even if they are your oppressors, you should not hate them, because that hatred is also harmful to you. Instead of hating an oppressor, one should try to understand the oppressive system and try one's best to change it, with the help of good friends who also want to overcome suffering and obstacles in the way of cultural and spiritual development — as well as social and economic development. If these four aspects of development — the cultural, spiritual, social and economic — could be integrated, then there could be real human development.

Unfortunately, over the past two centuries, universal love in world religions has declined so much that institutionalized religions seem to be, on the whole, the norm. Most churches tolerate or support the political status quo no matter how oppressive the present regimes may be. (There are, of course, exception.) And since the rise of capitalism, Protestantism, Catholicism, Buddhism and Hinduism as well seem to cater to the rich, while religious leaders pay lip service to the poor. At best, they offer some social welfare to the needy, but there have not been enough prophetic voices to transform the social and economic order to be more just and peaceful for all humankind. The rate of child malnutrition is on the rise, as is prostitution and sex tourism as well as militarism, materialism and consumerism.

Some religious leaders have tried to work with other secular leaders to make the world a more meaningful and peaceful place, but so far we have been unable to establish widespread basic changes which would ensure basic human rights for all and protect people from political and religious exploitation. Tibet, Burma and Bangladesh may be extreme cases, but such suffering, to lesser degrees, exists everywhere. As well, the lack of food, shelter, clothing and medicine for the majority of people in many countries is appalling — not to mention the suffering caused by polluted air and water.

Indeed, the rise of the secular intellectual has been a key factor in shaping the modern world. Seen through the long perspective of history, it is in many ways a new phenomenon. It is true that in their earlier incarnations as priests, scribes and soothsayers, intellectuals have guided society from the very beginning; however, their moral and ideological innovations were limited by the cannons of external authority and by the inheritance of tradition. They were not, and could not be, free spirits, or adventurers of the mind.

With the decline of priestly power since the 18th century, a new kind of mentor emerged to fill the vacum and capture the ear of society. The secular intellectual might be deist, skeptic or atheist. But he is just as ready as any pontiff to tell mankind how to conduct its affairs. He has proclaimed, from the start, a special devotion to the interests of humanity and an evangelical duty to advance them by his teaching. And he has brought to his self-appointed task a far more radical approach than his clerical predecessors, as he has felt himself bound by no corpus of revealed religion.

The collective wisdom of the past, the legacy of tradition, the prescriptive codes of ancestral experience exist to be selectively followed or wholly rejected as his own good sense might decide.

For the first time in human history, and with growing confidence and audacity, men have arisen and claimed that they could diagnose the ills of society and cure them with their own intellects: moreover, that they could devise formulae that, if followed, would not only change the structure of society, but the fundamental habits of human beings for the better.

Unlike their sacerdotal predecessors, they were not servants and interpreters of the gods but substitutes. Their hero was Prometheus, who stole the celestial fire and brought it to earth.

One of the most marked characteristics of the new secular intellectuals has been the relish with which they have scrutinized religion and its protogonists.

The intellectuals have examined how far these great systems of faith have aided or harmed humanity and to what extent these secular popes and pastors have lived up to their precepts of purity and truthfulness, of charity and benevolence. The verdicts they have pronouced on both churches and clergy have been harsh.

Over the last two centuries, the influence of religion has continued to decline, and secular intellectuals have played an ever-growing role in shaping our attitudes and institutions. Yet when examining the records of these great intellectuals who have shaped the world since the French and Russian revolutions, right through to the cultural revolution in China and the Pol Pot regime in Cambodia, I have come to the sad conclusion that the secular high priests, too, have all failed us — whether he be a Rouseau, Karl Marx, Tolstoy, Brecht, Bertrand Russell or Mao Tse Tung.

In particular, if we focus on their moral and judgemental credentials as intellectuals fit to tell mankind how to conduct itself, the way these secular intellectuals ran their own lives, and their relationships with family, friends and associates, were, on the whole, appalling — not to mention their sexual and financial dealings.

One must also ask whether they told us the truth, and how their systems stood up to the test. Indeed it seems that they all contributed so much to the suffering of humankind, although it is also true that they may have helped to create some beautiful literature and sharpened our way of thinking somewhat.

In my opinion, the secular gods failed because they too became intolerant and arrogant. In many cases, ideas and the direction of humanity became more important to them than the individual men and women they encountered. They, too, lacked the commitment of personal transformation, although Tolstoy tried but failed. Yet, he had a direct positive influence on Gandhi and Martin Luther King.

As a Thai, I regard my national hero, Phya Anuman Rajadhon, whose centennary was recognized by UNESCO last year, as more important than the world's leading intellectuals, even though he was not as well-known, nor was he a great genius. But he was so humble and so selfless that he regarded himself as an ordinary man, who had time to respect everyone, and encouraged others to be better than he. Yet he could live in, explore and preserve his national culture, as well as integrate it meaningfully with those of our neighbours. I feel that if we know our limits and respect others, we will usually not go wrong. We should develop individually and socially by understanding and appreciating our cultures — including our spiritual traditions — and then economic development will not result in such a wide gap between the rich and the poor, with neither the rich nor the poor being happy.

Although Buddhism with a capital "B" can be tribal in a very negative sense, and can legitimize dictatorial regimes or immoral multi-national corporations, if we were to direct our efforts towards universal love, we could spell it with a small "b"; i.e. we should try to follow the Buddha, as our Christian friends try to follow Christ and our Muslim friends submit their egoes entirely to God.

The first law of Buddhism with a small "b" should read: "Do not be idolatrous about, or bound to any doctrine, theory or ideology, even Buddhist ones. All systems of thought are guiding means; they are not absolute truths."

This would certainly be a sharp contrast to the dogmatic teachings of quite a number of secular intellectuals who contributed to revolutions, upheavals and human sufferings in the past.

Thich Nhat Hanh, a Vietnamese Buddhist monk, writes: "If you have a gun, you can shoot one, two, three, five people, but if you have an ideology and stick to it, thinking it is the absolute truth, you can kill millions ... Peace can only be achieved when we are not attached to a view, when we are free from fanaticism." The more you understand this and try to practice it, the more you will appreciate the importance of a diversity of religions and beliefs.

Yet to unite those of different views, if we are truly of good will, we must not avoid contact with suffering, but find ways to be with those who suffer. We must also avoid accumulating wealth while millions are hungry.

These may not be high ideals, but if we practise them, it may result in a consciousness of, and a precedent for, social justice and peace work. However, in order to do so with awareness, we should not lose ourselves in dispersion and in our surroundings. We should learn to practise breathing in order to regain composure of the body and mind, to practice mindfulness, and to develop concentration and understanding.

This approach to development is non-dualistic, in that one must be peace to make peace in the world.

We should stress the continuity of "inner" and "outer", calling the world our "large self" so that we actively care for it.

I hope this concept will help guide us in our work on social justice and peace issues and will challenge each person to examine his or her behavior in relation to the needs of the larger community while freeing him or her from limiting patterns. I believe this concept is relevant to the growth of mind, spirit and body — the whole of human development.

To me, in order to build understanding and respect between people of diverse religions or beliefs, one needs an alternative to living by ideology. Socially engaged spirituality must be free from the bondage of ideology. As someone said: "The greatest religious problem today is how to be both a mystic and a militant; in other words, how to combine the search for an expansion of inner awareness with effective social action, and how to find one's true identity in both."

On the one hand, there is the prevalent social engineering mentality which assumes that personal virtue can be more or less conditioned by a radical restructuring of society. The opposite view is that radical social improvement is wholly dependent upon personal and spiritual change and changes in lifestyle. But a growing number of spiritually-minded people recognize that the "inner" work is massively discouraged by the social conditions which are the consequence of individual delusion and fear. Thus an American Zen Buddhist poet and activist, Gary Synder, remarks that the so called "free world" has become economically dependent on a fantastic system of greed that cannot be fulfilled, sexual desire which cannot be satiated, and a hate which has no outlet, except against oneself. Under these conditions, the odds are heavily against a spiritual lifestyle. Yet the so-called socialist societies have, almost without exception, wanted to join the so-called "free world".

Therefore, this vicious circle must be broken socially as well as personally — a socially engaged spirituality is essential.

Social activism in the past has been mostly preoccupied with what is "out there" Opening up to what is "in here" and sharing it with others can bring great relief, but it also brings a disconcerting awareness of how much "I" need *my* business, *our* certainties or rationalizations and *their* malevolence. Just to maintain awareness of the boredom, frustration, indifference, anger, and hostility experienced by the activist without being carried away or cast down is an invaluable spiritual practice. But this is only possible if there is an adequate balance of daily meditation and periodic retreat, as well as being aware of social ills outside ourselves.

These practices slowly dissolve the self-need that feeds on hope, allowing us the freedom to do just what the situation demands of us.

Through deepening awareness comes acceptance, and through acceptance comes a seemingly miraculous generosity of the spirit and empowerment for the work that compassion requires of us. We can even take ourselves less seriously. With this critical self awareness, we can genuinely understand and respect others of diverse religions and beliefs. We can even join hands with them humbly and knowingly in trying to develop our spaceship earth to be peaceful and just.

An address at a conference on Building Understanding and Respect between People of Diverse Religions or Beliefs, 14-18 May 1989, Warsaw, Poland.

II
RECONCILIATION AND RELIGION:
A BUDDHIST REFLECTION ON RELIGION'S CLAIMS AND THE REALITY

1

I am greatly honoured to be invited to address such a distinguished audience. It is very generous indeed of the Centre for International Christian Peace Research to have a Buddhist speak at this very important and timely gathering. However, a talk after a reception, like an after dinner speech, should be light — certainly not academic, which is beyond my ability in any case. If possible, it should stimulate the listeners to think on the subject of our seminar which will be taken seriously from tomorrow onward. From a Buddhist point of view, if a speaker can awaken his listeners, that is a great achievement — literally and spiritually, especially after so much food and drink.

As for the topic of our discussion, no one needs to be reminded that every day people find themselves in conflict, ranging from minor discomfort to serious confrontations. It can flare up over back fences or national borders; over cleaning up the kitchen or cleaning up the environment. It can involve our most intimate relationships or the briefest interactions. When people cannot tolerate moral, religious or political differences, conflict is inevitable, and often costly.

Conflict can open avenues of change and provide

challenges. Conflict-resolution skills do not guarantee a solution every time, but they can turn conflict into an open opportunity for learning more about oneself and others.

Conflict can be both positive and negative, constructive or destructive, depending on what we make of it. Certainly it is rarely static — it can change any time. The Buddhists would call this *anicca*. Nothing is permanent. Everything is changing. Yet in many conflicts people are so attached to their views, and tend to blame the other side without examining their own position critically.

However, we can sometimes alter the course of a conflict simply by viewing it differently. We can even turn our fights into fun. Transforming conflict this way is an art, requiring special skills. Indeed skilful means *(upāya)* is a keyword in Buddhist terminology.

There is no need to declare oneself a Buddhist, but it would do no harm to develop skilful means to understand oneself and others, as well as the world situation.

Violence is a sure sign of crisis, as is a heated argument where people hurl abuse at each other and become overwhelmed by their feelings. During crises, normal behaviour goes out the window. Extreme gestures are contemplated and sometimes carried out.

The first thing we must learn is that crisis, tension, misunderstanding, discomfort and conflict are part of life, and that it is a mistake to try and avoid them.

Life can be less painful if we learn to anticipate potential conflict and manage it constructively.

Conflict resolution depends greatly on awareness, and there are clues which range from the obvious to the subtle.

The first step in the art of resolving conflict is to regard conflict as an opportunity to apply skilful means.

Generally, when people think about conflict, they believe that there are only three solutions: compromising, winning and losing. From the Buddhist viewpoint, the end result is not as relevant as the means, which should always be peaceful and nonviolent.

I will now tell you three incidents from the life of the Buddha that illustrate how he dealt with conflicting situations, two of which directly deal with armed conflicts. You may regard these as winning, losing or compromising; it is up to you. But for me, skilful means were used compassionately and mindfully, with patience and a certain degree of detachment all along.

2

The first incident arose from a difference of opinions between two monks on a minor issue of interpreting Buddhist discipline. But these two monks happened to be experts in different fields of studies with a large number of followers. A small conflict became more serious and more people became involved, until the two groups accused each other violently, in words if not in actions. However, it clearly shows that their minds were polluted. Each group stuck to its own position of righteousness, which meant that the others were wrong. The Buddha went to their monastery and told them that each should ask for forgiveness from the other, letting go their past opinions, so that they could live harmoniously together in the future. He told them a story of the past to show how conflicts could grow from a small misunderstanding to a serious crisis — as in the case of two birds fighting, which eventually involved the demise of the King Elephant, Lord Protector of the Jungle. He also told them another story of a king and queen who had been killed by another ruler. Their small son, who survived, witnessed the killing of his parents, who had asked their son to be patient and to forgive the enemy. The son eventually joined the enemy's service and became his royal page. Once the two were alone in the jungle. The King was asleep and the page drew his dagger many times to revenge his parents' deaths, but their words of caution came to his mind, so he could not commit the act of regicide. The King awoke, saw the drawn dagger in the hand of his page and learnt the whole story. All were forgiven, and the page ended up as the royal son-in-law, who succeeded to the throne.

These two stories are often retold in Buddhist countries, to remind us of the nonviolent way of solving conflicts. Yet they made no impact on the quarelling monks, although the stories were preached to them by the Buddha, who saw no alternative but to go away from them and spend the whole three months of the rains retreat in the forest. He was happily looked after by an elephant and a monkey, and his mind was calm, compassionate and detached. Soon after the Buddha's departure to the forest, people found out that the monks were misbehaving very badly, without even due respect to the Buddha, the founder of their own religion. So lay people refused to give alms to the monks, whose livelihood depended entirely on lay support. The monks then came to their senses, after being hungry for many days. They then went to pay respect to the Buddha and asked for forgiveness. They also let go their views and opinions and were willing to accept others as they were. The incident taught them not to be so pious, nor to be so full of self-righteousness and self-importance.

Put this in a modern setting. One may say that through deepening awareness comes acceptance and through acceptance comes seemingly miraculous generousity of the spirit and empowerment for the work that compassion requires of us. We can even take ourselves less seriously. With this critical self-awareness, we can genuinely understand and respect others of diverse views and ideologies. We can even join hands with them humbly and knowingly in trying to develop our spaceship earth to be peaceful and just.

At least this is the conclusion I drew from the first example of conflict resolution during the time of the Buddha. You may see it differently. However, let me tell you the second one, which directly concerns armed conflict.

3

The King of Kosala wanted to be related to the Buddha, so he asked for a princess from the royal Sakya family to be his Queen. The Sakya, the clan from which the Buddha was born, was very caste conscious and refused to allow marriage outside their related clans. Although they regarded Kosala as a mightier Kingdom, they still did not wish to regard that royal family, castewise, as equal to theirs. However, a compromise was reached by sending a princess born of a slave girl to be the Queen of Kosala.

Vidhudhabha was the son of this Queen. Neither he nor his father knew that the Queen was an outcaste.

When the young prince went to visit his maternal grandfather and his maternal relatives among the Sakya clan, he accidentally found out that they all looked down upon him behind his back because his maternal grandmother was a slave girl, so the young prince vowed to kill all members of the Sakya clan in revenge.

When Vidhudhabha succeeded his father to the throne of Kosala, he marched the army northward. The Buddha knew of the situation. He went to sit at the border of the two kingdoms thrice and was able to stop the warlike King. Yet the Buddha could not convince the king to get rid of his own hatred and desire for revenge. Eventually the king managed to kill almost all members of the Sakya family, yet on his return home, Vidhudhabha and most of his troops were drowned in the river.

One could draw many conclusions from this incident. However, if we believe in the law of Karma, we should realize that each individual, each family, each nation will reap the benefits or otherwise from their own deeds, speeches and actions. Although the Sakya clan produced such a wonderful person who eventually became the Buddha and who preached that people should get rid of caste and class barriers, they held views in opposition to his teaching. They also deceived the king of Kosala who was much mightier than them. As for Vidhudhabha, his thoughts drove him to bad action and his life ended tragically.

You may think that this incident does not solve the situation in armed conflict. But for Buddhists, the Law of Karma reminds us that when faced with violence, we must not react against it violently.

Those Sinhalese who want to solve armed conflicts in Sri Lanka by violent means may claim to be Buddhists. However, they are no different from Vidhudhabha and the Sakya who honoured the Buddha and listened to his sermons, but thought, spoke and acted violently. But at the same time, there are many Sinhalese and Tamils who do not consider themselves Buddhists, yet are compassionate and full of forgiveness towards others.

They are the ones who will in the long run resolve

the conflicts on that island, which will not be easy. We need Buddhists, Hindus, Christians, Muslims, Marxists, etc. to face the situation mindfully, to understand the structural violence and to avoid blaming any ethnic or religious community. Then we can surely find a skilful means to patiently and nonviolently solve the conflicts.

Take Tibet as another example. However violent and ruthless the Chinese aggressors have been to them and their country, His Holiness the Dalai Lama and all the spiritual leaders of that Buddhist tradition have never said any harmful word against China. What they did was to ask the Tibetans to refrain from armed struggle and to examine themselves and their cultural traditions in order to understand what led to a situation where many of their monks and lay people were killed, their monasteries and homes destroyed.

Indeed, not long after the bloody incident in Lhasa last year, the Tienanmin massacre in Peking followed. This time the Chinese killed and harmed their own people as badly as they had done in Tibet. Yet no spiritual leaders among the Tibetans in exile ever said that it served the Chinese right or that the law of Karma had now punished China.

In fact, the Tibetans who practise Buddhism are always full of compassion toward the Chinese and hope that one of these days the conflict over Tibet will be resolved. One cannot help but admire their attitude. Although they have been in exile for almost 30 years now, they are still very positive and hopeful, yet realistic. Their teaching on how to be aware of oneself and how to meaningfully improve one's community as well as their perceptions on nature and the environment have positively influenced the world at large.

Their most precious contribution is perhaps their meditation practise, which is common to all schools of Buddhism. In conflicting situations, it is good to begin your contemplation on the person you hate or despise the most.

Contemplate the image of the person who has caused you the most suffering. Use this person's image as the subject of your contemplation. Contemplate the bodily form, feelings, perceptions, mind and consciousness of this person. Contemplate each aggregate separately. Begin with the bodily form. Contemplate the features you hate or despise the most or find the most repulsive. Continue with the person's feelings. Try to examine what makes that person happy and suffer in his daily life. When contemplating perceptions, try to see what patterns of thought and reason this person follows. As for the mind, examine what motivates this person's hopes and aspirations and what motivates his actions. Finally, consider his consciousness. See whether his views and insights are open and free or not, and whether or not he has been influenced by any prejudices, narrow-mindedness, hatred or anger. See whether or not he is master of himself. Contemplate this way until you feel compassion rise in your heart like a well filling with fresh water, and your anger and resentment disappear. Practise this exercise many times on the same person.

This is only one of many meditation practices. You can of course meditate on yourself, on the suffering caused by the lack of wisdom and on detached action. We should always remember the Buddhist saying:

In the time of war
Raise in yourself the Mind of Compassion,
Helping living beings
Abandon the will to fight.
Wherever there is furious battle
Use all your might
To keep both sides' strength equal,
And then step into the conflict to reconcile.

Take another example from Vietnam. During the colonial period, the Buddhists were not only exploited by the French, but by their Catholic compatriots who looked down upon them. During the American period, some Buddhists tried to work on reconciliation between the North and the South, between the Left and the Right. The Ven. Thich Nhat Hanh, a well known monk, founded the School of Youth for Social Service in Saigon, so that young students could do useful work to help war victims. Yet the Vietcong regarded these youngsters as CIA agents and the American advisers took them to be communists, as they served all, without siding with any ideology. One night, five of them went out to work in a village and four of these brave and compassionate students were treacherously killed.

Thich Nhat Hanh sat in deep meditation all night and wrote a wonderful play called *The Return Journey Continues,* which was full of forgiveness and loving-kindness for those who killed his best friends.

After the war, many Buddhists were persecuted by the new regime; many boat people who had left their country were robbed and many women raped by Thai pirates. Yet Thich Nhat Hanh wrote a powerful poem — "Please Call Me By My True Names".

> I am a frog swimming happily in the clear water
> of a pond,
> and I am the grass-snake, approaching in si-
> lence, feeding itself on the frog.
>
> I am the child in Uganda, all skin and bones,
> my legs as thin as bamboo sticks,
> and I am the arms merchant, selling deadly
> weapons to Uganda.
>
> I am the twelve year-old girl, refugee on a small
> boat,
> who throws herself into the ocean after being
> raped by a sea pirate,
> and I am the pirate, my heart not yet capable of
> seeing and loving.
> I am a member of the politburo, with plenty of

power in my hands,
and I am the man who has to pay his "debt of
blood" to my people,
dying slowly in a forced labor camp.

My joy is like spring, so warm it makes flowers
bloom in all walks of life.
My pain is like a river of tears, so full it fills
all four oceans.

Please call me by my true names, so I can hear
all my cries and laughs at once,
so I can see that my joy and pain are one.

Please call me by my true names, so I can wake
up and so the door of my heart can be left
open, the door of compassion.

This piece of poetry has influenced his compatriots
and others very positively toward reconciliation, especially those who have resettled themselves in new
countries. It is essential that they free themselves from
mental turmoil and hatred, replacing these negative
thoughts with wholesome ones like love, joy and
equanimity.

4

The last episode from the life of the Buddha that I
will mention took place about five years after the

Buddha gained Enlightenment, when he went back to his hometown and found his mother's tribe, the Koliyans, and his father's tribe, the Sakayans, at war.

The dispute had been triggered when Sakayan and Koliyan farmers could not decide who should be first to divert the Rohini River into the fields. Both sides insisted that their crops would ripen with a single watering and then the other side could divert the river. The farmers began to insult one another's tribes and the tribes' warriors rushed out, enraged by the insult, preparing to avenge their honour.

At this point, the Buddha intervened. The warriors dropped their weapons in embarrasment as their Enlightened kinsman questioned them about the cause of the quarrel. When the Buddha discovered that the cause of the dispute was water, he asked them whether water was worth as much as warriors. They answered that warriors were beyond price, and the Buddha said "It is not fitting, then, that because of a little water, you should destroy warriors who are beyond price".

In this case, the conflict was resolved. The lesson to be drawn from it is that creating peace must go beyond eliminating, or at least reducing violence. One has to go to the root cause of the conflict.

If Buddhists are to play a meaningful role in the world for justice and peace, besides resolving armed conflicts we need to be bold enough to question the unjust structures in our societies, not only the single violent acts of individuals and countries.

We need cooperation between Christians, Hindus,

Muslims and those of other ideologies. Although our stand is clearly nonviolent, we must cooperate with others in answering certain basic questions like: why is it that people do so little for the basic needs of the common man and woman everywhere. And why are people so good at producing far too much and so bad at helping where there is "too little"?

Of course there is not much money to be made on basic needs, but much on basic greed. As a consequence, precious resources are wasted, not only on arms, but also on luxury goods for the few.

Buddhists should be able to see through this with the help of friends like those of you who have come to this seminar — and together we should be able to bend these structures in other directions.

In this day and age, whether we have more Buddhists or not is not very relevant, but I do think the world needs Buddhist ethics, Buddhist meditation and Buddhist experiences, especially in critical self awareness. Buddhists also need good friends from other religious traditions and ideologies who care for social justice. Together we can help in resolving conflicts, from the personal to the international.

A keynote speech at a seminar on Reconciliation and the Role of Religion in Situations of Armed Conflict, 16-21 November 1989, Life & Peace Institute, Uppsala, Sweden.

III
OPENING REMARKS TO THE PACIFIC
YOUTH FORUM

On behalf of the participants from overseas, I should like to thank the International House of Japan and the Yamagata Perfecture for being so kind in inviting us to come here.

It was very appropriate that we had our Pacific Youth Forum in Morioka in 1985. Morioka associated itself very closely with the late Inazo Nitobe and, as you know, Nitobe was the founding father of internationalism and the pioneer of peace study in Japan. He had a great influence to Mr.Shigeharu Matsumoto, the founder of the International House of Japan.

In 1987, we had our Pacific Youth Forum in Hiroshima to commemorate the International Peace Year declared by the United Nations. At that meeting, Mr.Soedjatmoko, the then Rector of the U.N. University, joined us. We all had a wonderful time.

This year we are having our meeting in Yamagata. Again, it is very appropriate because Yamagata Prefecture is very well known. Yamagata Prefecture has been immortalized by Basho, the famous poet. Many of his beautiful haiku were written here. Even people like me who don't understand Japanese are captured by the beauty, simplicity, and elegance of Basho. So it is indeed a great honor to be in the prefecture of the great poet.

It is appropriate that the Youth Forum is taking place here because this is for you, and for all the youths. I'm very young — at least at heart — and the young are looking toward the 21st century. They are looking for something new, something challenging, whereas the old like the powerful participants of the Summit Meeting in London, they don't look for anything new. They want to maintain the status quo. It is the club of the rich, the club of the powerful. We can not entrust the future in their hands alone. I think we must entrust the future to the people, to the farmers of Yamagata. I think it is wonderful that the people of Yamagata are doing something new at the prefectural level, doing something to change the international order. The Yamagata farmers themselves are doing something wonderful for the people of Japan and the people of Asia and the Pacific. And I think this is where the top leaders must look and listen. They should not only talk about money and power. They must talk about the people, aspirations of the people, the concerns of the people.

Our first session being held at the Life-Long Learning Center is something extraordinary. Nowhere else has been so appropriate as here to hold our forum. This facility is open to public from 9 o'clock in the morning to 9 o'clock in the evening. It is a place to help people, to help people adjust to new life-styles. I think this is where other countries, other cities, and other prefectures should learn from Yamagata. I think it is also wonderful that the youth should learn from this. To the young, eventually you will become old and you must also have life-long commitment to learn. You must learn from your birth until you go to the grave. I think this is where this Life-Long Learning Center can help us all, particularly those of us who come from overseas.

My opening remark focuses on the challenges and opportunities for the 21st century. Indeed, the challenges and opportunities for the 21st century should come from the young. The only good thing perhaps for me as an older generation is to look back in order to prepare for the future. As there is a Sanskrit poetry which says: "The longer you can pull your bow back, then the arrow will go forward to the front directly through darkness, through light, to something bright in future."

So I think if we look back a little bit perhaps, we can prepare ourselves for the future. I do not want to bore you with history, but I want to remind you there is one very famous and perhaps controversial article by an Japanese-American, Francis Fukuyama. Last year, he wrote an article called"The End of History" referring to the end of an ideology. He meant, of course, the end of socialism, particularly the fall of the Berlin Wall and Mr.Gorbachev's new detente.

He also said that it is now the end of the British Empire. He also mentioned the end of the American Empire. What he tried to point out is the rise of a small and enterpreneurial country like Japan. It is something new, that the end of history is the end of an ideology. In a way, capitalism is the answer. Even Mr.Deng Xiaoping believes in that. He may not say so, but the implication is quite clear. The echo is very loud among those who look to the 21st century.

People even say that if Japan is going to be No.1, then you have to look at the other four small dragons, namely Taiwan, Hong Kong, South Korea, and Singapore. Indeed, Singapore is already the "little Japan" in Southeast Asia. The Association of Southeast Asian Nations(ASEAN) closely follows. This is the rise of something new, that is the rise of pragmatism, the rise of capitalism, no more ideology, no more socialism. Even the former Indo-chinese communist states have to join the capitalist world. What about the Chinese? Are they joining the capitalist world? This argument seems to end there. What about South Asia? What about the great civilization of India? People like Francis Fukuyama have no concept, and I feel that if we Asians are not aware of our continent, we will be only concerned about money and power. That could be dangerous. This is my remark about Mr.Fukuyama's article.

Another book, this time written by an Anglo-Saxon American, Robert Elegant, entitled *Pacific Destiny: Inside Asia Today*, was also published last year. His conclusion is that the West must change or the control of the world will belong to a resurgent Asia. He did not say what a "resurgent Asia" means, but he said Asia is going to replace the West unless the West changes. I was in Norway last year. There was a leading Norwegian ecologist who said that unless Scandinavia changes fundamentally within this decade, Europe will not exit as it has been known in history.

The West to me is changing. When you look at the West, do not look at the summit. The summit represents those people who do not want change. They do not want to have a new international order. They want to let the rest of the world die, be exploited ecologically, remain poor. They mean to remain industrialized at the expense of the agricultural countries. Even farmers in Japan realize that. The farmers here are left behind at the expense of industrialization.

What do I really mean by the changing of the West, I refer to those people from the West who care for something humane, who are conscious about ecological issues, who care for ethical issues, and even spiritual issues. I think there is now this new movement in the West which wants to look to and study the 21st century carefully.

Even when the Noble Peace Prize was given to the Dalai Lama, nobody in the East, nobody in Asia cared about him. The Chinese would do anything to let the Dalai Lama remain unknown. Even the leading Japanese Buddhists went along with the Chinese in not inviting the Dalai Lama to Japan.

Two years or three years ago, when they had the Summit Peace Prayer at Mt.Hiei, they did not invite the Dalai Lama because the President of the Chinese Buddhist Association said no. The leading Buddhists of Japan preferred to please the leading Japanese industrialists, kowtowed to the Chinese political leaders and ignored spiritual issues. But look at Norway, a country of four million, giving importance to the Dalai Lama. The King of Norway received the Dalai Lama in spite of diplomatic pressure from the Chinese Ambassador and the Chinese Foreign Office, that is something which we should look at carefully.

On the 11th of July, the Parliament of Europe gave the Human Rights Prize to Aung San Suu Kyi, the lady who had been detained in Burma for two years. She is the daughter of a nationalist leader, the founding father of Burma, and yet she is under house detention for two years already on orders of the ruling military junta. And yet, nobody cares in Asia. The Japanese Government was the first government to recognize the military junta. The Thai Government was the second government to recognize the military junta. It even sent Burmese students back to Burma so that the Thai entrepreneurs could buy teak wood from Burma so that those wood would come to Japan. Unfortunately, the Burmese students were killed. Most of us only care for money. We do not care for human rights. This is where the West is changing and we are not responding properly.

The West is thinking of the global village. Even the Green Party is now thinking of the spiritual side of man as well as environment. There are not only human rights group in Europe and America. There are now those newly converted Buddhists in Europe and America who care for the rights of animals. They are protesting that animals are being treated severely by companies which make perfume and other luxury items especially for women. In the East, we are supposed to be Buddhist and yet we ignore this very fundamental issue.

So we should closely observe what is changing in the Weat. We in the East, particularly Japan, feel that we have been imitating the West since the last century. But we are only poor copycats, and what we have imitated are only the technological advances.

The industrial revolution came on the heels of the decline of religion in the West. Formal and structured religion will decline everywhere, but the spirit of religion will always be there. That is, the spirit of man. Love in Christianity, peace and submission to God in Islam, compassion and wisdom in Buddhism. All of them are wonderful. However, formal religion could become capitalistic. It could become chauvinistic. It could work against human beings. If you want to look to the future, you must look at religion at its best. The World Council of Churches in Geneva is now asking us, Buddhists and Muslims, to think together, that we must do away with the financial debt of the poor countries, material debt of the poor peoples. Majority of the people in my country are farmers. If you go and ask them about their future and if they tell you they have a future, they are telling you a lie. We have no future because we are in debt. We sell our daughters to become wives and prostitutes in Japan, in Germany. Our people go to work in the

Middle East and now they are also coming to work in Japan. There will be no future for all of us in the 21st century unless these issues are dealt with fundamentally.

In my opinion, one of the challenges of the 21st century is how to overcome consumerism. The lure of advertisement has built in all of us this consumerist attitude. In Buddhist terms, consumerism is a personification of greed, which is one of the root causes of evil. There is also the problem of how to overcome militarism. In Buddhist terminology, this equates to hatred. Worst of all, most of us do not realize that we are so attached to the new form of education. Education that is only at the head level. We become clever. We become sophisticated. But we become narrow-minded. We do not care about social justice. We have no time for our spiritual growth, for beauty which people like Basho had experienced. We have to change the educational system because it does not serve anymore the purpose of stimulating further pursuit of knowledge.

If you want to move to the 21st century, I would like to call your attention to the words of Soedjatmoko, the founder of our Pacific Asrama, the founder of our Pacific Youth Forum, the second Rector of the UN University. He said,"If humankind is to survive, the 21st century must be the return to the sacred." This means that we have to go back to the formal spiritual religion to care for one another. We must challenge the American writer Fukuyama. History has not come to an end. We must go back to the ideal. We must go back to socialism at its best, not socialism as practiced in China, in the Soviet Union or the Eastern bloc or by any communist party. Socialism at its best means brotherhood of all human beings, liberty, fraternity. The state must become less and less relevant. The people will become more and more relevant. This is where we should look to.

We only have three or four days of working together. We cannot solve the problems of the 21st century. But if we can forge friendship here especially among the young people, trust could be established. We would live as Asian, we would be all human beings living together.

Ananda, the cousin of Buddha, told the Buddha, "Lord, friendship or good friendship is half of the holy life." The Buddha said, "No, Ananda, good friendship is the whole of the holy life." In this world, what we need is friendship, what we need is to develop critical self-awareness, critical of ourselves, critical of our country, critical of our way of living. This is where the Life-Long Center, Education Center on this very site is very important. If you can develop critical self-awareness, you can change your lifestyle to be more simple, to be aware of the sufferings of other peoples and, then, we can move to the 21st century more meaningfully.

I hope these opening remarks will make you think hard. You need not agree to all of what I have said, but they may be useful perhaps in the future.

From Proceedings of The Asia-Pacific Community in the 21st Century: Challenges and Opportunities for Youth , 17 July 1991 Yamagata, Japan.

SEEDS OF PEACE : A BUDDHIST VISION FOR RENEWING SOCIETY

In Buddhism, peace does not only mean the absence of war. Peace is a means and an end in itself. It is also the ultimate happiness — as the Buddha says there is no happiness other than peace, which is equated with freedom.

A leading Thai Buddhist monk, Ven. Phra Depvedi (P.Payutto), explains that freedom is threefold. First, people should enjoy the basic freedom of life in the absence of fundamental insecurities and dangers that threaten their existence, e.g. poverty, disease and calamities, like drought and famine. Second is social freedom — the absence of human oppression and exploitation. Included here are tolerance, friendliness and benevolence. And the final freedom is of man's inner life, that is, freedom from mental suffering and from greed, hatred and delusions which corrupt the mind and cause people to commit all kinds of evils.

I am sure most religious traditions and ideologies would agree with the above explanation. The differences lie in the means to achieve peace and freedom.

The dominant approaches of our times, capitalism and socialism, have used social engineering strategies in their own ways. However, I think these methods employing social engineering have failed to create the conditions for human development.

Capitalism does not merely make use of human greed, but glorifies this human weakness as a great virtue. It celebrates self-interested behaviour and it encourages the accumulation of wealth, but does not easily allow for the fair distribution of it. It subordinates human development to accumulation by putting the economic objective above all else. It has evolved into a new religion of consumerism and has already ruined many countries in the world, including former socialist ones.

The equalitarian ideology of socialism is wonderful, but in reality it has led to state capitalism and authoritarianism. Hence the failure of the so-called Second World.

Capitalism permits some individual freedoms while denying a fair distribution of wealth. The former socialist states tried to ensure a fairer distribution, but denied basic freedoms. I do recognise the merits of Marxist class analysis and the contribution of Marxism to the debate on social development, but I am entirely against the Marxist-Leninist-Maoist approaches to social change, since they are violent and bloody. Unfortunately, the Greens, on the whole, have not yet learnt to cultivate peaceful minds among themselves.

Now, turning to Buddhism, the most crucial difference it has with capitalism is that it does not seek to make a virtue of self-interest and self-agrandisement. In fact, Buddhism condemns greed, which can easily lead to aggression and hatred, and shows how to be content by changing oneself first. That is, it requires one to cultivate seeds of peace within ourself in order to transform one's consciousness. Then one can strive with one's fellow human beings to improve everyone's well-being.

Unfortunately, Buddhists have failed to deal with problems in that spirit. We have failed to deal with the injustice of feudalism and capitalism. In the past, we have compromised ourselves with Hinduism and Confucianism. Now, we need to understand the socio-cultural realities of our societies and their tensions and develop appropriate approaches so that no section feels discriminated against.

As a Buddhist, I am an advocate of the middle path of development — avoiding the extremes and violent means of all sorts. We cannot turn the clock back to the time of the Buddha, but we could go back to his essential teachings, which I call Buddhism with a small "b." It is beyond sectarianism and nationalism. Buddhists have long been involved in state-making and have often compromised their principles for the sake of patronage from states that oppressed people. State patronage tends to divert the Buddhist community from the truly Buddhist course and co-opts it into supporting and justifying the violation of people's rights. However, I do not propose that we condemn Buddhism with capital "B." We should be aware of its strengths and its weaknesses. My late teacher, Ven. Bhikkhu Buddhadasa, set a very good example in Siam for the last sixty-one years. One could call his reform movement a Buddhist Theology of Liberation, although he called it Dhammic Socialism. The three main aims of his life are indeed a good model for the World Parliament of Religions. He said 1) Those who adhere to any religion should understand and try to practise its essential teachings, which are basically peace, love, liberaton and justice as well as spiritual progress; 2) Those who belong to a religion should respect all other religions; 3) All of us should unite against materialism which is linked closely with greed, hatred and delusion.

Those of us who cultivate seeds of peace within should not look down upon those religious leaders who represent the oppressive system and who sometimes unknowingly exploit themselves and others in the name of religion. In fact, we should encourage dialogue with them. We should also try to have dialogue with those who oppress us.

The traditional Buddhist method for cultivating seeds of peace is to start with *dāna*, which means generosity or charity and is basic in most religions. One can begin by giving what one does not want, gradually giving what is very dear to us — giving our time, our energy, our thoughts to those who need them. Ultimately we can even give up selfishness or even selfhood itself.

Once one sees the value of giving as more important than taking or acquiring, then one can really be content. One can limit greed and practise a simple lifestyle. One will see that it is wrong to acquire wealth while the majority are malnourished and homeless. Our aim in life will therefore not be fame, profit, wealth or sensual pleasure. We can really share our time, energy and material resources with those who are in need.

The practice of *dāna* on the one had cultivates seeds of peace within and on the other radically undermines consumerism and capitalism.

The next step in cultivating seeds of peace is the practice of *sila*, which is usually translated as the precepts or moral code. In fact, it means how to be normal – not to exploit oneself or others.

The most basic ethical precepts in lay Buddhism are the five vows to avoid killing, stealing, sexual misconduct, lying and intoxication.

In Buddhism, all killing is bad. If we understand liberation as an impulse which seeks to enhance life in all forms, then the norm of non-killing becomes a precondition for social liberation and world peace.

To generate peace and to bring about liberation requires eliminating, or at least reducing, violence. The problem is that there are several kinds of violence. The clearest is direct violence as described in the first precept, which states that five factors are involved in killing — not only life, but the perception of life, not only the thought of murder, but also carrying it out and the resulting death.

There is also structural violence, violence which kills slowly and is built into a social structure. Of the five factors noted, only three apply here: there is life and the perception of life, but there is no thought of murder and hence no follow through. Death, however, is the end result. But the result of what? Death does not result from direct violence but from a desperately unjust social structure that gives too much to the few and too little to the many. How does a modern Buddhist deal with this form of violence?

The second precept, abstaining from taking what does not belong to one, seems relevant here. Again the five elements are involved: someone else's belonging, and awareness of the fact, the thought of theft and the act of carrying it out, with theft as the outcome. However, theft is not quite the same as structural violence. Something is taken, but there is no awareness of a theft having taken place.

A landowner has land, but the landless have only their ability to till the land. The landowner says "You may till my land, but you have to give me 70% of the harvest." (A figure fairly typical in most SEA countries.) The landowner may feel he is being generous, since the alternative is to use a tractor to till the fields. Or he may sell the land for a golf course at a tremendous profit. The peasant may feel grateful, for the alternative may be starvation or selling his daughter as a prostitute or migrating to a city to work as a cheap labourer.

Surely there is something morally wrong in this arrangement. To maintain on oppressive structure of this kind, something else is needed. The usual capital "B" Buddhist explanation of the law of *karma* is that the peasants are now reaping the results of their bad deeds committed in the past while the landlord obviously cultivated much merit by building temples and Buddha images. Hence both the rich and the poor must support the material aggrandisement of the monkhood for the future welfare of each other.

Buddhism with a small "b" is certainly against this kind of wrong teaching. If the landlord practises *dāna,* he will feel it is wrong to get 70% out of the land, while the landless labourers lack enough to live on. Buddhadasa's Dhammic Socialism is an approach that emphasizes not taking more than is needed and at the same time is in accordance with the laws of Nature, since people would share whatever extra they had out of compassion and loving-kindness. People would set aside for themselves only what they needed; anything in excess of that would be left for society.

A third type of violence, cultural violence, is any element in the culture, particularly religion or ideology, that legitimizes direct and/or structural violence. One can see it very clearly in the mass media, especially in advertising. Of course, there are Buddhists past and present, and there will be some in the future, who commit direct violence and participate in structural violence. They will not, however, find any support for this in the Buddhist scriptures. To claim this support would be a violation of the fourth precept which is against false speech. Although that precept is more concerned with lying in the conventional sense than in legitimizing violence, if Buddhism is invoked in defense of violence, it constitutes an act of lying.

From the above arguments, one can conclude that Buddhhism contains a very strong ethical system supportive of peace. Its precepts against violence represent a liberative impulse. But there is a weakness: strength in personal commitment is combined with the silent mechanisms of evil. The larger a structure is, such as a nation state or a large corporation, or a merging of the two, the more we become accustomed to it, the more violent it becomes. Can a Buddhist fulfill the obligations of military service? Should Buddhists remain silent when the government continues to increase the national budget for military armaments at the expense of basic health and education? Some might argue these issues are more political than moral. Of course, they are both. The major question is exactly how the ethical inspiration of Buddhism might enlighten politics by being courageous enough to question a socially unjust society — not merely the individual acts of people or their government.

If Buddhists understand structural violence and its roots in hatred *(dosa)* and learn how to eliminate it mindfully and nonviolently, Buddhism will not only be relevant to the modern world but could be a source for its liberaton. Similarly, consumerism is linked directly or indirectly to greed *(lobha)* and lust *(rāga)*. One can see this clearly in advertisements and the mass media, which exploit women's bodies to artificially created needs.

Modern education deals almost exclusively with the

heads, not the hearts, of students. The clever ones are recognized and rewarded materially and financially, although they need not be generous or aware of social ills. Most of the rich and powerful are not happy either. Their exalted positions rest directly or indirectly on mass poverty and ecological destruction. This is indeed ignorance *(avijjā)* or delusion *(moha).*

If Buddhists are to make a meaningful contribution to world peace or the liberation of the modern world from violence and oppression, they must confront the three root causes, which are found not only in the individual but also in the social structure. Therefore, these roots of evil must be dealt with by Buddhists. The moral precepts must exist not only for moralists. All practising Buddhists must develop right-mindfulness.

Right-mindfulness, *(bhāvanā or samādhi)* is indeed freedom from greed, hatred and delusion, which corrupt the mind and cause people to commit all kinds of evils. In their place, we can plant the mind with seeds of peace. This is the practice of mindful living in daily life. One can practise this at every moment of one's life — while breathing, eating, drinking, washing the dishes, gardening or driving a car.

Once one practices mindfulness, one has peace and happiness inside, and one can share that way of life with others. The present moment is a wonderful moment.

Traditionally, the first part of training the mind is to achieve tranquality *(samatha).* This will allow us to plant seeds of peace within. The second is based on a technique for understanding the true nature of one's psychophysical constitution and of the world. This is called *vipassanā* or insight meditation, which is an analytical method for exploring causal relations and problem-solving. It develops into an internal factor for wisdom or right understanding by fostering detachment. In Pali, this is called *yonisomanasikāra,* critical self-awareness, which leads to selflessness. Maintaining *yonisomanasikāra* helps one to be earnest. It helps generate energetic effort and it helps reduce selfish desire.

The Buddha says that the foundation for real understanding *(paññā)* is equanmity for developing self-cultivation and critical self-awareness.

Understanding is different from intellectual knowledge, since it comes from both the head and the heart. It helps one to be aware, to be humble, to know one's limits. At the same time, it promotes loving-kindness and compassion, allowing us to share in the suffering of others and to work to eliminate its causes.

Of course, when one tackles the causes of suffering, especially in an oppressive social system, one usually gets hit by those who wish to maintain the status quo. Here mindfulness again helps one to understand one's danger and to forgive one's enemy.

The important thing is to bring out the awareness of one's anger in order to surround it with mindfulness. Then the anger is transformed into compassion. Thich Nhat Hanh says that anger is like a closed flower. The flower will bloom when the sunlight penetrates deeply into the flower. If one keeps breathing and concentrating, mindfulness will infiltrate the anger. When sunshine penetrates a flower, the flower cannot resist. It has to open itself and shows its heart to the sun. If one keeps breathing on one's anger, shining one's compassion and understanding on it, one's anger will soon crack and one will be able to look into the depths and see its roots.

One can deal similarly with greed, lust and delusion. *Bhāvanā* is a powerful tool to work against capitalism, consumerism, sexism, militarism and the like.

Critical self-awareness can also be used to examine our own society, nation-state, culture — even our own Buddhist tradition. With this attitude, one will not hate the oppressors, the capitalists or the dictators. Yet one must use one's understanding to dismantle the oppressive system and its inherent violence.

H.H. the Dalai Lama has really inspired many of us to love our enemy by cultivating seeds of peace. I am positive that one day Tibet will be free from China's domination and destruction. Perhaps the Tibetans may even be able to offer us a new future by building a Buddhist democracy or practising Dhammic Socialism.

The Burmese military junta may be able to keep Aung San Suu Kyi under house arrest, but the tremendous moral courage of that woman will one day free the peoples of Burma.

After more than 20 years of war and senseless killing, no one believed that peace could be re-established in Cambodia. When I first assisted Ven. Maha Gosananda in the Khmer refugee camps, it was very hard. But the Venerable was very determined to plant seeds of peace with his thoughts, words and actions. He asked us to conduct reconciliaton and meditation for rival Khmer monks and lay people. Twice he led peace walks through war zones. All these efforts should really be known.

I myself have been privileged to work for peace in Siam as well as to work with good friends in the International Network of Engaged Buddhists(INEB). The network is linked to the Buddhist Peace Fellowship in the U.S.A. and with similar organizations in Europe and Japan — working to free ourselves from the root causes of suffering and to challenge the oppressive systems.

Despite social and political oppression and the destruction of the evironment in Asia, my vision for renewing society and for human liberation is realisable because many of us work together as good friends or *kalayānamitta.*

The Buddha says *kalayānamitta* is important for everyone. We need to have good friends, good companions and good friendships. We can learn from others to develop ourselves and to help our society to be peaceful and just, starting with ourselves.

Once we can transform our consciousness to be less selfish, then with help from good friends we

294

can transform our societies to be free from human oppression and exploitation. It may not be easy, but it is possible.

Those of us at INEB are trying. No doubt we need many more good friends, non-Buddhists too, to help us critically as well as collaboratively, so that we may sooner rather than later liberate ourselves and our fellow sufferers. With seeds of peace and proper cultivation, I am sure this will be achieved. May it be so.

A major presentation at the Parliament of the World's Religions, Chicago, 1 September 1993.

V
PRESENTATION OF FOUNDER'S AWARD
TO SULAK SIVARAKSA

Born in Siam (or Thailand) in the 1930's, you were
trained in the traditional values of Siamese culture and
Theravada Buddhism. Like other privileged young men
of your generation, you were sent abroad for Western
education to England, where you received both Bach-
elor of Arts and Law degrees. Many Asians educated
in the West turned against the traditional values of
their own cultures and pursued Western dreams, either
remaining in the West to become rich or returning to
their country in positions of monied, powerful, exploiting elites. You did not follow either of these
alternatives, but returned to Siam as a humble university professor. There you observed the increasing
degradation of your culture and the suffering of your
people as a result of the impact of the West. You
watched as Western influence increasingly led to
militarization, the violation of human rights, the dis-
ruption of cultural values, the cancerous spead of
materialism and the growth of inequality. In the face
of this, you did not remain silent, but began to speak
out and write against .the corruption and social decay
you saw around you. In 1963, you founded the *Social
Science Review*, which quickly became the leading
intellectual journal in Siam, and in the 1960's and
'70's, you yourself became the central reference point
for those who sought to reverse the downward course

of your country. Your writing in time would come to include innumerable essays and some fifteen books in English and many more in Thai, books which have now been translated into many languages, profoundly affecting people all over the world.

In your speeches and your writing, you have pointed clearly to the dangers of seeking happiness solely through materialism, physical force and violence. You have ably showed the great power of the Buddha's teaching of self-respect, non-aggression and compassion. You have called for a Buddhist-type humananistic development emphasizing popular participation, social justice, human rights, basic needs and reverence for life in all its forms. Your latest book, *Seeds of Peace,* is an eloquent plan for a renewal of society through Buddhist values.

You have not only encouraged all of us to take active responsibility for the agonies that afflict our world, you have showed us how. You are an indefatigable activist and organizer, and over the past decades have founded such important and influential organizations as the Asian Cultural Forum on Development, the Thai Inter-Religious Commission for Development and the International Network of Engaged Buddhists. You have spread your message of peace and compassion in the course of an energetic and wide-ranging teaching career, not only at Thammasat but at other universities abroad, acting as visiting professor at Berkeley, Cornell University, the Universities of Toronto and Hawaii, and other institutions. Many human rights organizations rely on your guidance, and as a board member you continue to help chart the course of the Buddhist Peace Fellowship, the Institute of Asian Democracy and the International Campaign for Tibet, to mention just a few. You continually affirm the role that mutual understanding among religions can play in bringing peace to the world, and you are a major voice in interreligious dialogue.

Your fearless proclamation of the truth and call to justice and compassion have not always been accepted by the powers-that-be. In fact, there have been a number of attempts to silence you. Although you have been a consistently moderate voice in Siam and have always preached non-violence and tolerance, in 1967 and again in 1984 you were charged with treason by the military dictatorship. There have been several occasions when you have had to flee your country or face imprisonment and death. Most recently, on August 22, 1991, you gave a talk at Thammasat University in Bangkok in which you gave voice to the unethical and illegal way in which the military had seized power in a coup in February 1991, and you drew attention to the economic exploitation of the country and its poor by the military dictatorship through lucrative contracts made with multinational corporations. Charges of treason were again drawn up against you and, facing imprisonment and fearing that you would "disappear" while in prison, you were again forced to flee the country. This set off a pro-democracy movement in your country and resulted in recent elections.

Last winter, you returned to Siam to face the legal charges against you, in the attempt to help the struggling and still shaky democratic movement gain strength and momentum. When you return to Siam after visiting us here at Naropa, you will once again be putting yourself at risk to benefit others.

Sulak Sivaraksa, your words and your example uniquely embody the deepest principles of Buddhism and the best values of the world's other great spiritual traditions. And they exemplify the values that underlie and inform the kind of training and education that our founder, the Ven. Chogyam Trungpa Rinpoche, asked us to provide here at the Institute. Looking at you, our students can see clearly and without mistake what we would like them to become.

In recognition of your courage and clarity, of the insight, compassion, and great impact of your life, on behalf of the Naropa Institute and its founder, the Ven. Chogyam Trungpa Rinpoche, I would like to present you, on this 10th day of September, 1993, with the Founder's Award. May your vision of human dignity and enlightened behaviour, which you bring from your Buddhist upbringing and culture, take root in the hearts of all, and may you succeed in your quest to bring peace and harmony to the world.

John Whitehouse Cobb
President, The Naropa Institute,
Boulder, Colorado.

VI
SULAK SIVARAKSA'S SPEECH

It is indeed a great honor to receive the Founder's Award from the Naropa Institute, especially at this time of my life, as I being prosecuted by my government for being a naughty boy with the gloomy prospect of 15 years imprisonment. An honor like this is very timely as it encourages me to feel that one's work and effort are, after all, recognised.

I have been admiring the Founder of this Institute for a long time, although I did not have the fortune to meet Trungpa Rinpoche. However, I have read quite a number of his books both in Thai and in English. He was indeed a man who inspired many people. He must have had a unique mind and personality that were extraordinary. He must have had a particular gift of being able to communicate diverse and unusual ideas from his tradition in a simple, straightforward way that went straight to the heart of the matter. I think he was one of the most, if not the most, successful Dhammaduta to the west. Of course, he was controversial and in many ways unconventional. In a small way, perhaps, I follow in his footsteps — only in being controversial and unconventional. In fact, great minds in any traditon must always be controversial and somewhat unconventional. My own late teacher, the Ven. Buddhadasa Bhikkhu, was in fact a conservative Buddhist monk, but he was so radical that many Sinhala Theras called him a goat and not a monk. Some Thais regarded him as a non-Buddhist or even a communist. Yet of all the contemporay Theras in the whole of the Southern School he was the most profound and contributed more positively to the world than most. He was even regarded by some as the Nagarajuna of Theravada tradition.

Another teacher of mine, the Ven. Thich Nhat Hanh, is perhaps the most well-known among those involved in engaged Buddhism all over the world. Yet he was not liked by many senior monks in Vietnam. Even the late Secretary-General of the World Conference on Religion and Peace regarded him with suspicion. Of course there is a great similarity between his thinking and that of His Holiness the Dalai Lama.

My point is that controversial and unconventional behaviours are sometimes necessary or even essential. It is up to us to be skilful in understanding such behaviours and activities with unbiased views, with mindfulness and with compassion.

With such controversial and unconventional approaches Trungpa Rinpoche did so much for Buddhism and alternative lifestyle in the west, and the Naropa Institute is one product of his creative mind and positive energy.

The Institute is not old and is not big, but after all small is beautiful; besides it links directly with the great *mahasiddha* of the most renowned Nalanda University of ancient India. The Venerable Naropa himself was also the link with his great teacher,

Tilopa, and through his Tibetan student Marpa, the central doctrine of the Kagyupa school is very much alive now. The Venerable Trungpa Rinpoche made it possible that we all benefit from this wonderful lineage.

I regard the Naropa Institute as a unique place of learning. I am glad that it does not impose Buddhism on its staff or its students, but provides a Buddhist background for those who care to grow intellectually as well as mindfully.

My main criticism of educational institutions all over the world is that they tend to concentrate on the heads but not the hearts. The more research the professors do, the better they are supposed to be. If you do not publish, you will perish. The more research you do, the more expert you become and the more compartmentalized it is. So you dig yourself deeper into your own grave of knowledge which need not be moral or spiritual. Students, too, are encouraged to use their heads like bank accounts. The more they accumulate knowledge, the better they will be. The clever ones are rewarded materially and financially, although they need not be generous or aware of social ills and how to get rid of them nonviolently.

I believe the Naropa Institute is different in the sense that it encourages teachers and students to be friends and to learn from each other.

I myself regard my students as my teachers, too. I also believe that the Institute offers opportunities for all to develop both their heads and their hearts. Through

302

meditation, one can become mindful. With mindfulness, one can have a real understanding of oneself and the world. With understanding comes humility and compassion, not haughty knowledge and arrogance.

The world nowadays needs so much understanding and compassion. I believe the Naropa Institute in a small and beautiful way is offering that unique opportunity for these seeds of peace. I hope they will grow and multiply.

I am indeed very privileged to be accepted as a member of this unique institute. With humility I gladly accept the honor bestowed on me. Please regard this honor as not only for me, but also for my family — especially my wife, who sometimes endures more hardship than me (I am happy that she is represented here by our eldest daughter) — as well as for my many friends and supporters and for all sentient beings who struggle non-violently for peace and justice.

VII
STATEMENT FOR THE STATE GENERAL
FOR THE PLANET

I should like to congratulate our hosts for looking back to the 1788 State General which permitted the different parts of society and the representatives of different regions to express their hopes, claims and proposals and which helped lay the foundation of a new society. Indeed, soon after that came the French revolution with the ideals of liberty, fraternity and equality.

One wonders why these three ideals were not realized during the past two centuries. Unless we look back to learn from our mistakes, our search for humanist solutions, despite our hope, our dream and our efforts, will fail again as we will soon enter the 21st century of the Christian era.

If I am not mistaken, it was at the Sorbonne in 1749 that Turgot proposed the idea of human progress. Prior to the 17th century, development from the harmonious environment was regarded as destruction. You could take the Taoist approach in China, the Hindu idea in India or the ancient Greeks in Hellas. If the golden age is interfered with, out of proportion, it will deteriote into the silver age, the iron age, etc.

Indeed, it was in 1620 that Francis Bacon claimed in his *Novum Organum* the supremacy of the new knowledge. He stuffed guinea pigs with snow to find out how the wretched animals could stand the cold so that our scientific enquiry would be ascertained. No text books mentioned that Bacon died because of pneumonia, besides being disgraced as a corrupt judge.

Further, Isaac Newton proclaimed that our knowledge could in fact be observed and experimented with. Hence the supremacy of natural science and the social sciences must follow.

Even our Chinese colleagues now want the Western paradigm of progress. If you don't catch up with the West, you are nobody. Hence the Chinese Four Modernizations, which for me is very dangerous. Indeed we must go beyond the Newtonian physics, the Western Industrialization and even the Western Renaissance. Would I be unpopular to challenge the Eurocentric paradigm?

If I may say so, it all goes back to Rene Descartes, who said *"cogito ergo sum"*: I think therefore I am. So we stress so much on our thoughts. The philosophers, the scientists, the economists and the technocrats enjoy the day at the expense of the masses.

The more one accumulates facts, the more clever one is supposed to be. One is rewarded financially, politically and socially. Whether one is at the same time good or not? That is irrelevent. As G.E Moore said, goodness can not be proved scientifically or logically. Hence, the head is separated from the heart.

If one wants a humanist perspective for environment and development, one should not only go back to the State General of 1788, one has to go back to Descartes and question the phrase *cogito ergo sum*. "I think therefore I am" means that we put the whole value on thoughts, on the philosophers, the intellectuals, the clever ones. Many people still feel that scientific knowledge and technology will solve the world's problems. I feel science and technology have created problems more than solved them, especially now scientific research has become very complicated and expensive. Scientists depend almost entirely on arms merchants and multinational corporations. How could the outcome of their research serve the masses and the environment?

Why don't we change from Descartes's formula. The Buddhists would say, "I breath therefore I am." Without breathing we shall all be dead. If we breath mindfully, we can syncronize our heart and our head. We will not be arrogant intellectuals; we will be humble and see the value of all beings — no class differences, no inferiority or superiority. The same is true for race, sex and culture. Indeed, we would relate equally to the non-human species. We could listen to and learn from animals, plants, earth, mountains, rivers and oceans. Our understanding would then become our compassion. We would really care for those who suffer, and we would surely want to eliminate the cause of suffering.

What we need nowadays is to limit our greed, our hatred and our delusion. However, these three root causes of evils must not remain abstact. We must know how greed has become the new religion of consumerism. Hatred links closely with power and centralization. Delusion is the arrogant intellectuals who think social engineering will solve all social ills. What is good for General Motors need not be good for the general public. Indeed we need to care more concerning the basic necessities of humankind. Then we could be humble and mindful. To tackle the environmental crisis is to deal with our own personal crisis. Most governments are not able to tackle fundamental problems because political leaders have no seeds of peace within. Despite their rhetoric, they are alienated from the grassroots. They are bound to lose more and more of their legitimacy, even though many governments have democratic forms. In essesse,they serve the rich and the powerful — not the poor — and they really don't care for social justice or the natural environment.

If the greens and the socialists are peaceful and mindful, they could work wonderfully. The mistake in the past was not communism or socialism. But it was the violent approach. Hence dictatorship and totalitarianism,plus top down development process.

If one could be peaceful and mindful, one could restructure one's ego to be less selfish, and perhaps one could reconstitute the society to be nonviolent and just and to care for environmental balance.

Violent structure, violent culture and greedy motives are all over the world. Without knowing who we are and how we should relate harmoniously with ourselves and our environment, we are really deluded. With seeds of peace within, breathing mindfully, I am sure we could really tackle the seemingly insurmountable problems with hope.

27 September 1993, Vizelay Group, with the support of the Foundation for the Progress of Humanity, Abbaye des Vaux de Cernay, 78720 Dampierre-en-Yveliness, France.

VIII
BUDDHADASA BHIKKHU

The Venerable Buddhadasa Bhikkhu who passed away at the age of 87 on July 8, 1993, was perhaps the most well-known and controversial monk in the contemporary Theravada tradition.

Although adhering strictly to the Vinaya rules of the tradition, which is conservative, he remained radical all through his life. He claimed that to practice religion seriously, one had to be both conservative and radical. Hence for his 84th birthday, a festscrift was published to honor him, with the title of *Radical Conservatism: Buddhism in the Contemporary World*. Contributors included H.H. the Dalai Lama, Thich Nhat Hanh, Bhikkhu Sumedho, David W Chappell, Lewis R Lancaster,Donald K Swearer, etc.

The traditionalists attacked him because he regarded Mahayana as important as Theravada. He even questioned some remarks made by the most famous Theravada commentator, Buddhaghosa. Besides, he praised authentic teaching in the Bible and the Q'uran.

His teaching was not only for personal happiness but for social justice and ecological balance. He proposed Dhammic Socialism as a Buddhist alternative to capitalism and communism.

Due to Buddhadasa's writing and teaching since 1932, young Thais have come to realize the importance of Buddha Dhamma once more. Previously they thought Buddhism linked too closely with superstition and the nation state. With his help, they now understand the essential teaching of the Buddha on selflessness, mindfulness, understanding and compassion. Even the subtle doctrine of Dependent Origination is practical for personal salvation as well as for overcoming suffering in the world. Buddhadasa also consented to be patron of the International Network of Engaged Buddhists, together with H.H. the Dalai Lama and the Ven. Thich Nhat Hanh.

Buddhadasa claimed that since Buddha was born in the forest, was enlightened in the forest and passed away in the forest, we should really respect and preserve the forest. Besides, the word "temple" or "monastery" in Pali means forest or park, so we should really live openly with our natural surroundings.

His place is called the Garden for Liberation. He sat all day underneath trees, surrounded by dogs and chickens, birds and bees, contemplating deeply, and gave much to the world through his lifestyle, teaching and writing. Donald K. Swearer called him the Nagarujura of Theravada.

Some of his works have been translated into several languages. Those in English are *Handbook for Mankind; Mindfulness with Breathing: Unveiling the Secrets of life; Buddha-Dhamma for Students; Keys to Natural Truth; Heartwood of the Bodhi Tree: the Buddha's Teaching of Voidness; The Buddha's Doctrine of Not-Self; Christianity and Buddhism; Practical Dependent Origination; Why Were You Born?;Why Dhamma?; Extinction without Remaining;*

Dhammic Socialism and *The First Ten Years of Suan Mokh*.

Suan Mokh is the place he founded in 1932 as the Garden for Liberation. Now meditation practice is available at Suan Mokh for English-speaking people from the 1st-10th of every month. Those interested in this and in any of his books may write to Dhamma Dana Foundation, Suan Mokh, Chaiya, Surat Dhani 84110, Thailand; or Wat Buddha-Dhamma, 8910 S. Kingery Highway, Hinsdale, IL 60521, U.S.A.

Although Bhikkhu Buddhadasa passed away before the World Parliament of Religions in Chicago which took place from 29 August-4 September 1993, his book on *No Religion* was distributed widely to the participants. The book was dedicated to understanding peace and cooperation among the world's religions.

After his 80th birthday, he kept on saying that his mother was the most important person in his life, yet he had not done enough for her. So he wished to form a new religious order for women called Dhamma Mata, which would avoid controversy regarding the ordination of Bhikkhuni. However, if members of this order are well trained spiritually and educationally, they will contribute positively for the welfare of their sex as well as for the whole of humankind.

When he was seriously ill in the past ten years, he refused western medical treatment with advanced technology. He wanted to die a natural death and to face death meaningfully as a Buddhist monk should. The doctors who closely looked after him were amazed with his courage in facing death mindfully, and his exemplary life inspired them.

Before he became unconscious, he asked his monk attendant to read to him the Thai edition of Thich Nhat Hanh's *Present Moment: Wonderful Moment*. He told the monk to practise according to the teaching contained in the book. He said he too would practise accordingly — to be mindful all the time. Those were his last words.

From *Tricycle* : *The Buddhist Review* USA
Winter 1993. Vol.III, No.2

IX

BANGKOK: CITY OF MANY VILLAGES
An Interview with Sulak Sivaraksa

One of Thailand's leading social thinkers and activists, Sulak Sivaraksa, founded the International Network of Engaged Buddhists. He has served as Chair of the Asian Cultural Forum on Development and has taught at the University of California at Berkeley, the University of Hawaii, Cornell, Toronto and Swarthmore. In his work, he draws on his study and practice of Buddhism to approach a wide range of subjects, including economic development and environmental issues. He is a lawyer, a scholar, a publisher and the author of more than sixty books in both Thai and English.

Last March, when Sulak was a guest speaker and workshop leader at the "Revolution of Hope" conference sponsored by the Omega Institute in New York city, he took time out from a very overbooked schedule to discuss his city of Bangkok for this issue of PARABOLA.

– Virginia Baron

PARABOLA: Is there a particular historical significance to the name Bangkok?

SULAK SIVARAKSA: Bangkok is the name known in the West. It was originally the name of a small village along the Chao Phraya River where French troops were garrisoned in the 1680s. "Bang" is a village and "kok" is a kind of tree. It dates back to the 16th century as a small town, but it became the capital only two hundred years ago. The city is really an amalgamation of villages. Bangkok is one village and the district where I live is Bangrak, village by a rak tree, and there is Banglampoo and many others. They are all villages.

The official name of the capital in Thai is Krung Thep. "Krung" means the capital city and "Thep" the gods or angels. In English it is translated as the City of Angels, but Krung Thep is only an abbreviation from a much longer name which means "city built by a god in order to worship the Buddha."

P: Are there myths related to the city?
SS: Bangkok is not very old as a capital. It took the place of Ayuthia, which was the old capital and also the official name of Bangkok until we opened the city to the West. Ruler before King Mongkut (of *The King and I*), who became the ruler in 1851, called himself the King of Ayuthia. It was only Rama IV that the country became known officially as Siam. The Thai government called its country Siam in a treaty with the British in 1855 because that was what the Europeans called it.

P: You mean the name of the country was changed as a convenience to the West?
SS: Yes, to please the Westerners. It was then that Bangkok replaced the name of Ayuthia (or Ayodya,

according to our pronunciation of that city of India), which is the sacred city of Rama (Vishnu incarnated). He symbolized the Aryan race, the triumph of good over evil.

Ayuthia means the invincible city, although technically we were defeated there twice by the Burmese. When the Thais were converted to Indian civilization, not to Hinduism, we accepted the Indian myth that all our kings would become Rama (the present king is Rama IX) and Rama must reign over the capital city. Our culture relates to Indian culture and traditions in somewhat the same way that North America relates to Europe.

P: You mentioned that Bangkok is composed of many villages. What are the characteristics of a Thai village?

SS: It is in the village that Buddhism has the strongest influence. You have the family, the household, and there you will find the concepts of equality, fraternity and liberty. Long before the French Revolution, the Buddha preached about a harmonious way of living in which all creatures are treated as brothers and sisters. At the village level, you don't see much difference between rich and poor, and you see a respect for the environment. These are village concepts.

Unfortunately, we have adopted the Hindu hierarchical system where a king is all-powerful. He can confiscate your land or have your head cut off! This is not a Buddhist concept. Buddhism plays a role in trying to influence the king not to be too harsh on people.

In Buddhism, there are two wheels: the wheel of power is the city, the nation, the ruling administration; and the wheel of righteousness, which is the sangha, the monkhood, which tries to convince the powerful not to exploit their power. I try to restore the role of the wheel of righteousness whenever I can. Once we lost sight of the wheel of righteousness, Bangkok became the ugliest city in Southeast Asia. It has beautiful spots, palaces, temples, parks, but it is smothered in pollution.

P: Is it possible to trace the mistakes that led to the loss of balance between these wheels?
SS: A hundred years ago, our myths started to become unreal to us — when Bangkok became the city. Until then, Chiang Mai prided itself as equal to, if not better than, Bangkok. Villages took pride in being villages. They didn't want to become cities, to be near the seats of power. But because we were afraid of being colonized, we centralized the power, and we used education to subjugate people, to make villagers feel inferior.

This was under King Chulalongkorn, Rama V. He started with the best of intentions, but, because when you are afraid of something you don't understand, you imitate it, Rama V imitated the British colonial administration in Burma. The result is that today our administration is still colonial, hierarchical, not Buddhist, that is to say not offering respect to all. The process of centralization made the city important and in the process destroyed the villages, and even Buddhism became crippled under its effects.

One of the good things about Buddhism is that it teaches you about suffering. When you know you are suffering, you can renew and revitalize yourself. Today monks have come to the forefront in efforts to protect the environment. Some temples have opened as hospices for AIDS sufferers. People are working in alternative medicine, conservation, new methods of farming.

P: Is fear a factor of daily life in Bangkok as it is in many other large cities of the world?
SS: Fear in the city is the fear of being too close to power — which is autocratic and unpredictable. When you have good kings, you have less fear, but to tell the truth, good kings are rare in history. If you live in a village, in the country, the fear is of robbers, but of course, that is only if you are very rich. In our tradition, if you are wealthy, you are educated not to show off your riches. Buddhism teaches you to give rather than to take, so the differences between rich and poor are not so obvious. You are encouraged to spend more on the temple and monasteries. An Englishman's home is his castle, but a Siamese home is just a place to sleep. The temple becomes a kind of communal hall, a place for exchanges and education. It is the place where the common wealth is

displayed and whatever you do to make it beautiful is insurance for the next life.

P: The strengths and weaknesses of a culture can often be seen most clearly in its cities. Is this true in Bangkok?

SS: Every culture has its strengths and weaknesses. When you know what they are, you try to balance them off, but once you embrace another culture, without understanding it fully, you're in the soup! When we opted to follow the West, to imitate it blindly, we became colonizers ourselves without realizing it. We only knew one aspect of the West — materialism. Once we accepted the scientific advances, we also got the side effects — such as the weakening of spiritual traditions.

Unfortunately, the positive aspects of the West, which are as relevant today as ever, have not made it to us yet. Liberty, freedom of expression, and concern for those who are deprived–these, for me, are the great contributions of Christianity. We have them in Buddhism, too, but you have democracy. We must all work on having governments where everybody counts.

P: In your book, *Seeds of Peace,* you talk about the "Buddhist model of society." Can you see the possibility of this model transforming society in Bangkok, especially with the help of the younger generation, who are growing more aware of needs that are not being met?

SS: It may not be completed in my lifetime, but Bangkok is in the process of transforming. In the early Sixties, I tried and failed. I wanted to preserve the trees, the canals, the tram, and I proposed more public parks and a limit to the height of high-rise buildings. In the beginning, people thought I was a mad educator. They wanted "development" and more concrete buildings. Then more people became interested and we created new societies for conservation of national arts and the environment. We invited the king's eldest daughter to plant trees. Now we are beginning to see more trees and public parks, but we haven't yet reached the stage of stopping high buildings

In Chiang Mai, our second city, three years ago they wanted to build a cable car up Doi Suthep, the most holy place where the Buddha relics are kept. Some intellectuals tried to stop it but they couldn't. They came to me for help and I said if you have the Sangha, the monkhood, behind you, you can stop it. They asked me to give a public lecture in the city and many many monks came. They stopped the new cable car and now they've stopped high-rises, too. This is our first city to do this.

To come back to the Buddhist vision, I agree with Thich Nhat Hanh that if each individual is transformed, if we become more positive, our friends become more positive. Then these positive attitudes lead toward a more harmonious lifestyle and respect for the environment. In Bangkok, we could improve public transportation, raise gasoline prices ... but ideally, we must move the capital city away from Bangkok. It doesn't work any more. Now we are being destroyed by AIDS, consumerism and our own selfishness.

We must either undo what our ancestors did one hundred years ago and decentralize, or move the capital city elsewhere. We may have to do that anyway, because Bangkok is sinking. We could even have two or three capitals, one for the king, one for the government and one for commerce. Unfortunately, human beings being what they are, they think in eighteenth- or nineteenth-century concepts and keep repeating old patterns. But, just as the young people in the West are changing, so are ours. They are looking back to the village concept, where the future lies.

Now, the people who lost everything, who were gamblers and drug addicts and who lost hope, have come back to the four noble truths: to confront suffering mindfully, to find the cause of suffering and to overcome it — through the nonviolent way of thinking, speaking, living — and it's working. These are the people we need in Bangkok. As I said, when I was born, Bangkok was really a collection of villages, with wooden houses, trees, birds .... We need to feel as if we live in a village.

PARABOLA, The Magazine of Myth and Tradition, Vol XVIII, No.4 Winter 1993: the City.

X
BIOGRAPHY AND BUDDHISM IN SIAM

George Simson: Introduction

Professor Sulak Sivaraksa must be introduced at eye-level. Others either have or will tell you about him as a most modest, most generous, yet most illustrious and courageous figure bigger than life.

Three years ago I had never heard of Sulak Sivaraksa. But I was introduced to his mind in the best way: through an essay of his, "Global Problem Solving: A Buddhist Perspective," in a book edited by Glenn Paige — one of the truly great souls at the University of Hawaii — *Buddhism and Nonviolent Global Problem-Solving: Ulan Bator Explorations* — sponsored by the Center for Global Nonviolence and published by the Matsunaga Institute for Peace at the University of Hawaii.

The words of that essay leap off the page by beginning uncharacteristically for this kind of writing: "To be honest and to begin by getting right to the point, I must state plainly that there is no serious contemporary Buddhist perspective for global problem solving." A paragraph later, Achan Sulak writes, "Members [of the World Fellowship of Buddhists] meet every few years to reaffirm how wonderful we Buddhists are." But then later in the essay he shows his commitment to Buddhist principals such as "gener- osity of spirit" and the "interrelatedness of life" and the "caring for all existence" while at the same time dealing with contemporary realities through the activation of Buddhist principles, organization, and making common cause.

So I asked Glenn who Sulak was. Was he an Asian Buddhist? Yes, said Glenn. Well, I said, he reads like a British lawyer. Yes, said, Glenn, he's a British lawyer, too.

Then sometime after this, in 1992 I learned from a colleague in the English department that his PhD student from Thailand, Carina, recommended that a visiting scholar from Thailand might be interested in writing the Siam volume in our series on the histories of biography in Asia. One of the guidelines for our series is that they must be written by a person native to the culture being written about. Lo and behold, it was our Siamese Buddhist British Barrister. The extraordinarily skilled Professor Poranee Natadecha of UH arranged a meeting with Sulak when he was here in 1992. We agreed that he should write the volume on the history of Siamese biography. Two details of our meeting remain in mind: first, his enthusiasm for reading biography when he saw the books at CBR, and second his keen sense of the mutual understandability of the Asian and Western sense of what constitutes biography, or perhaps I should say, what constitutes the universality of the human personality. Then, in response to my rather shamefacedly admitting that we had not raised the money yet, he said it was the idea that counted!

I also learned at about this time that he had just barely escaped the clutches of the military dictatorship in Thailand, that he was one of the great spirits in world non-violence, but that the military in Thailand was trying its best to silence this voice of reason and compassion. He is now out on bail after being snatched when he returned home. (I use the gangster slang because the action deserves no better.) Then I learned that he had been nominated for the Noble Peace Prize, a nomination I heartily endorse. So I felt like Rick in Casablanca — what does one tiny volume matter when there is so much suffering, injustice, and violence in the world?

Achan Sulak answered the question when he mentioned that one of the ten relevant issues to be tackled by Buddhists is the relationship between society and the individual. If we emphasize the individual, we must study life-writing. Perhaps for atheists like me this proposed book could be one vehicle for that "secular spirituality" that Sulak sees on the road to peace and justice.

So in thought and in person, it is most fitting and proper for Sulak Sivaraksa to speak now — at eye level — on "Biography and Buddhism in Siam."

When I saw George the last time at his office, he very kindly lent me two books on biography. I read one through, and the other I read a great deal. Very useful. There's only one criticism I may make of these two books: I don't know why they left out Leslie Stephen, because after all he was the first compiler of the *Dictionary of National Biography* in England. But in *Biography as an Art: Selected Criticism* by James Clifford there's no mention of Leslie Stephen, and in *The Development of English Biography* Stephen is only mentioned by name. But I suppose we all leave out something. Anyhow the topic of my talk is "Biography and Buddhism in Siam"

Biography according to Harold Nicholson, who quotes the *OED*, is the history of the lives of individual men — because in those days, women were not counted — as a branch of literature. And he stressed three relevant words. By history he means truth. Then biography is about individual men — of course biographical writing is based on individuality. And as a branch of literature, he said it must be artistic, a distinct approach. It has to be beautifully written. So these are three elements in a biography. He went on to discuss pure and impure biography, and so on. Now, from the Buddhist perspective, the number one issue is truth.

But what do we mean by truth?

I think that is the big debate. As you may recall, when Aristotle mentioned his master Plato, he said he admired Plato a great deal and regarded him as a god, and yet, he said, because of the truth he must reveal Plato's weaknesses and shortcomings. And I think perhaps that set the tone of Western biographies. Whatever the shortcomings, they must be accounted for, because you want to reveal the truth.

Second is individuality, that is personality. Third is the art, which depends on the artist and how he can make the biography beautiful.

From the Buddhist perspective, what is understood to be truthful is very difficult. Why, I will try to explain. Individuality in Buddhism also is a rather difficult concept. If you are not careful, you are promoting egoism. So individuality in the Buddhist concept needs explaining, too. The history of the person *per se* should not be written merely for the sake of individuality — this is my interpretation of the Buddhist concept. Of course, my Buddhist perspective is only from the Pali canon, which is very much Southern school Buddhism. I will embrace a little bit the Sanskrit source, but very little, since I know very little about it. But in the Pali cannon you can see that even the life of the Buddha is not related to tell you about that individual who was born as a prince, who went out to seek liberation, or about his ministry of 45 years scattered all over the place. The reason for telling us about Buddha's life is not because of his individuality, but because relating episodes of his life would be helpful in teaching Buddhism. So there is no real compilation of the life of the Buddha. Certainly not during the Buddha's time, nor even some years afterward. I think that for Western scholars, that's a big difficulty, a big challenge. For example, there is the question of the Buddhist calendar. When I signed a book for the Center, I used the year 2536; this is the Siamese, the Thai, the Khmer and the Laotian reckoning. But to the Singhalese, the Burmese, and the Indian, it was the year 2537. The difference is because we count the year after the Buddha passed away, one year afterward, as number one, whereas the Indian, the Burmese and the Singhalese regard the day he passed away as number one. So that could be reconciled. That's easy. But then, if you go by the Japanese, the Tibetans, and the Chinese, there's a vast difference, the year the Buddha passed away. In fact three years ago, there was a meeting in Germany, called by Professor Heinz Bechert, the best-known German scholar on Theravada Buddhism. He called a meeting of all scholars interested in the history of Buddhism, in order to decide the precise date of the birth of the Buddha, the date of his enlightenment, and the date of his passing. Of course there was no concurrence. And Bechert being very Germanic, he asked for a vote, but of coure there was none — it was not possible. Regarding the perception of truth, can truth be voted in? How do you decide? The Western Julian calendar was decided on the basis of a cultural trend, and then later on it was changed into the Gregorian calendar. But at least people agree that this year is 1993. Is that the *truth* ? Nobody really knows. The Buddhists would call it a recognized truth, *sommottisacca*, conventional truth. It is useful for calculation. For the Buddhists, the Buddhist era could be 2536, 2535, it could be anything, provided that it is recognized as the convenient truth. But ultimately, in Buddhism, there is *paramatthasacca*, the ultimate truth. And the ultimate truth is very difficult to write about. According to the Tibetan tradition it is something that is revealed. And of course, in the Zen tradition, it's known only through *satori*. And in the Theravada tradition, you perceive the truths from the books, and you only get it form the conventional truth. We all know the four noble truths:[1] suffering, the cause of suffering, elimination of suffering, and the noble eight-fold path leading to the cessation of suffering. But that is only the truth as stated in the books. And you could only achieve that truth when you yourself are liberated. And once you are liberated it's not possible to communicate only through conventional truth. I think it is the same with biographies. If you're not careful, your biography could be hagiography, which, of course, in later Buddhist canon, there are. But earlier, in Buddhist literature, biographies were written to help the faithful or those who wanted to follow the Buddha to understand the truth. Thery were not the truth itself. I think that's the first important thing.

And the idea of learning about people's lives is two-fold. Number one is to learn about the most significant teaching of the Buddha, namely, the three signs or the three characteristics of all things, that is, *samanyalakshana*, or the *trilakshana*. First, everything has to confront suffering, *dukkha,* every being or non-being confronts suffering, or insufficiency, *dukkha.* Second, every being, every compounded thing is bound for change; nothing is permanent: *anicca.* Third, everything is without essence, souls; the soullessness, or rather egolessness, is *anattā.* I think that particularly the last Buddhist truth is the most difficult concept for anyone to grasp. So when you write or relate biographies, it's just to remind people or to help them understand the three essential elements which pervade the world. People don't tend to understand it, because people are afraid of suffering — they try to avoid suffering. You tell people life is changing all the time. Most people want their lives not to change. They want it to be permanent, particularly when they're happy, or they think they're happy, though they're not really happy. And ultimately there's nothing permanent. But of course in the Western concept biography is something to be permanent. When that person dies, the biography is supposed to remain there like a tombstone, but in the Buddhist view the biography is to remind those who read it or hear about it that they must meditate on suffering, change and impermanence, and that all things are essenceless. I think that is the first requisite in Buddhist biography, as I understand it.

The second requisite is to portray exemplary lives. The biographers give you examples of the lifestyle to imitate, because in the Buddhist view the best lives are those of the *Brahmacarya,* that is those who have noble or chaste lives. That's why the monks and the nuns are more important in Buddhism than the lay people. And their lives are exemplary lives. If they commit minor mistakes, they have to confess immediately. Otherwise their life could not be exemplary. If they commit a major offense, not only do they confess, but they have to ask the whole assembly to forgive them. And if they commit a serious offence, they are expelled straight away from the holy life. Even if they are not expelled, their robe only makes them hypocrites, not really having chaste lives. I think that for the Buddhist, that's essential. So the lives that are told are exemplary. They are not told chronologically as in Western biography; they are told in bits and pieces to remind the faithful that life can be regarded as exemplary. So in the Buddhist canons you can go to the *Theragāthā,* voices of the elders, or poems of the elders, which are utterances of monks, and *Therīgāthā,* voices of nuns. They just tell you bits and pieces of their lives, which is wonderful for those who want to practice the holy life, or for those who confront suffering; their life would help you. For instance, in the *Therīgāthā,* there was a lady who was betrothed to marry somebody, and she didn't want to. She ran away with a slave boy and had one son. She wanted to go home, because usually in India, the woman should return home when she wants to deliver a baby. It wasn't possible. So after the second son she wanted to return home. So at last they went. To make a long story short, one son was killed, the other son was killed, and her husband was killed, and of course she became mad. Then when she went to her home, which was the home of a rich family, the whole family had gone bankrupt and disappeared. Insane, she went to the Buddha. She heard the Buddha was somebody, the all-enlightened, the all-compassionate one, and she wanted her husband, her parents, her children, to come back alive. She asked the Buddha. Buddha said, 'Of course! Possible. Provided you get me a mustard seed from any household whatsoever which doesn't know death.' So she went from household to household. 'Yes, you could have a mustard seed, but do you know that my father died?' 'Do you know that my grandfather died?' And then she realized that death is inevitable. So she came to the Buddha, and then she became enlightened. This was just related as a few short verses that became very, very important for the Buddhists. Then that narrative provided a kind of prime resource for later biographies. So you can see from the Buddhist view the early biographies are just a scattering of anecdotes, of course, artistic and beautiful — I mean *Therīgāthā* was all done in poems, and so was *Theragāthā*. But for me they serve two purposes, that of showing exemplary lives, and to remind people of suffering, impermanence and essenceless-ness. Later biographies, particularly in the commentaries of the Pali canons, were written to show not only the two points I mentioned, but to prove certain Buddhist theories. And that means to me that the Buddhists must have become a little shaky, that they wanted to prove something or had been confronted by non-Buddhists. So the later commentaries explain more, the life of the Buddha, the life of various elders, and even lay people. The main idea was to prove, number one the law of karma, or rebirth. Because in the Buddha's time it was not essential to prove this! If it's helpful for you to believe, go ahead. If it's not helpful, there's no need to discuss it. But I think about 500 years later, they wanted to prove the law of karma, such as why one might be short-tempered, why one might be ugly, and at the same time powerful.

Ashoka the Great was emperor of all India, but he was supposed to have had very rough skin, and he had a very bad smell, and he had a very bad temper. All these could be explained by writing his biography, biography meaning not only this life but also including past lives. Ashoka became emperor because in a previous life when he was very young, as a boy, out of piety he offered earth to the Buddha, out of piety and sincerity. And he asked to become the universal monarch, the emperor. But the fact that he offered earth and not rice, which of course the Buddha took, and because that earth was so smelly and mixed with rice, and the Buddha had to eat earth and rice because he would not refuse, then that's why the boy born as Ashoka had a very bad smell and bad temper. And these were explained not in the Pali canon but in Sanskrit texts, the *Ashokāvadāna*. In Sanskrit they have a lot of texts known as, the *āvadāna* literature, explaining past life and present life, so biography is used to prove certain important points in Buddhism. I think that's very important.

The word *avadāna* refers to a story which explains the process whereby the seeker after the truth, in previous life, seeing the Buddha, performs various kinds of good actions and thus through the working of karma, leaps the fruit of enlightenment in a later life. Thus in the case where the hero finally becomes Gotama the Buddha, such a story is known as Jātaka. It describes usually the karmic process whereby the disciple of the Buddha attains enlightenment, through a series of existence.

Avadāna, on the other hand, is a legend originally a pure and virturous act, as the Greeks would call it an aristeia — afterwards a sacred story, and possibly a story the hearing of which purifies the mind. The word *avadāna* or *apadāna* (*v* and *p* are interchangeable in Pali and Sanskrit) means 'pure action, heroic action'. The book is a Buddhist *Virtue Sanctorum*.

In Buddhist terms, this word is used for stories relating to 'deeds' which are remarkable on account of their consequences (according to the law of karma) mostly ground deeds or glorious achievements of liberality or self-sacrifice, but also sometimes wicked deeds.

In Tibetan *avadāna* means 'the utterance of what is fully grasped'. It is a common designation for the recital of events of ideal life, full of instructive lessons.

Buddhist biography will tell you a truth, but as I

said, the conventional truth, not the ultimate truth, because ultimate truth cannot be told. Conventional truth, of course, is very difficult, too. Perhaps the main difficulty in the West occurs when you want conventional truth to be ultimate truth. That's why a lot of people rebel against Christianity. You no longer regard Genesis as truthful. God simply could not create the world in seven days. Another example is that the women's liberation movement does't like the idea that Eve came out of the ribs of Adam. This is perhaps where Buddhists can be helpful to the Christians. Because this is conventional truth, it was spoken in those days. You must not take it literally. It's the way people understood at that time and wrote that book. They could not know better. So you must go beyond the conventional truth. And for this, particularly, my teacher, Buddhadasa, a famous monk now 86 years old in the south of Siam — he calls himself the servant of Buddha, — Buddhadasa developed a theory called *pāsākhon pāsādham.*

Pāsākhon is human language, and *pāsādham* the Dharmic language, which he derived from the conventional truth and ultimate truth. We are bound by human language, we are trapped by human language, because language has its limitations. And sometimes we want to use language to express something which was at that time acceptable, but nowadays is not acceptable. Like the book of Genesis, it was acceptable perhaps two thousand years ago, and we try to use the standard of these days to judge two thousand years ago. And likewise in Buddhism, if you don't understand that, it doesn't make sense. Because some of the monks are flying around, you see, flying is part of the psyche of power. Another example is Mahakasyapa, the most senior monk, who presided over the first council and who, according to certain traditions, is still alive. He has reached the state of liberation, but his body is supposed to be functioning, in a state of trance somewhere, waiting for the future Buddha to come. Now, is it true, or is it false? It depends. Logically you cannot prove one way or the other. Of course by the Western approach nowadays it's not possible. But if you use the Buddhist concept, why not? If you reach the ultimate truth of Nirvana, you could not care less whether he's there or not! As things are changing, nothing is permanent, but it could last a little bit longer, to wait for the future Buddha to come! From the Buddhist point of view this is not very relevant. It is only relevant if you feel that it would be helpful to regard these stories, to see them as exemplary lives. Once you reach the ultimate, anything could happen. That's number one, and number two, even Mahakasyapa, he may last until the next Buddha, but ultimately he will also disinteagrate, subject to change. Even he's not permanent. I think that once you grant that issue, you can correctly understand Buddhist biography. Otherwise, when people tackle Buddhism they will find it's very, very difficult, because a lot of myth is involved, a lot of supernatural powers are involved. So you have to regard it as conventional truth, human language, and not the ultimate truth. So whatever interpretation you take of Buddhist biographies, they are to help you see that the life is exemplary, and at the same time to help you to understand about suffering, impermanence, and essenceless-ness. I think that this approach has its strengths and its weaknesses. You mustn't regard Buddhists as having all the answers. At the same time I feel that the Western approach doesn't have all the answers either. But I think if you take the two, perhaps we can learn from each other. That's my point.

Now coming more to Thai biography, until recently, obviously, the influence was mostly from the Buddhist approach. As I said, you may write biography to show an exemplary life. If you're not careful, it becomes hagiography. And if you're not careful all these supernatural powers and so on come into play, which of course some of the younger generation find very difficult to swallow. Since a biography may be to prove the law of karma—rebirth—those people who don't believe in rebirth find this a little bit difficult. For me, there is a lot of evidence, a lot of material. For those who follow the Buddhist tradition strictly, biographies are only to show exemplary lives or to remind you of the three characteristics. Otherwise a biography is not meaningful.

The late supreme Patriarch of Bangkok, Prince Jinavara Sirivaddhana, who died about fifty years ago, wrote about his mother in two lines. He did not even mention her name, even though she was a princess by marriage. He mentioned the date she was born and the date she passed away, and that his mother lived to the age of 92; the idea of course was that even though she lived to the age of 92 she passed away. Impermanence is very important. In our custom, we always produce cremation volumes. Books are published particularly at cremation to be distributed free of charge. And at his mother's cremation, he published a Jataka, a story of a previous life of the Buddha. And for his mother's life, only two lines, And you can go on. Phya Anuman Rajadhon, my teacher, wrote when his mother died and when his father died. When his mother died he said that sometimes creamtion volumes also have some biographies of the deceased, sometimes not. He said, 'I chose the latter because my mother was just an ordinary woman. But the most important person for me and my brothers and sisters. And I'm very privileged to be born her son. And her life was very important for me, but not for anybody else. I decided not to write about her.' I mean Phya Anuman was a great writer who wrote many, many books, including biographies. Similarly, when his father died, he said, 'my father was an ordinary human being'—the Buddhist word is *puthujana,* that means, you are not yet a stream-winner,[2] you are not yet a noble person, you are not yet destined to be enlightened. A *puthujana* is an ordinary weakling. Hence, he has virtues and faults. 'If I mention his virtues, it is not right for the son to praise his father. But if I mention his faults it's not right for the son to mention the father's faults either. So I decided not to write about my father.' Period. That reminds you of Sir Edmund Gosse who wrote the famous book *Father and Son.* Conflict between father and son and so on. And here again, you see, from the Buddhist view, the conflict between father and son is certainly not admired, not encouraged. Because the father and mother are the most important persons in your life. The Buddha said your father and mother are to be regarded as enlightened persons, *arahants;* they're your first teachers. And I think the whole process works that way. And you must realize that, you know, it is very important. Because even during the time of the Buddha, he was born in the period where most of the rulers were killed by their sons, usurping the throne. Even King Ajatasattu who patronized the first council, killed his father, Bimpisara. So it's usual. In Buddhism, the teaching tried to work with that, and I think it worked, particularly in the Thai concept. My son is now rebelling against me, which is wonderful. But up to my period, I have not heard of a son rebelling; it is not possible culturally, because such a son would be rebelling against the most enlightened person in your family. I can't recall any such biographies, whereas in the West many are written by a son or daughter, but in our context I have never seen one. Partly because, as I said, in Buddhism biographies are of exemplary lives and to remind you of impermanence, suffering, and essenceless-ness.

Biographies that have been written in the contemporary period have been influenced somewhat by the West, but at the same time the Buddhist influence is still very strong. The one written by Prince Patriarch Vajirañāna has been translated into English by Craig Reynolds. I think Prince Vajirañāna's memoirs have a very good translation and a very good introduction. But the Buddhist influence is there again; he wants to show—he said very clearly, 'I want my life to teach my stdents. I want you to know my failings as well as my achievements. And my achievenments, he said, are not because I was a prince, but because I worked hard, and what I tried to do I devoted for the whole of the Buddhist religion.' Of course, as a critic I can see that he didn't show all his failings, which is understandable; those of us who write autobiography never show all our failings. Sometimes we don't know them; sometimes we want to hide them. And this is where autobiography is perhaps different from biography. But autobiography in the Thai context always avoids individuality as understood in the English concept, in which one regards oneself as the writer distinct from the subject one writes about. But in the Thai context, under Buddhist influence, you have to relate more to others, in order not to hurt others. I think that makes Thai biography, compared to Western biography, rather, less harsh. Anything of conflict you avoid. The other prince who wrote his memoirs was a brother of Prince Vajirañāna, Prince Damrong, and when he went to England, George V said,

"Damrong, when are you going to be damm right?"
And he wronte his memoirs. Then like Phya Anuman,
Prince Damrong wrote many, many books, and in fact
he was the one who wrote the most modern biographies. Why? Because he was the one who started the
tradition of giving books at cremations, and later on
people even gave books at birthdays. The idea of this
all goes back to Buddhism. The offering of Dhamma
is the best of all gifts. First he published books on the
Pali canons, and then on Buddhist prayer. Later on he
started to publish literary books. Because the government didn't have enough money, he published books
on old Siamese literature, Siamese chronicles. For
cremations, he would write a biography of the deceased,
avoiding any shortcoming. From the Western point of
view that is not appropriate, and younger people in
Siam also attack him on that issue. Just a week before
I came here one student asked me whether we could
regard Prince Damrong's biographies as trustworthy. I
said yes, up to point. And I said you must use the
Buddhist standard. The Buddha said, don't believe
anything, not even those works claimed to be words
of the Buddha. Don't believe anything even if it
comes from the sacred books of Buddhism, and even
so with Prince Damrong's writing. Damrong wrote
nothing that is false; he would never write anything
that is known to be false. But of course he doesn't tell
all the truth. Because I mean all the truth connot be
revealed, particularly when you write a book about the
deceased, and more so if it is paid for by someone

wanting to publish a big book. But I think it's useful information. Damrong wrote his own memoirs, and his memoirs end at the age of 13. He lived to the age of 81. And he was a great historian. And we would have had a wonderful book. But at the age of 13 he witnessed a court case in the palace. His father, King Mongkut, known to the West in the *King and I,* had many, many concubines, and one of them was charged with adultery. Damrong was called as a witness. He had become a novice in the monastery, and after he left the monkhood he was called as a witness. Had he written beyond the age of thirteen, he felt that he would hurt a lot of his cousins, half-brothers, and other relatives, so he refused to write. I think for me that is in accordance with the Buddhist view that if you cannot tell the truth, you must not write anything at all. And of course this is both a strength and weakness. Indeed, a grandchild of this lady who was called to the court on the charge of adultery became the first Asian president of the U.N. general assembly, Prince Wan, a very famous man. And I knew him quite well, towards the end of his life, and I asked him to write his memoirs. He went through the Second World War, First World War, and was the Siamese minister to the Court of St. James's at the early age of 34. As a lad he went to Oxford, to Marlborough College in England, and to Paris too as a graduate. But he just wouldn't write. I said, "OK, Your Royal Highness, if you won't write, why don't you allow me to interview you? Let me...." I just wanted to imitate

Boswell. He said no, perhaps because as a Buddhist he would not want to reveal secrets—and he'd known a lot of secrets. He was educated at Oxford, but he refused the Western approach to biography. Most politicians or statesmen in the Western European tradition write their memoirs to justify their lives' work. But he refused. His cousin, Prince Dhani, also went to Oxford. I pushed him so hard that eventually he worte a book called *Seven Cycles of Life,* which he published at the age of 84. In our tradition one cycle consists of 12 years. I have just completed five cycles recently; I am now 60 years old. Now *Seven Cycles of Life* is a mere minimum. He himself is effaced. And again I think in a way that's very Buddhist. To tell people how wonderful you are is not right in the Buddhist view of egolessness. And for me I think that's a contradiction: if you want to write autobiography, you must mention your ego somehow, and you must also get your ego out, to show to yourself and to people. You must at the same time make fun of your ego. That's what I did in my own book, *Phases of Life,* which, if I may so claim, is a little bit unconventional by Thai standard. But I think in my father's generation, the ego had to be abliterated. And so it was even in the book of Phya Anuman, my teacher, who, like Prince Damrong, wrote many, many books, including biographies. But he would never write his memoirs. I pushed him and I even went to see him every week with a tape recorder, until he got fed up and said, "All right, I will write". And he wrote four volumes.[3] And yet, even though it's a wonderful book on the social history of Bangkok, you get a minimum of him. I think that is subconsciously the Buddhist influence. It's not permissible to talk about oneself, not even one's family, such as how his wife and mother suffered. They were very poor. He came up to the top echelon and yet, with nine brothers and sisters, he had to help them all survive, but you don't get those personal matters at all. You get a beautiful picture of Bangkok, sixty years ago, eighty years ago. It's a wonderful social setting. But there is no psychological revelation about the man or his family.

The only biography between that generation and my generation, which I feel is very, very important, is by a woman who also went to Oxford. Her father was a Siamese minister at the Court of St. James's. He came from a very distinguished family. He had a wife, but in those days when you went abroad, you did not take your family. He ran away with a seventeen year old English girl. Her father became very, very upset and petitioned the King of Siam, and the minister was recalled from London. So his career was finished. A girl was born to this seventeen year old woman and the Siamese minister — in those days we had no ambassador. The minister died and the girl became an orphan. And yet, because of her intellectual ability and her deligence, she was the first Siamese woman to win the King's scholarship to Oxford. And she wrote her memoirs, *Life Like a Dream,* which it was, and she married a Prince Charming. This prince was adopted by King Prajadhipok, the last of the absolute monarchs. After their marriage in London, he husband died in the Second World War. And she's still alive; she's over 80. She is perhaps the richest Siamese woman now. Her memoirs were in two volumes, telling you even of her love affair, and how she betrayed her second husband, and so on. But obviously these have a certain English influence. But yet the Buddhist influence is there, because although she had been an agnostic, and when her father died was raised by missionaries and became Christian and then again became agnostic, in her old age she became Buddhist. Subconsciously, she came back to Buddhism and she said that she wanted to write to show her failings, to show that life is just like a dream, it's not really true. With all her wealth now she feels very lonely and the only thing which comforts her now is Buddhist meditation, Buddhist practices. These are glimpses of the Buddhist concept of biography as found in my country.

So far I have mentioned only biographies and autobiographies written in Thai. There are three memoirs that I know of that were written in English, one by Prince Chulachakrabongse called *Brought up in England.* Later the author also wrote in Thai. A princess, Rudee Voravan, also wrote in English and published in the U.S. Another volume published in the U.S. was by Mr. Kumut Chandruang called *Boyhood in Siam.* I hope my own too will be published in the U.S. perhaps next year.

Thank you for your patience. Now perhaps we can have some questions and discussion.

Questions and Answers

Questioner: So the implication of not doing biography is that you don't want to move yourself out of the present, that you want to stay in the living moment ?

Sulak : In a way, yes.

Questioner: That that's a really important feeling about life.

Questioner: Was there a big impact, say around the middle of the nineteenth or beginning of the 20th century, on Thai biography because of Western influence?

Sulak: Yes, I didn't develop that theme. I mentioned briefly Prince Damrong was the one. He is more or less known as the father of modern Thai history; in fact he would be the father of modern Thai biographies. I think there was obviously certain English influence, but subconsciously the Buddhist influence is there. So I think this would be a theme I'd like to tackle at the deeper levels. If you're not careful, you know, you could say, well he didn't go through, penetrate deeply enough. But, you see, for us as Buddhists life is only a cycle to get out of. Life, birth and death, is a cycle, and the point of Buddhism is to tell you how to be detached from, how to understand, and how not to be trapped in that cycle.

Questioner: Besides the fundamental assumption behind it though, were there some differences in biographical technique in a more Western style of demanding text and corroboration and witnessing in the kind of rudimentary way that the English do?

Sulak: I think that is coming. But so far, up to the present, there's not much of that available. The art of biography form the English tradition is not yet developed. And you must realize even in England it's something new. So, people writing, so far, it's only one level, you know, you don't have that psychological depth. I think that I would say that far yes.

Questioner: Are there popular journalistic biographical sketches the way there are in the West?

Sulak: Oh yes.

Questioner: And are they condemned by serious people or are they taken as confections and left alone? Who reads them?

Sulak: Most of the biographies now are on rather popular levels. But I mentioned one lady who wrote a serious one, though it was not so very well written, despite the fact that she's very revealing, partly because she's not a very good Thai writer. She gives too much detail, and the print is too small—it's two big tomes. On the whole most biographies are rather popular and for me it's rather hagiography. I mean all the kings—this is where my difficulty comes—all the princes have done wonderful things and nothing negative. I tried to mention negative elements about Rama the Fifth. He was a wonderful king, but he had quite a few negative elements. Also Rama the Sixth. That's why they charged me eight years ago for defaming dead kings. If my case had been a conviction, we could not even write history. Luckily, the case was withdrawn, so it was never proven in court. Unfortunately, I think we still think that some people are sacred, and we don't have a real appraisal. There is one biography of a very important monk. It's translated into English now, in two versions, *The Life of Achan Man.* He's supposed to be the last Arahant, the last enlightened person, in my country. And this is by Achan Maha Bua, the most senior meditation master. It is a fascinating book. It was reviewed by Kukrit Pramoj, a most well-known journalist, and he tore it to pieces. And yet it was translated by two people, one a Thai, one an American lady at Berkeley, published in two versions. Tambiah, in his book *The Forest Saints of Thailand,* made use a great deal of this book.

Questioner: One of the great changes in the last, say, hundred years in biography in the West is that everybody gets a serious biogrphy: the bottle-washer, the carpenter, the baseball player, the ditch digger—somebody, someplace writes something serious about one of these. Biographies are written about individuals form a very broad spectrum of statuses and classes. Of course it's still mostly kings and generals and other power people. Is there such a motion in Thailand—to write about every kind of person in a serious way?

Sulak: No, I think that, again, to come back to me, my case of *lese-majeste* shows that open criticism is not yet possible. And I think unless you have open criticism you cannot have serious biography. Even kings' and generals' biographies are all positive, with no negative elements. And then you go back to the Buddhist view, that only your life is less exemplary. I had one wonderful great writer who was my teacher's teacher, Phra Dhammanidesduayharn; he was a very well-known writer, but he said nobody shall write my biography, because my life is not pure, not free from smoke or fire. So he prohibited it. Another case is a very famous monk and great Pali scholar, the Ven. Phra Dhammacetiya, former abbot of Wat Thongnopakhun, where I was ordained as a novice. He wrote instructions for his cremation, and I was one of the five committee members he appointed. He said, "When I die, nobody shall write anything to praise me, because I have devoted 45 years in the holy order, and what I have done is known to those who follow my career." Period. But anyhow, disobeying his instructions, although I did not write any praise in his cremation volume, I wrote an official biography of him. And I also wrote a book on the monk named Dhammacetiya; I used the subjective elements I knew about him, and I criticized the whole Sangha, the whole hierarchy. The book became very controversial, and I must say, rather unBuddhist. I wrote another book like this on Dr.Puey Ungphakorn, the former Governor of the Central Bank of Thailand and former President of Thammasat University—a wonderful man who was badly treated in the *coup* of October 1976. He is still alive. The book has gone to many editions and was translated into Japanese.

Questioner: Do you think this is the direction, say, like blending East-West mind sets or perceptions, that biography would take?

Sulak: I think that, yes, I think that's a very good point, and that's how I see it. And I see myself as one of those. And I get a lot of criticism because they said I claim to understand the Thai tradition, yet I rebel against that tradition. And I try to bring the Western tradition into biographies.

Questioner: The appraisal?

Sualk: That's right. And people are reluctant to ask me to write memorial volumes, cremation volumes, because they find—they fear that however beautifully I talk about the deceased, I'm bound to have at least one or two paragraphs that they don't want to be heard. And I feel it's essential to have this. My English barrister's training.

Questioner: We'll have to have you come here regularly, to keep you out of trouble, I guess!

Sulak: One princess, Chongchit Thanom Diskul, Prince Damrong's eldest daughter, wouldn't write her memoirs. I had interviews with her, all on tape, and on her centennial had it published, by the Diskul Foundation. Her sister asked to see it, and she deleted quite a number of passages. Then it came back to me, so I told the printer to ignore what she deleted. Oh, she became very furious! But it was all true. And I failed—perhaps, you know, looking back, perhaps I should not have been that impatient, perhaps I should have let the first edition go that way. I should have waited for the second edition, but I was too inpatient. But for me, it was very, very important. Because the princess who died was wonderful; she talked to me openly, because she knew me. And she knew the tape recordings were being made. I was surprised she told me everything. And she was wonderful, and it's on the record now.

Questioner: Is it published in English now?

Sulak: No, it's only in Thai, unfortunately. The English versions of Thai biography are not, so far, very successful.

Questioner: My Thai is *nit noi*.

Sulak: Prince Chula wrote his own memoirs, *Brought up in England,* a wonderful work. He wrote Thai history in the form of his ancestors' biographies, called *Lords of Life*. It was all positive, which made it difficult, of course. Even our friend, Walter

Vella, when he did the book *Chaiyo: King Vajiravudh and the Development of Thai Nationalism,* told me it was very difficult. He went to interview a lot of the King's courtiers, and they said to him, "I will tell you the truth, provided you don't write about it." What can you do? In *Chaiyo,* I think Walter Vella tried his best in the American tradition; at the same time he tried to obey the Thai tradition. It's the best book on that topic, at present. But it's certainly not the best book, for people like me, because it's not revealing enough. But, luckily, I think in a way Walter Vella got the best of both worlds. He got it published here, by the University of Hawaii Press. They would not publish it if it were superficial, yet at the same time he got the prize given by the Thai king for the best book of the year and he was invited to receive the prize form the crown prince on the centennial of King Vajiravudh, Rama VI. Perhaps he did not do a good enough work so the Siamese gods punished him: he was killed just the day before he was to receive the prize. I'm being unkind. Poor Walter—he was staying in a hotel, and he knew Bangkok so well, and his Thai was superb. He was among the first Americans to learn Thai in the Second World War, and he knew Bangkok. But Bangkok changed into one way streets. And he knew that. But he didn't know that they allowed buses to come two ways, so he was killed by the bus. But anynow, regarding his books—he wrote another one on Rame III, called *Siam Under Rama III*. I published the Thai translation of this. I think they're certainly very good, but of course there's a lot of room for improvement.

Questioner: I have a question. If a mother writes her autobiography but in it there are things that would hurt her adult chidren, feelings perhaps, should she leave that out or should she put it in?

Sulak: Ah, that's a very...ticklish question, isn't it? I think it depends on individual judgment. Do you want, number one, the truth, or do you want the feeling? Or sometimes people don't care whether it's truthful or not; they want their books to be sold. *Goodbye To All That,* by Robert Graves, caused his parents to be very hurt. And it was not only that it disturbed their feelings, but they said that what Robert wrote was not true. But Robert Graves could not care less.

Questioner: Maybe to them it was not true but to him it was true.

Sulak: We have to realize, of courese, particularly those who write autobiography, that sometimes we have a little nervous problem ourselves. Sometimes we want to prove that we are so wonderful at other people's expenses. I also belong to that group—you know, a little bit neurotic.

George: Sulak, thank you very much.

Notes:

1. The beginning and most fundamental of the Buddha's teachings.

2. Stream-winner, or *arya* (usually translated as "Noble" or "noble one") refers to a specific attainment whereby the individual enters the "path of seeing," referring to the direct perception of ultimate truth. Such an individual approaching enlightenment is recognized as having achieved a sublime state.

3. In English, *Looking Back* by Sthirakoses, Chulalongkorn University Press, Bangkok 1992.

Presented at the University of Hawaii, April 30,1993

XI
A THAI PERSPECTIVE ON SOCIALLY ENGAGED BUDDHISM: A CONVERSATION WITH SULAK SIVARAKSA

This conversation took place between Sulak Sivaraksa and Donald Rothberg at Berkeley, California, in July 1992.

Work and main influences
Rothberg: How did your own work in Siam develop?
Sivaraksa: I started very small. In 1962, I started working with the University Press in Bangkok. I started a journal called the *Social Science Review* in 1963 and got many people to write for it. Now my country was under a dictatorship since 1947, which had become much more severe since 1957; most social studies available were nothing but government propaganda dominated by American capitalism and militarism. Overnight, this journal became the central intellectual journal. Young people were attracted to it, although I had originally intended it for my peers and for those educated abroad. I started meetings for young people, using a temple in Wat Bovornives [a monastery in Bangkok, also housing a Buddhist university].[1] We explored alternative ways of thinking, and these young people began to become political; many of them were successful in changing the government in 1973. I also started a bookshop, which also became a meeting

place. Everywhere I went, I started publications, printing presses, magazines and books. I gave lectures and I made many more friends, as well as more enemies. This is how I work.

I start in my own country with Buddhists, then worked with Christians, Muslims, and agnostics. Later, I expanded to my neighboring countries — Southeast Asia, South Asia, Japan and America. My work has developed by interconnections on the basis of friendship.

I organized the Komol Keemthong Foundation in 1971 in order to promote the idealism of the youth; it was named after one of the young people working with me that I admired very much, who was killed by the Communists. Of course, this notion of promoting youthful idealism is too abstract; we actually use a number of concrete ideas taken from many places — from Thich Nhat Hanh, Ivan Illich, Paulo Freire, Dr. Ariyaratne of Sri Lanka. We still often work with this foundation. I also founded the Sathirakoses-Nagapradipa Foundation, named after two of my teachers, which works on environment issues, on questions of conservation and nature resources, and also attempts to help artists and poets. At the Wongsanit Ashram outside Bangkok, connected with this foundation, young people and artists can come for retreats, for periods of reflection and learning, as well as for meditation.

I have also founded ecumenical organizations, like the TICD [the Thai Inter-Religious Commission for Development], in which we work with Christians and

Muslims on questions of alternative development, and the CGRS [Coordinating Group on Religion and Society]. I'm good at starting organizations; this is my strength. I like to give ideas to people; I find committed people, and soon I often have little to do with the organization!

Rothberg: What have been the main influences on your own connection of Buddhism with social action?

Sivaraksa: I have been very much personally influenced by Thich Nhat Hanh. He has suffered more than have most monks and has been involved more for social justice. In Vietnam in the 1950s and 1960s, he was very exposed to young people, and his society was in turmoil, in crisis. He was really in a difficult position, between the devil and the deep blue sea — the Communists on the one hand, the CIA on the other hand. In such a situation, he has been very honest — as an activist, as a contemplative monk(not unlike Thomas Merton), as a poet (again like Merton), and as a clear writer. Most important to me have been his teachings on "interbeing" (Nhat Hanh 1987a), and poems like "Please Call Me By My True Names" (Nhat Hanh 1987b, 63-64). Of course, his work really rests on the traditional Buddhist teaching of *paticca samuppāda* ["dependent origination," the inter-relatedness of all phenomena] brought into a very contemporary setting.

I have also been very influenced by Gandhi and by the Quakers. Gandhi experienced and responded to the dreadful suffering connected with the British occupation of the subcontinent. His radical approach was to be with the poor and to use nonviolent approaches, to use spiritual. Later, I came across the Quakers. I was especially interested in the radical Quakers and the idea of a religious society of friends. The Quakers regard friendship as central, just as did the Buddha. I was also very attracted by the Quaker notions of the sacredness of a human being and nonviolence. I found the Quakers more articulate than Buddhists on the need to question and resist the powers of the states, to question the status quo; Buddhists have been coexisting with the state for too long.

The new Western Buddhists and groups like the Buddhist Peace Fellowship really have been good for me. Particularly helpful have been people who have had a radical (and sometimes Marxist) background before they become Buddhists, who come to Buddhism with critical social awareness. For me, the Marxist systemic analysis of society, of the seeds of oppression, is very useful, provided it is placed in a nonviolent context. Perhaps radicals (including Marxists) can learn from Buddhists to be more humble, more mindful, to have some spirituality.

Johan Galtung,[2] a European who became a Buddhist, was the first one to lead me into serious thinking that Buddhists must take on the system rather than focus on individuals. Schumacher(1973) helped us in particular to think about the development of economic systems not based on greed and consumerism. Here, radicals and Marxists can also learn from us; we hate the dreadful system, not the people. In Christian language, we hate sin, not the sinners.

A Buddhist approach to social action in the contemporary world

Rothberg: In your essay on "Buddhism and Contemporary Internation Trends" (Sivaraksa 1992b), you wrote that traditional Buddhist approaches and categories have not yet been adequately translated into modern terms. What do you think has to be done to make Buddhism relevant for modern social problems?

Sivaraksa: In making Buddhism more relevant for the contemporary world, it is important not to compromise on the essentials, such as the ethical precepts (*sila*).[3] However, these ethical precepts need to be rethought in order to make sense of life in contemporary societies. Buddhists traditionally have lived in rather simple societies, largely agrarian, as is still often the case in Southeast and South Asia. In such societies, ethical issues may also be simple. One can say,"I am a good person. I don't kill. I don't steal. I don't commit adultery. I don't lie." But, when the society becomes much more complex, these simple interpretations of ethical norms don't work so well.

For example, to follow the first Buddhist ethical precept, to refrain from killing living beings, is not so simple now; social reality in the modern world has become much more complex and interconnected. We have to ask questions like these: Do we allow our tax money to go for armaments? Do we keep ourselves seperate from the political realm and not challenge the government? Should we breed animals for consumption?

Our understanding of the second precept, to refrain from taking what is not ours, must also be extended. We may not literally steal in our face-to face interactions, but do we allow the rich countries to exploit the poor countries through the workings of the international banking system and the international economic order? Do we allow industrial societies to exploit agrarian societies? The First World to exploit the Third World? The rich to exploit the poor generally?

We can ask similar questions on the basis of the third precept, to refrain from improper sexual behavior. We need to think not just about adultery and hunting others, but also to think more broadly about other sexual and gender issues, about male domination and the exploitation of women. For instance, we use women for advertising in ways that promote sexism, lust, and greed.

In fact, to participate in the system of consumerism is already to violate the first, second, and third precepts. Following the fourth precept, to refrain from improper speech, is also very difficult. Think of all the advertising and all the political propaganda, all the lies and exaggerations in the media and in education. We have to challenge all this even when it is legal. Buddhists in Asia often have liked to coexist side by side with the state and legal system. I think we have to rexamine ourselves.

Buddhist social ethics traditionally have been entirely personal. We have not looked at the system that is violent, that is oppressive, that in fact, involves theft.

The Buddhist notion of enlightenment and understanding [or wisdom, Pali: *paññā*] also need to be extended so that enlightenment is not always internal enlightenment; here also Buddhism has been weak. *Paññā* must involve a real understanding of yourself and of society. If your society is unjust, exploitative and violent, how do you respond? With all the *pāramitās* [or "perfections"] of a Bodhisattva, one dedicated to the liberation of all beings: humbly, seriously, without much attachment, with awareness, with vigor, with patience, with a great vow to change things.[4] But Buddhists have too often been "goody-goodies" and not really responded to all the suffering in society.

We also need a different understanding of suffering and the course of suffering (the first two "Noble Truths" taught by the Buddha). Suffering at the time of the Buddha was certainly often dreadful, but it was simpler to understand; the interrelatedness of all phenomena that is a main teaching of the Buddha was simpler then and is much more complex now. We Buddhists need help from the social scientists: from sociologists, phychologists, antropologists, etcetera. We should be very open and translate the findings of these disciplines into Buddhist understandings. Of course, one must have the right view of things and use these sciences to help against greed, hatred and delusion; otherwise, all these methodologies and sciences could lead one astray. But without the work of these disciplines, we may become deluded and think that Buddhist practice can solve everything. It doesn't. Without transforming the Buddhist sense of wisdom to bring in understanding of, and respond to, social reality, Buddhism will not be so relevant and might only appeal to the middle class. If we are not careful, it will become a kind of escapism.

Rothberg: Sometimes when I read Buddhist texts or talk to Buddhists, even many socially and politically concerned Buddhists, they often suggest that the basis problem is internal greed, harted, and delusion, as if working on the individual is most fundamental. According to this way of thinking, whatever problems there are with societies or systems are just an expression of what is "inner." There is little sense of a more "dialectical" relationship of individual and system, of how greed, hatred, and delusion are formed by systems, while the systems are then supported further by greed, hatred, and delusion. Of course, there is much traditional Buddhist emphasis on *sangha* [community] and ethics, but the assumption commonly is that changing the inner leads to outer change. How might we develop a vision of socially engaged Buddhism as integrating inner and outer work more fully so that the one informs the other?

Sivaraksa: Ambedkar, the leader of the

untouchables in India, who became a Buddhist at the end of his life, challenged the Buddha in a wonderful way.[5] He said that it was not enough to speak of the course of suffering as being greed, hatred, and delusion; that is only to speak of more "internal" causes. The social structure is also a course of suffering; as an untouchable, he could see that very clearly.

The Buddha's intention was certainly to change individuals; the ultimate aim was liberation. However, he intended to help liberate not only individuals but the whole society. His method was to create the *sangha*, the community, as a kind of alternative society within the larger society that would influence the larger society indirectly.

But we should also remember that the larger society at that time was not all that wicked. The system wasn't too rigid. One changed individual could make a big impact. A rich man, a kind of banker at the Buddha's time, Supata, who became Anāthapiṇḍika, became the supporter of all the poor in the region. In our time, you can get one good banker and nothing particularly changes. Now you have to change the whole system of banking! We must be very demanding in transforming ourselves, but I think we would be deluded unless we also have a clear understanding of how to change the oppressive society.

The Bodhisattva vow to save all sentient beings is a very special challenge to all Buddhists. Without that vow, we may become very selfish. We may not be able to change the word right now, but we can begin by encountering, understanding, and sharing the suffering of others, and wishing to help. Of course, we must do this with equanimity and detachment. This is compassion, *karuṇā*, our basic attitude guiding both our more internal and our more external work. There must be a balance of the internal and external; to stress one at the expense of the other is for me a betrayal of Buddhism.

Rothberg: When I visited earlier this year the monastery of Pah Ban Tat (in northeast Thailand) founded by Ajahn Mahā Boowa, I had several conversations with Bhikkhu Paññāvaddho, an English monk who is probably the senior Western monk in Thailand. He questions whether it was really possible for persons socially engaged to live fully the spiritual life, no matter how helpful they might be. For him, to live this life is to work for liberation by uprooting the "defilements" that block one's basic love and understanding. However, this requires living in a highly supportive environment, like that of a *wat* [monastery]. The life of social engagement will very likely not have the spiritual depth that is possible for a monk in such an environment as a monastery.

This is a major concern for many people in the West. Our intention is to work socially in a way that brings much spiritual depth, as well as social depth, rather than somehow act superficially in dimensions.

Sivaraksa: Of course, it is great danger that those who are socially engaged lack spiritual depth, inner calm, and peace; some activist Buddhist monks (for instance, in Sri Lanka and Burma) have sometimes even become violent. But what Paññāvaḍḍho said is applicable only to a small minority of monks, those who are convinced that their prime duty is to get rid of defilements. It is unrealistic to expect that all monks should have these intentions. Even at the time of the Buddha, many monks did not. Monks should act somewhere between the minimum(following the basic ethical precepts) and the maximum (practicing for liberation); most are in between. Beyond following the minimal ethical precepts, the monk should make some contribution. In the Theravādin Buddhist tradition, there is the custom of having town monks, who help and lead the people in various ways, for instance, in education and medicine; this is traditional expression of socially engaged spirituality.

Without the spiritual dimension, however, those working socially will burn out. We must have joy, peace, and rest for ourselves, in our families, among our neighbors. If we are to connect ethical norms and social justice, we must have time for spiritual development, time to meditate, time to integrate head and heart, and then time for renewal and retreat several weeks a year, sometimes with teachers who help us and question us. This is why centers of renewal like Buddhadāsa's Suan Mokh, the"Garden of Liberation" [in south Thailand], Thich Nhat Hanh's Plum Village [near Bordeaux, France], or the center I muself started, the ecumenical Wongsanit Ashram, are so important.

Without this kind of inquiry and practice, those

trying to transform society will be more likely to be greedy, wanting to be big shots, or full of hate, wanting power, or deluded, wanting an impossibly ideal society or being a naive do-gooder. Meditation and critical self-awareness help one to see these questionable motivations or at least to ask oneself: "Am I doing that out of greed or hatred?" even if there is no clear answer.

But meditation alone is not sufficient — because people suffer so much. One must also act; one must do what one can.

The basic understandings of the three founding patrons of the International Network of Engaged Buddhists [INEB, founded by Sulak], the Dalai Lama of Tibet, Thich Nhat Hanh of Vietnam, and Buddhadasa Bhikkhu of Siam, are all very relevant.[6] Each of them, representing one of the three main Buddhist traditions (Vajrayāna, Mahāyāna, and Theravāda), meditates regularly and is very concerned about developing "*dhammic*" societies, societies based on wisdom and compassion. Each of them has faced suffering very directly and responded very fully, in ways from which we can learn.

The Dalai Lama has been exiled for over thirty years from his native Tibet. He uses meditation and compassion, teaching us to love the Chinese government and Chinese individuals who have often committed atrocities against the Tibetans, killing, destroying temples, and so on. His teaching is very relevant for my young *bhikkhus* [monks] in Sri Lanka, in the middle of a civil war; how can they learn to love the Tamils? I have not been successful yet. But many of these monks are now starting to meditate and joining in traditional monastic practices, like collecting alms.

Thich Nhat Hanh has also been a great help. In Siam, for example, he helped the Vietnamese refugees, who have often been very badly treated by Thais in their refugee camps; some of the refugees have been raped by Thai pirates. Thich Nhat Hanh worked with them, teaching them not to hate Thais. He has also helped the refugees when they've settled in America and in Australia, helped them especially with their wounds from the war. For Thich Nhat Hanh, to help others is to help oneself. Those of us who have been to Plum Village, the spiritual community in France that Thich Nhat Hanh started, can see how meditation and social awareness both flourish there.

Buddhadāsa may not have been persecuted as much as the other two leaders, but he has been often attacked. He has been called a Communist by some; some Sri Lankan monks called him a goat and a propagandist for the Christians. A well-known Buddhist scholar critized him as a non-Buddhist and called him, a senior monk(now eight-seven) all kinds of names, largely because he was open to approaches from outside the Buddhist tradition. Buddhadāsa is very much based in Buddhist tradition, of course; he is very strict in following the Theravādin ethical precepts. At the same time, he has embraced Vajrayāna and Mahayāna Buddhism as valid paths. His Holiness the Dalai Lama

went to visit him. He has also admired the work of
Thich Nhat Hanh.

The importance of community

Rothberg: A life integrating social engagement
and spiritual work in the West is quite hard for many
reasons, especially because there are not so many
support structures. At the Buddhist Peace Fellowship
summer institute in July 1992, you spoke about
community as an important form of nonviolent re-
sistance, as a support for questioning consumerism
and the structures of domination and oppression.

Sivaraksa: It is important that daily life be lived
in community. The present daily life in industrialized
societies, so much based on seperation, individualism,
and consumption, is not conductive to socially engaged
spirituality. The Buddhist tradition, on the other hand,
emphasizes the centrality of community life based on
simplicity. There is the old tradition that monks should
not have more than three robes, only one bowl, one
thread, one needle, and one pair of sandles. We are
also taught not to be attached or give great significance
to money (even if we lay people need money for
survival). The more we are self-reliant, growing our
own food, and so on, the less money becomes important. Whatever we grow we are willing to share
with others. That is why I think that you need to live
close to nature and be with people. In our traditional
society, it has always been like this. Whatever you
cook, you share with others. It would be good for this

approach to come back. I think that this is possible, if people think seriously and question consumerism, promoting nongreed, nonharted, and nondelusion, educate people about alternatives to materialism and about how to make capitalism more sane.

In our society, especially in the countryside, we still have extended families in most of the country, except in Bangkok, which is just like any Western city. We still respect our parents and grandparents and have feelings for the poor, the blind, and the mentally retarded; we don't feel ashamed if we have mentally retarded people in the family. We have to reinforce what is positive in the traditional approach (in areas like agriculture, medicine, food, and dress); otherwise, modern trends will wipe everything away.

Rothberg: In the United Stated, Buddhism is often interpreted very individualistically. Gary Snyder (Ingram, Gates, and Nisker 1988, 5) once said that *sangha* is the least developed of the "Three Jewels" of Buddhism [the "Three Jewels" are the Buddha, or the example of the liberated person; the *dhamma*, or basic teachings about liberation; and the *sangha*].

Sivaraksa: When my teacher, Ajahn Buddhadāsa, reached the age of eighty-four, the end of the seventh cycle of his life according to our custom, I produced the book *Radical Conservatism* (Sivaraksa, Hutanuvatra, Chaemduang, Sobhanasiri, and Kholer 1990). I think that the title is important. As a Buddhist, if one is not radical and does not work to eliminate suffering, one may end up only taking a little bit of Buddhism for one's individual ego. But Buddhism is not often radical; it coexists too easily with capitalism and consumerism. If Buddhism is not radical here in the United States, it will one day simply become a kind of Americanism and not make much of a contribution, just as Buddhism is often a mere decoration in Japan.

Many intentions to create community in this country have failed, largely because individualism has become so strong and because communities have not been firmly based on ethical guidelines. I think of Locke, and your Declaration of Independence, that would make possible "life, liberty and the pursuit of (what they call) happiness." Too often, of course, the pursuit of happiness is really the pursuit of property. The traditional member of the Buddhist *sangha* has no property whatsoever. All members are equal economically and socially. Lay people can look at the *sangha* as a model and try to have less property, not be so attached to what they do have, and work for greater economic and political equality.

The community must also be based on ethical precepts. Of course, ethics is not just about not killing or stealing or abusing another sexually; it is also about respecting others, sharing our resources, seeing how we can contribute, living harmoniously, and so on. If we can develop Buddhist communities that rest on simple living, are close to nature, and that encourage serious thinking that challenges consumerism and the status quo, that would be an important contribution.

First World and Third World:
working and learning together
Rothberg: At the present time, there is much
more interaction of "First World" and "Third World"
socially engaged Buddhists. How can we best work
with each other? What can we learn from each other?
Sivaraksa: Again, the essential point is that each
person must develop critical self-awareness, humility,
seeds of peace, and then dialogue is possible, listening
is possible, good friends are possible. Once we work
together, particularly in relation to suffering, then the
gaps between rich and poor, First World and Third
World, North and South, are gone; we become partners and friends. Alone you can't do very much, but
with your friends, you can do a great deal. If you
want to gain exposure to the South, then you need
people from the South to help you. If I want to go to
Sri Lanka or Burma, then I need friends from those
countries to help me, so that I can learn from them,
and they can learn from me, I need to respect them,
be genuine and sincere, and be at their level, not wear
a big cap.

The conditions in the United States for socially
engaged spiritually are difficult. Consumerism, greed,
loneliness, manipulation of political power, and hatred
have become so strong. Worst of all, the people are so
deluded, most of the time unknowingly. Working with
us in Asia may be helpful, working for half a year, or
a year, helping the Tibetans, or the Ladakhi, or the
Thai, or the Burmese. But this shouldn't be escapism.

You might work in Asia and see that the source of suffering there is perhaps in the First World. When you come back here, after you have lived with them in community and close to nature, you may have more motivation to live like this in your own country.

I can also be helpful to be exposed to a society where it is clearer that there is delusion, where power is clearer. In my society, for example, you can see that the generals kill people openly. In this country, the generals never kill your people. They're much more clever, and the people stay deluded; the wars are all supposed to be just, great for the American flag, for the open society, the liberal West, and so on.

Oppression, reconciliation and the middle path
Rothberg: Although engaged Buddhists may identify systems of domination and oppression, they often question the tendency among many leftists to polarize oppressors and oppressed; Buddhists more often emphasize reconciliation. How do we identify systems of oppression, as well as those concrete persons who are in many ways responsible for oppression, without forming a rigid distinction between "good" people and "bad" people?
Sivaraksa: This is the most difficult question. This is where you need serious spiritual practice. It is easy to condemn the·oppressors, but actually when you condemn others, you condemn yourself. Right now in my country, this difficult problem is very central [following the demonstrations and killings of hundreds

in the streets in Bangkok in May 92]. Of course, it is very easy to pass judgement and bellieve in right on one side and wrong on the other. But here you have to have a deeper understanding that is often difficult to explain, of karma and interdependence over vast periods of time and space. We must cultivate this deeper understanding, thinking also about the nature of social system, rather than just focusing on the persons.

If you get attached to right and wrong, you become so tiresome and full of hatred, and ultimately you may have to kill; in Christian terms, you become God. We must develop more mercy and compassion. Here, the West can learn from Buddhists. Our ability to forgive is our strength. But, of course, you have to practice; you have to go deeper and radicalize yourself, going beyond thinking about "an eye for an eye."

Acknowledgements

I wish to thank Joyce Rybandt and Veronica Froelich for their aid in transcribing this conversation and Wim Aspeslagh for his helpful comments on the manuscript.

Notes

1. Explanatory phrases within brackets have been added by the interviewer.

2. Johan Galtung is currently a political scientist and peace researcher at the University of Hawaii.

3. The five basic ethical precepts in Theravāda Buddhism include guidelines to refrain from killing, stealing, "false" speech, improper sexuality, and intoxicants that cloud the mind. See Saddhatissa1987).

4. Traditionally, there are six *pārāmitas*: giving or generosity (Pali:*dāna*), ethical integrity(*sila*), patience(*khanti*), vigor(*viriya*), meditation(*samādhi*), and wisdom(*paññā*).

5. Dr. B. R. Ambedkar (1891-1956), after a careful survey of the world religions, came to the conclusion that Buddhism was best suited to meet the ethical, social, and spiritual needs of both the untouchables in particular and the contemporary world generally. He converted publicly shortly before his death, and since then perhaps twenty million former untouchables in India have followed in converting to Buddhism. For a short account of Ambedkar's life, see Queen(1993).

6. For representative works of these authors, see Dalai Lama (1984, 1990), Nhat Hanh (1987b, 1992), and Swearer (1989). Buddhadāsa (1906-1993) may be the least known of these three figures in the West, but he is probably the best-known monk in Thailand of the twentieth century. He is the founder of an innovative as well as highly traditional community of forest monasteries and is known for his questioning of religious orthodoxy, his deep interest both in meditation and in social change, and his prolific writings.

References

Dalai Lama, 1984, *Kindness, Clarity, and Insight*. Ithaca, N.Y.,: Snow Lion Press.

——, 1990. *A Policy of Kindness*. Ithaca, N.Y.: Snow Lion Press.

Ingram, C., B. Gates, and W. Nisker. 1988. Chan on Turtle Island: A conversation with Gary Snyder. *Inquiring Mind* 4 (Winter): 1, 4-5, 25. Available from Inquiring Mind, P.O.Box 9999, Berkeley, Calif. 94709.

Nhat Hanh, T. 1987a. *Interbeing: Commentaries on the Tiep Hien Precepts*. Berkeley: Parallax Press.

——. 1987b. *Being Peace*. Berkeley: Parallax Press.

——. 1992, *Touching Peace: Practicing the Art of Mindful Living*. Berkeley: Parallax Press.

Queen, C. 1993. The great conversion: Dr.Ambedkar and the Buddhist revival in India. *Tricycle: The Buddhist Review 2* (Spring): 62-67.

Saddhatissa, H. 1987. *Buddhist Ethics: The Path to Nirvāṇa*. London: Wisdom Publications.

Schumacher, E. 1973. *Small is Beautiful: A study of econimics as if people mattered*. London: Blond and Briggs.

Sivaraksa, S. 1985. *Siamese Resurgence: A Thai Buddhist voice on Asia and a world of change*. Bangkok: Asian Cultural Forum on Development.

——. 1986. *Religion and Development*. 3rd ed. Bangkok: Thai Inter-Religious Commission for Development.

——. 1988. *A Socially Engaged Buddhism: By a controversial Siamese*. Bangkok: Thai Inter-Religious Commission for Development.

——. 1990. *Siam in Crisis*. 2nd ed. Bangkok: Thai Inter-Religious Commission for Development.

——. 1992a. *Seeds of Peace: A Buddhist vision for renewing society*. Berkeley: Parallax Press.

374

——. 1992b. Buddhism and contemporary international trends. In K. Kraft, ed., *Inner Peace, World Peace: Essays on Buddhism and nonviolence.* Albany, N.Y.: S.U.N.Y. Press.

Sivaraksa, S., P. Hutanuvatra, N. Chaemduang, S. Sobhanasiri, and N. Kholer, eds. 1990. *Radical Conservatism: Buddhism in the Contemporary World: Articles in honour of Bhikkhu Buddhadāsa's 84th birthday anniversary.* Bangkok: Thai Inter-Religious Commission for Development.

Swearer, D.,ed. 1989. *Me and Mine: Selected essays of Bhikkhu Buddhadāsa.* Albany, N.Y.: S.U.N.Y. Press.

American Friends Service Committee
National Office
1501 Cherry Street
Philadelphia, Pennsylvania 19102

January 21, 1994

Geir Lundestad, Director
Den Norske Nobelkomite
Drammensveien 19
Oslo 2
Norway

Dear Geir Lundestad:

The Board of Directors of the American Friends Service Committee nominates Sulak Sivaraksa of Thailand for the Nobel Peace Prize in 1994.

Sulak Sivaraksa has throughout his life been a courageous and articulate voice for peace, human rights and social justice. Rooted deeply in his Buddhist faith and the traditions and indigenous culture of Siam. Professor Sulak has created organizations and publications which have helped to form and nurture a community of persons dedicated to non-violence in a region particularly torn by violence and war. While reaching out to the West both through organizations and writings, Sulak has also spoken out clearly against the dangers of Western materialism which threaten both the natural environment and the indigenous cultures of Thailand.

His public statements on behalf of democracy in Thailand have drawn criticism and legal action against him. Even the current charge of *lese majeste* he faces was brought by a general Sulak criticized for engineering a military coup rather than supporting the emerging civil society of Thailand.

Born in Bangkok in 1933, Sulak Sivaraksa graduated

from the Assumption College in Bangkok, and was further educated at St.David's College, Lampeter, Wales and Middle Temple, London, where he became a Barrister-at-law. After completing his education, Sulak returned to Thailand where he began both his work as publisher and editor and his work with the Thai Buddhist Order (Sangha), two efforts which have characterized thirty years of work on behalf of non-violence and social justice.

In 1963, he founded and edited *Social Science Review*. This magazine heralded the beginning of a new renaissance among Thai intellectuals following the earlier 1957 arrest, killing, and exile of progressive writers, academics, politicians, artists, and social activists.

The *Social Science Review* was the first to publish information about the US military bases in Thailand and their involvement in the Vietnam War. The magazine helped to form a bridge between Thai activists and the anti-war movement in the West. After the Vietnam war, Sulak was a member of one of the first groups of Thai people to visit Indochina.

Much of Sulak's work has involved publications. He has founded and edited at least seven magazines in Thai and English, and published more than one hundred books on culture, development, Buddhism, non-violence and humanitarian principles. His work as a publisher not only has given an outlet for his own writings, but has provided an extremely important vehicle for the expression of alternative views in Thailand. For example, after the coup of 1976, *Pajarayasara*, one of the magazines Sulak had founded, became a forum for people who were interested in nonviolent social change. Since the eighties, it has been the only journal initiating and promoting discussion of alternative ideas among the Thais.

Professor Sulak has revised and now reissued his important book *Siam in Crisis* with many new articles.

These articles express his ongoing concern for the future of indigenous Asian cultures. He sees these cultures consistently being eroded by increasing Western influence. Professor Sulak has advocated both in his writings and lectures that Asian peoples must be selective in what they choose to adopt from Western cultures. He sees that an unexamined embracing of everything"Western" has already led to a new"religion of consumerism" and a loss of cultural identity.

Traditionally in Thailand, the monk has been at the center of community life and education. Western cultural influences have eroded this aspect of Thai culture.

Sulak interprets the tremendous spiritual and cultural power of the Thai Buddhist Order(Sangha), and calls the Sangha's search for a new role in modern society an identity crisis.

In 1966, Sulak collaborated with Thailand's two Buddhist universities to create a program for training monks in community development. The program developed awareness of modern social problems and knowledge of such basic tools for community work as skills in health care and community organizing.

Based on this work, Sulak created the Thai Inter-Religious Commission for Development (TICD), which generated programs that reach out to other religious groups to work in community development. TICD has also specialized in identifying monks with special aptitudes for community development, indigenous health care and environmental preservation. In the past 15 years, the network has expanded to include more than 200 monks, with such well known success stories as the environmental work of Phra Prachak in Burirum Province, the Buddhist cooperative programs of Luang Po Nan in Surin Province and the herbal treatment center of Phra Somnuk in Nakhon Pathom province.

Another important NGO which Sulak helped to found is the Coordinating Group for Religion in Society, one of the first human rights organizations in Thailand.

The Coordinating Group helped to create a non-violent alternative to the increasingly violent and polarized extremes of the left and right.

When the bloody *coup d'etat* of October 6, 1976, returned the military to power, thousands of university students went into exile, into the jungle, or to prison.

The Coordinating worked to save the lives of countless students and political activists. Subsequently, Sulak founded other NGO's which provided constructive opportunities for Thai youth. Many students who were released from prison or who came back from the jungles under the Amnesty Decree went to work for the benefit of society within this NGO structure, non-violently and to great effect.

Sulak has a deep understanding of the role that non-governmental organizations can play in providing structures that help communities respond to problems, in providing opportunities for young people to learn and gain constructive experience, and in building international networks of people whose common concerns transcend the separateness of region, culture, and distance. There are now over 100 NGO's in Thailand, many of which Sulak encouraged or helped to start. Participatory models of decision-making, strategies for the resolution of conflict, and new education models continue to develop.

As the Thai government continues to become more democratic and inclusive the NGO's work more closely with the authorities.

In 1989, Sulak, co-founded the International Network of Engaged Buddhists (INEB). It was the first international Buddhist network to link socially active Buddhist individuals and groups worldwide to support one another. It also serves as a clearinghouse for information and for creative solutions to local, national and international problems. Its greatest concern is empowering Buddhists and people of all denominations in areas under great duress, such as Bangladesh, Burma, Cambodia and Sri Lanka. Recently, INEB has conducted trainings on socially engaged Buddhism for Sri

Lankan, Cambodian, Burmese and Napalese monks. By helping to create leaders at the local level skilled in nonviolent social and political interaction, alternative economics, ecology and spiritual development, INEB seeks to empower local communities to solve their own problems and create strong, wholesome societies.

Sulak's active involvement for peace, social justice and human rights, and his criticism of indiscriminate acceptance of Western materialism has brought him into conflict with the military leaders of the country. At various times he has been arrested for criticizing the government. In 1976 many of his books were confiscated and burned. He has been forced into exile at times.

He now faces trial and possible imprisonment on a charge of *lese majeste* brought by the head of a military regime he had criticized. Despite these pressures, Sulak has been courageously consistent in his writings and public speaking on behalf of freedom of expression and social justice.

This is a critical time, both for Sulak Sivaraksa and for Thailand. A commitment to peace and non-violence in the fullest sense, are at the core of his life and writings. He not only advocates peace and justice, he creatively builds the institutions and structures which will create the environment in which peace and justice can grow and flourish. He is a rare person, who combines a brilliant analytic mind, articulate expression, courageous leadership, and a deeply loving spirit.

We commend Sulak Sivaraksa to the Nobel committee's consideration for the 1994 peace prize. We are most grateful for the opportunity to propose candidates for the Prize.

Cordially yours,

Kara Newell
Executive Director

EXCERPTS FROM REVIEWS

Sulak Sivaraksa is well-known in Thailand as an exponent of change to a more Buddhist and just society. Sometimes his words have provoked anger and suspicion that he is a Communist and while some of his earlier remarks and writings were rather extreme, lately he has become more moderate.

Bhikkhu Khantipalo
Wat Buddha Dhamma
Sydney, Australia

Sulak is unpopular in certain circles, but even a cursory reading of *A Buddhist Vision for Renewing Society* will make it abundantly clear that many of the criticisms levelled against him are without basis. ...It would do less than justice to Sulak's integrated "vision" to attempt to analyse all the distinctively Buddhist strands of his world-view. He thinks, speaks and acts as a Buddhist whose "passionate moderation" represents a new Middle Way. At times he draws consciously on traditional Theravadin themes, but it is clear that he has been strongly influenced by Mahayana and Zen Buddhism, and the imaginative "this worldly" ethic of Buddhadasa (Putatat). His radical critique of western patterns of development parallels Schumacher, and his advocacy of non-violence, while fully Buddhist, is also very Gandhian.

David L. Gosling
Journal of the Siam Society, Bangkok, 1983

Sulak forcefully argues against the materialistic attitude which is prevalent in the present Thai society and against development programmes which are emphatically geared towards material improvements — such programmes and attitude, according to Sulak, fail to pay adequate attention to the fundamental value of man's human qualities. One may disagree with him over the means to overcome social problems but it cannot be denied that the question which he poses gets to the very heart of what matters.

A. Buchongkul
Asian Action
September-October 1981

LIST OF OUR PUBLICATIONS

DHAMMIC SOCIALISM, by Buddhadasa Bhikkhu, 142 pp., Bht 120 locally (abroad US$ 6 post free).

LOOKING TO AMERICA TO SOLVE THAILAND'S PROBLEMS, by Phra Rajavaramuni, 94 pp., Bht 120 locally (abroad US$ 6 post free).

THAI BUDDHISM IN THE BUDDHIST WORLD, by Phra Rajavaramuni (Prayudh Payutto) 178 pp., Bht 100 locally (abroad US$ 5 post free).

MONUMENTS OF THE BUDDHA IN SIAM, by H.R.H. Prince Damrong Rajanubhab. Translated by S. Sivaraksa and A.B. Griswold., 60 pp., Bht 100 locally (abroad US$ 5 post free).

POPULAR BUDDHISM IN SIAM AND OTHER ESSAYS ON THAI STUDIES, by Phya Anuman Rajadhon, 216 pp. Bht 300 (hard cover), Bht 200(paper back) locally (abroad US$ 15 hard cover, US$ 10 paper back, post free).

SOME TRADITIONS OF THE THAI, by Phya Anuman Rajadhon, 196 pp., Bht 200 locally (abroad US$ 10 post free).

ESSAYS ON THAI FOLKLORE, by Phya Anuman Rajadhon (new edition), 422 pp., Bht 400 locally (abroad US$ 20 post free).

FUA HARIPITAK'S DRAWINGS: A STUDY AND RESEARCH ON STYLE OF THE OLD NORTHERN THAI ART (1964-67), Bht 400 locally (hard cover). US$ 20 abroad post free.

ANGKARN KALAYANAPONG; A CONTEMPORARY SIAMESE POET, 82 pp., Bht 80 locally (abroad US$ 4 post free).

RELIGION AND DEVELOPMENT, by Sulak Sivaraksa, Thai Inter-Religions Commission for Development, Bangkok, 2530/1987 90 Baht locally (abroad US$ 5 post free)

SIAMESE RESURGENCE, by S.Sivaraksa, 492 pp., Bht 260 (hard cover) Bht 180(paper back) locally (abroad US$ 10 post free).

A SOCIALLY ENGAGED BUDDHISM, by S. Sivaraksa, 206 pp., Bht 300 (hard cover), Bht 200 (paper back) locally (abroad US$ 15 post free).

SIAM IN CRISIS, by S. Sivaraksa, 2nd ed., 371 pp., Bht 300 locally (abroad US$ 15 post free).

SEEDS OF PEACE: A BUDDHIST VISION FOR RENEWING SOCIETY, by S.Sivaraksa, 193 pp. Bht 200 locally.

FIVE CYCLES OF FRIENDSHIP, by Friends of Sulak Sivaraksa, 132 pp. Bht 200 locally (abroad US$ 10 post free).

RADICAL CONSERVATISM: BUDDHISM IN THE CONTEMPORARY WORLD, A volume in celebration of Buddhadasa Bhikkhu's 84th year written by: Thich Nhat Hanh, Gabriel Lafitte, Phra Debvedi, Bhikkhu Sumedho, Lewis R. Lancaster, Sulak Sivaraksa, John A. McConnell, G. Lubsantseren, David W. Chappell etc; 576 pp., 750 Bht (paper back), 1,200 Bht(hard cover), locally (US$ 35.00 (paper back), US$ 60.00 (hard cover) aboard post free.

DR. AMBEDKAR: THE LIBERATOR, A **Souvenir** *Publication On His Centenary,* 56 pp., Bht 40 locally (abroad US$ 4 post free).

SEARCHING FOR ASIAN CULTURAL INTEGRITY: Papers from Inter-Cultural Seminar in Bangkok 1990, 222 pp., Bht 200 locally (abroad US$10 post free).

BUDDHIST PERCEPTION FOR DESIRABLE SO-CIETIES IN THE FUTURE: Papers prepared for the United Nations University edited by Sulak Sivaraksa et al, 1993 pp. 228 Baht 300 locally (abroad US$ 15 post free.)

WHEN ROYALTY DEMANDS DISSENT: Sulak Sivaraksa and the charge of lese majeste in Siam

1991-1993, 350 pp., Bht 500 locally (abroad US$ 20 post free).

LIFE WITHOUT A CHOICE, by K. Kusalasaya, The autobiography of a Thai interned in India during the Second World War who is now a well known Buddhist scholar. 304 pp., Bht 320 locally (abroad US$ 16 post free).

SEEDS OF PEACE, Thai Inter-Religious Commission for Development. 3 issues/year, suggested minimum subscription rate US$ 15 per annum. If you could afford more to help this worthy publicattion, please do so. Vols 2, 3 & 4 (1986-92) bound in hard cover Bht 400 locally (US$ 20 abroad each).

Please send your orders to Suksit Siam
113-115 Fuangnakhon Rd., Opp.Wat Rajabopit, Bangkok
10200 Tel: 66-2-225-9531/225-9532, Fax: 66-2-222-5188
Personal cheques from UK & USA made in the name of Suksit Siam are accepted.

BOOK-REVIEWS

Seeds of Peace

Sivaraksa's recently published book, *Seeds of Peace*, I am using for the second time in a course on "Democracy and Nonviolent Social Movements," offered at the University of Colorado. In this course we concentrate on movements worldwide (outside the USA) that seek democracy by nonviolent means. The students are all upper-division undergraduates (in their final two years of study for a bachelors degree) involved in an intensive program focused on voluntary public service nationally and internationally. In this course we study writings by and about figures like Gandhi, Adam Michnik, Aung San Suu Kyi, and Adolfo Peres Esquivel, as well as Frantz Fanon (to understand his advocacy of violence). We look at recent and contemporary movements in Latin America, South Africa, Eastern Europe, Israel/Palestine, the Philippines, China, etc. Of all the reading we do, the one book that consistently touches and stirs the students most deeply is Sivaraksa's *Seeds of Peace*.

From the academic standpoint, this book melds into clear exposition complex theories and practices from a vast corpus of writings on development, democracy, religious studies, history, sociology, anthropology, etc. As one who moves about in this terrain, I am amazed not only at Sivaraksa's wide reading and deep understanding but more so at his ability to compress so much learning into elegantly clear, eminently readable, quietly convincing prose.

The prevailing top-down neocolonial model of development has many critics. But none reach students from the USA quite as well as Sivaraksa. Students, like local Buddhists (Boulder has one of the larger Buddhist communities outside Asia) and activists for nonviolent change, recognize that Sivaraksa's "middle-path" approach to development is pervaded with a profound commitment to social justice, ecological harmony and self-rule. Students, activists and others — notably the global network of engaged Buddhists — also are deeply affected by his insistence that the way to lasting social change is via nonviolent means, yet that nonviolence has efficacy in the social realm only if first it is seated in the hearts and lives of those who seek change. Of course, the fact that Sivaraksa's life is on the line for true rather than sham democracy in his own country gives credence to what he says.

LeRoy Moore, Ph.D.

Rocky Mountain Peace Center
P.O. Box 1156, Boulder, CO 80306 U.S.A. (303) 444-6981

Religion and Development

I first encountered his ideas while I was doing research on modernization and the Buddhist religion in South and Southeast Asia. His seminal work, *Religion and Development,* helped me to formulate a qualitative foundation for my study. Many years later I was given the opportunity, by Sulak himself, to edit and revise a new edition of this work. After accomplishing this work — going from reading his works to working with him personally — I felt that I had reached a major milestone in my research on Thai studies. But more than this, I had made an invaluable spiritual friend, a *kalyānamitta,* that has lasted up to this day.

Sulak Sivaraksa *continues* to play an important role as a nurturer. I never cease to be amazed by the number of valuable projects he has fostered — the most recent being the International Network of Engaged Buddhists (INEB). If he sees potential in people, he encourages and helps them to bring their unique talents to fruition. He has sponsored more articles, books and other forms of literature than I am able to mention here; and he has directed grassroots programs and non-governmental orgainzations that seek to preserve a meaingnful spiritual dimension to the development and modernization process — both nationally and internationally.

Sulak has made great sacrifices in his own life. At various points in his life, his critical comments have obviously placed him in great danger. When I last saw him in May of 1992, he was still in exile because of his critique of the military's role in Thai politics, and he remains on trial now. Yet as he travels around, he works to bond people for the purpose of justice, awareness and peace.

Grant A. Olson
Research Associate/Editor
Northern Illinois University
DeKalb, Illinois 60115-2854, U.S.A.
Center for Southeast Asian Studies

When Loyalty Demands Dissent:
Sulak Sivaraksa and the charge of lese majeste in
Siam 1991-1993

Today Sulak Sivaraksa, well-known writer, intellectual, publisher and social critic, is scheduled to appear in court to face charges of *lese majeste* and defaming a former general and the latter's associates. If found guilty of *lese majeste,* Sulak may face a maximum prison sentence of 15 years. Sulak is now 60 years old.

Concerned civil rights lawyers including Thongbai Thongpao, Sampas Pungpradisth, Vasant Panij and Somchai Hom La-Or are representing Sulak. The case is not expected to be resolved quickly and could drag on for years.

Those interested in the background and development of the Sulak case may be gratified by the timely publication of a new book *When Loyalty Demands Dissent: Sulak Sivaraksa and the charge of lese majeste in Siam 1991-1993.*

When Loyalty Demands Dissent is not Sulak's latest book. Rather it is a book about "Sulak Sivaraksa and the charge of *lese majeste* in Siam 1991-1993" as the subtitle indicates. It also contains many articles, interviews, lectures and reflections of Sulak, but not exclusively. The publishers — Sathirakoses Nagapradipa Foundation, Santi Pracha Dhamma Institute and Ashram Wongsanit — have included many articles, interviews, news items and petitions relating to Sulak's arrest, as well as a large array of international documental concern expressed on his behalf.

The book was published on the second anniversary of Sulak's fateful lecture at Thammasat University, 22 August 1991, which subsequently became the albatross around his neck. Unfortunately, the text of the speech "Democracy and the coup d'etat," on which the charges against Sulak were based, was not included among the collection of articles and lectures in the book. Those who cared about Sulak's fate, but were not present at Thammasat University on the day the lecture was delivered, would want to know exactly what he said that heaped trouble upon his head. Many participants in the Democracy Movement of May 1992 claimed that the speech was a historic event because it represented one of the earliest signs of courageous dissent against the illegal NPKC-sponsored government which eventually snowballed into the mass demonstrations against military rule during May 1992.

The book takes the position that Sulak's trial is political. It claims that the NPKC bore the brunt of Sulak's attack. To the extent that Sulak's speech can be said to have caused damage, it caused damage to the former military-sponsored government, which was installed following a coup d'etat by a military faction. From hindsight, there appears to be some substance to the claim. The NPKC regime had to bow out following the May event of 1992. As to the claims, of the anti-Sulak camp, that other national institutions were also damaged, the historical evidence is certainly less clear.

The book is not just about Sulak. The articles, arguments and petitions often refer to critical national issues and appeal to deep national values in refreshingly new ways. The conventional separations between state and society, religion and politics, culture and power, are not respected. If there is indeed a fundamental message of the book, it appears to be that crises bring together fundamental values, politics, religion, culture and power in new ways. It is a great mix of great issues, great values and great institutions. Read the book to get a feel of the crossroads of ideas in Thailand.

Jeffrry Sng
Bangkok Post
October 8, 1993

Printed in Bangkok by

Ruan Kaew Printing House (Mr. Theera Jiaraditarporn)
947 Arunamarin Rd., (opp. Siriraj Hospital)
Bangkok 10700 Tel. 411-1423, 412-6552